AF291810

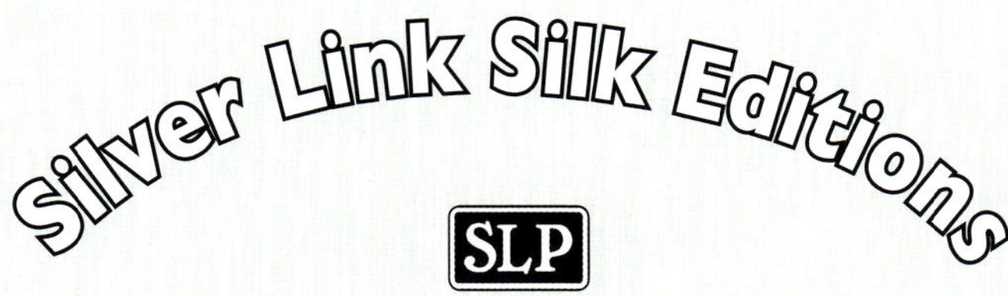

Steam Reminiscences
SOUTHERN

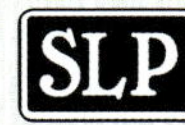

Silver Link Books

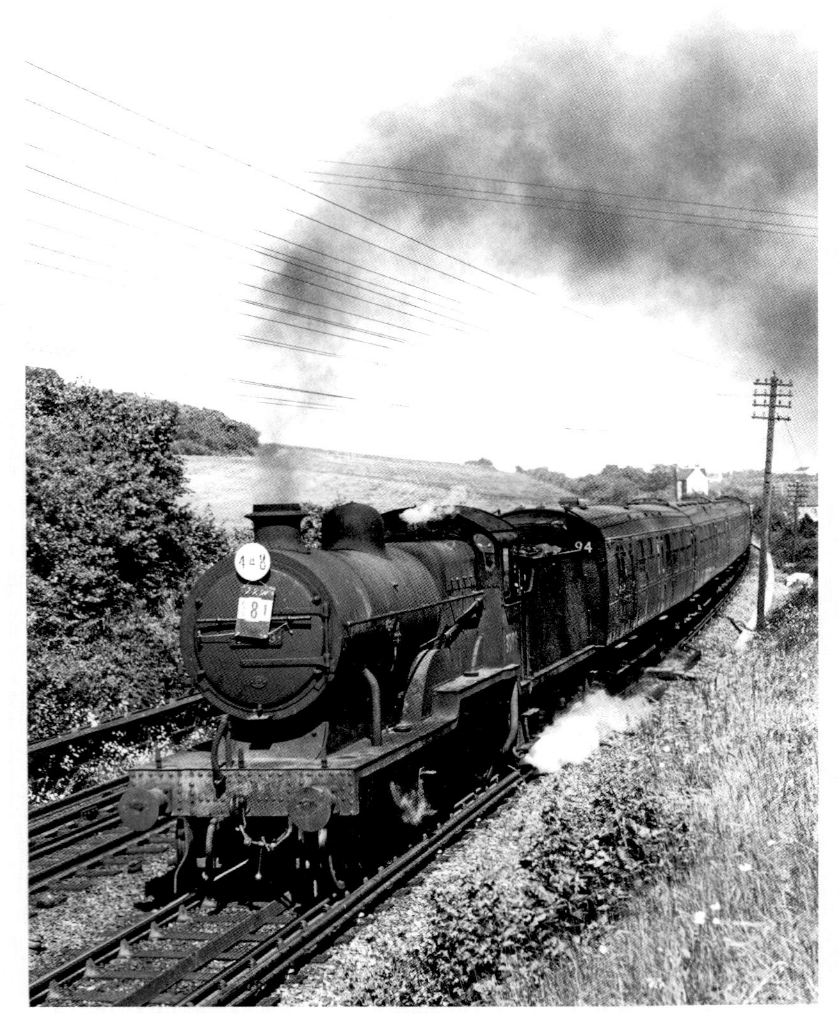

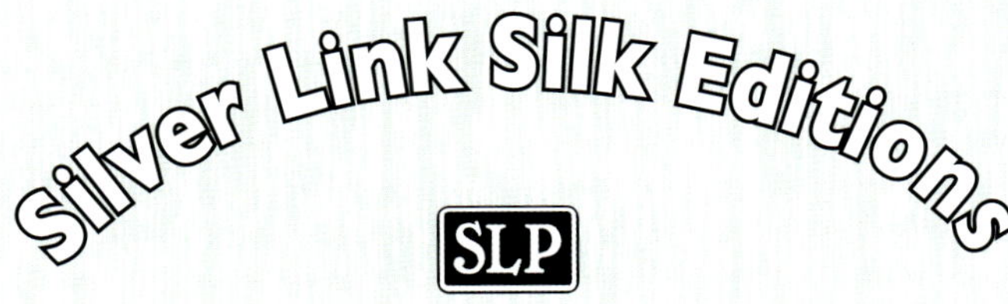

Steam Reminiscences
Southern

John Beckett

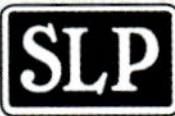

Silver Link Books

First published in 2021

British Library Cataloguing in Publication Data
A catalogue record for this book is available from the British Library.
ISBN 978 1 85794 547 8

Silver Link Books
Mortons Media Group Limited
Media Centre
Morton Way
Horncastle
LN9 6JR
Tel/Fax: 01507 529535

email: sohara@mortons.co.uk
Website: www.nostalgiacollection.com

Printed and bound in the Czech Republic

Contents

Frontispiece: **SOLE STREET BANK** 'L1' 4-4-0 No 31788 starts to climb the bank out of the Medway valley at the head of the 2.25pm Faversham-Victoria (a regular working for an 'L1') on 13 June 1959, the last Saturday before the Phase I Kent Coast electrification came into effect.

Introduction

I was born and bred in Sussex, by the Brighton main line. In 1945 I started to attend grammar school in Horsham. This involved a daily return journey by (electric) train, but also brought into sight the locomotive sheds at Three Bridges and Horsham and three steam-worked branches: Three Bridges to Tunbridge Wells, and Horsham to Brighton and Guildford. In a teenage (just) boy this, not unnaturally, produced an interest in railways.

Not until I was on National Service could I afford to buy and use a camera. Then postings to Cambridge and Bodmin allowed me to practise its use, and three years at Cambridge thereafter to achieve some success. (I did study Russian and Classics at the same time!) I was up at Cambridge just in time; by graduation in 1958 the local railway scene was being motorised at a great rate.

There followed a year in Surrey as a salesman of ethical drugs, with a company car, then some years associated with computers. During this time I used a succession of second-hand 120-size film cameras for black and white work. Not until 1961 did I buy a new camera, and that was only used for colour films.

This book contains a selection of shots taken on the Southern Region of British Railways between 1956 and 1968. Some have been selected because they show a point of interest, others because I hope they will be 'pleasing to the eye of the beholder'. They are small part of the black and white negatives I have from that period. I have included the former Somerset & Dorset Joint Railway and the nascent Bluebell Railway for the sake of completeness.

The book starts with the lines into Kent, then continues in more or less geographical succession through to Cornwall. Each area is arranged more or less in the 'down' direction for London (or Bath) to the coast, with the exception of the Bluebell Railway.

The author wishes to thank Ruthanne Smith for her skill and patience in typing, Mike Hudson for his many corrections to the text, and Messrs Townsend and Adams for the use of their design and editorial skills.

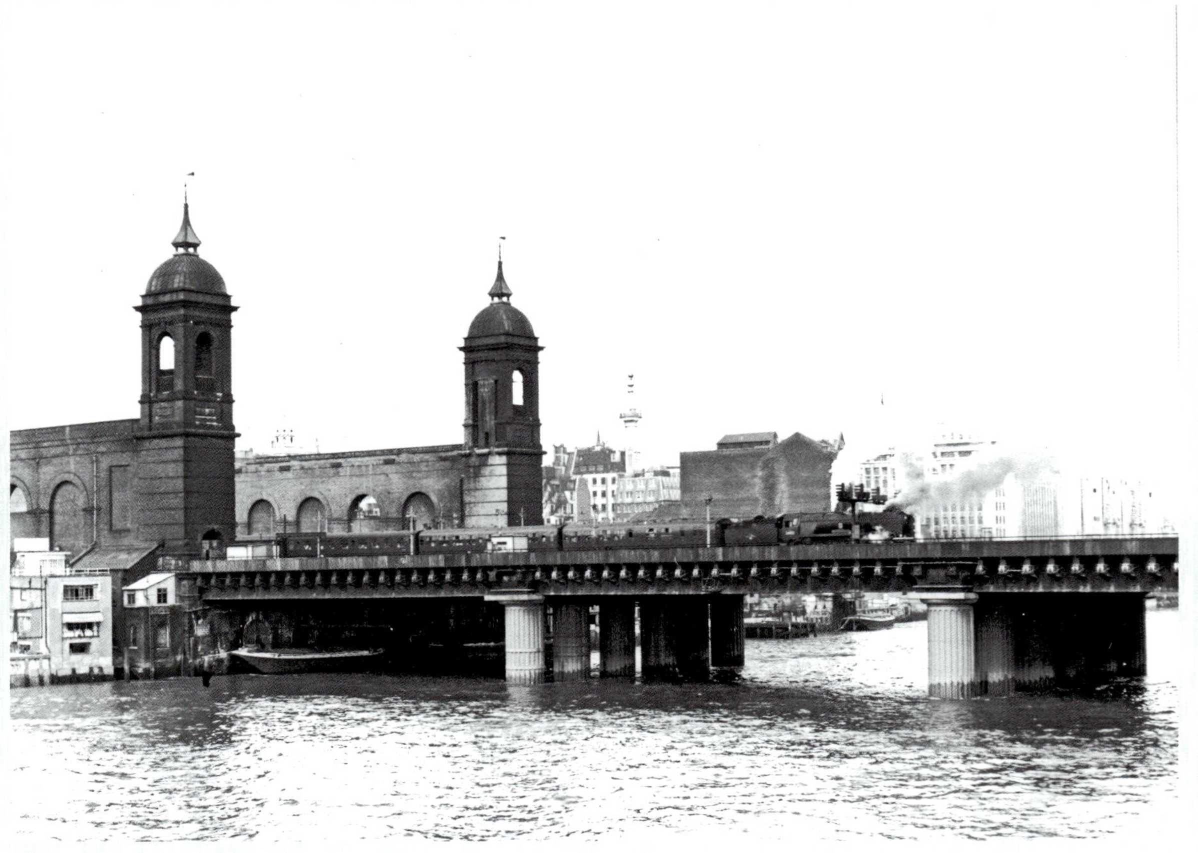

Left and right: **LONDON CANNON STREET** The evening rush hour: 'West Country' 4-6-2 No 34012 *Launceston* eases the 6.25pm to Ramsgate out of Cannon Street station and into the approach to Borough Market Junction, the junction with the line from Charing Cross to London Bridge and Kent, on 2 June 1961. The station is still in its post-war condition – without a roof and with its towers. Southwark Cathedral is in the background of the second shot and the Monument is in the background to the first. The wind, which carries away the engine's smoke on the north bank of the Thames, on the south bank is caught in a back-draught from the buildings and tosses the smoke high. The riverside quays are still in use.

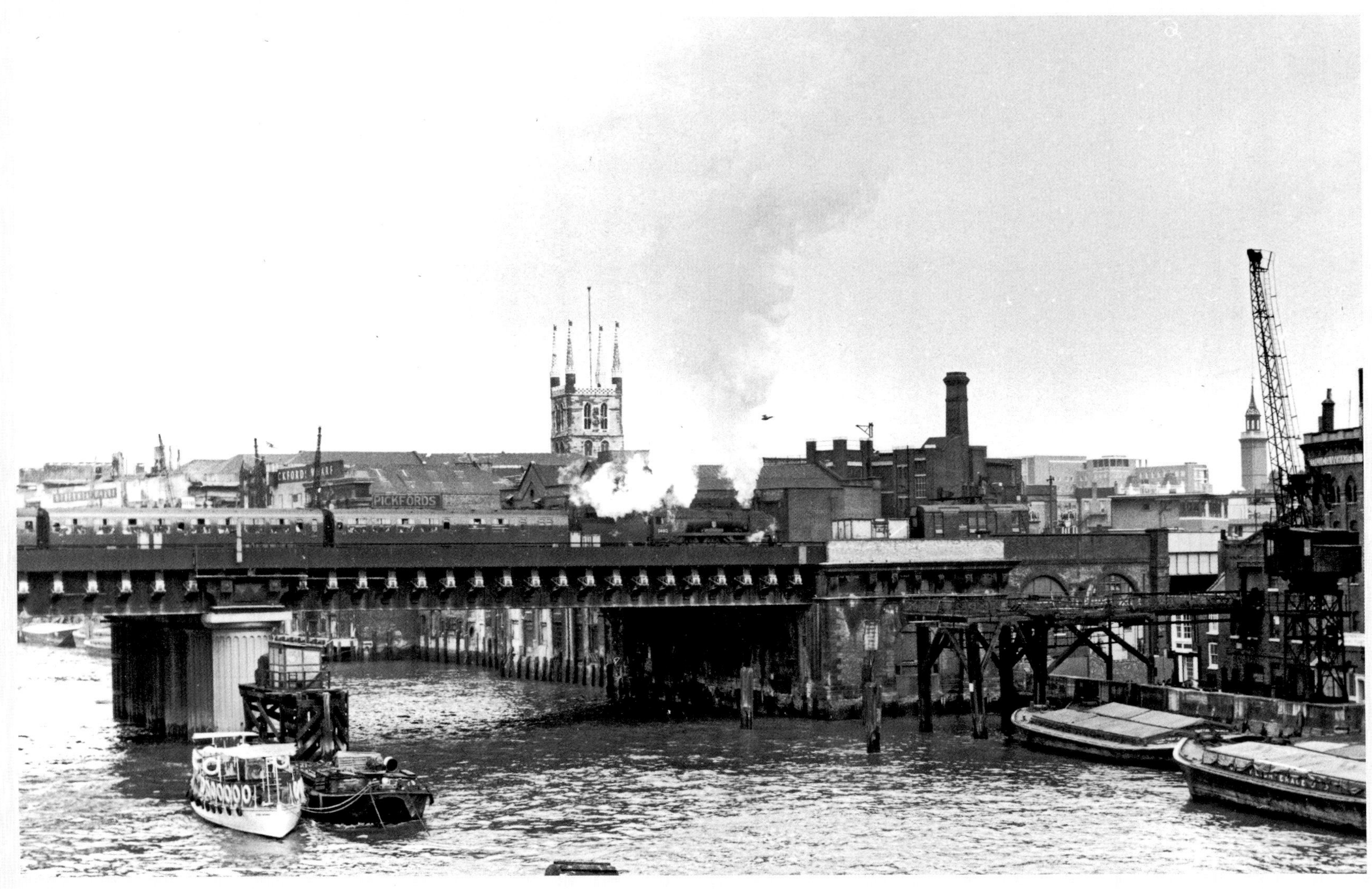

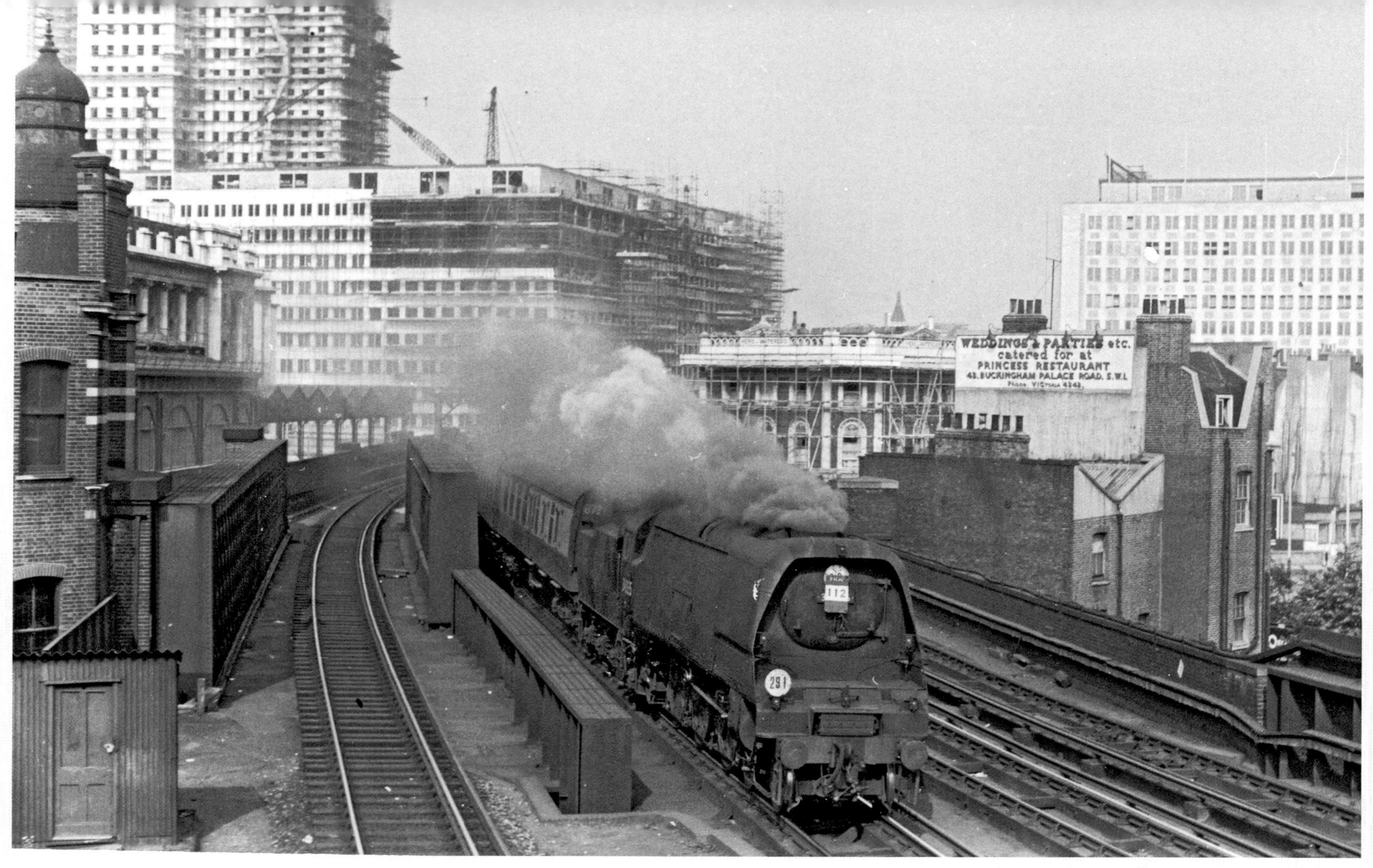

LONDON WATERLOO (EAST) 'WC' 4-6-2 No 34035 *Shaftesbury* approaches at the head of the 9.36am (SO) Charing Cross-Kent Coast on 27 August 1960. Steam has been shut off for the imminent station stop; the air-smoothed casing of the locomotive, modified by widening above the buffer beam, is struggling to lift the smoke.

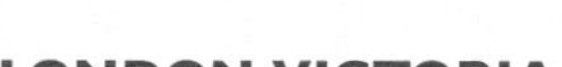

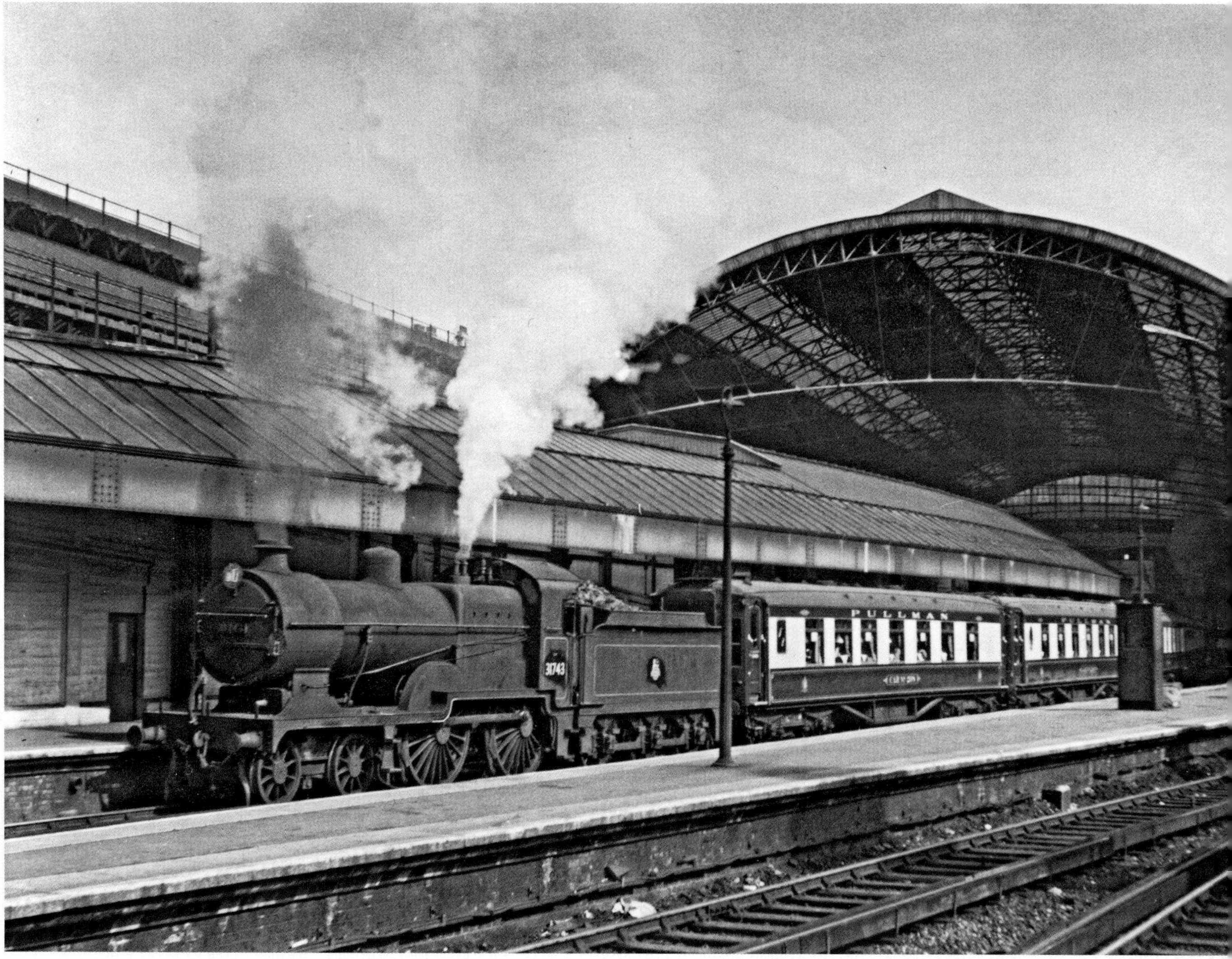

LONDON VICTORIA

'D1' 4-4-0 No 31743 emerges from the Eastern section of Victoria station on 19 August 1958 at the head of five Pullman cars – a special boat train for Swan's Hellenic Tours. The Hellenic tours were transported round the Mediterranean on a small, dedicated cruise ship and were escorted by eminent Classics dons on tours of Greek and Roman ruins. Swan may have hired an all-Pullman car train, but an entirely clean locomotive was too much to expect in mid-August.

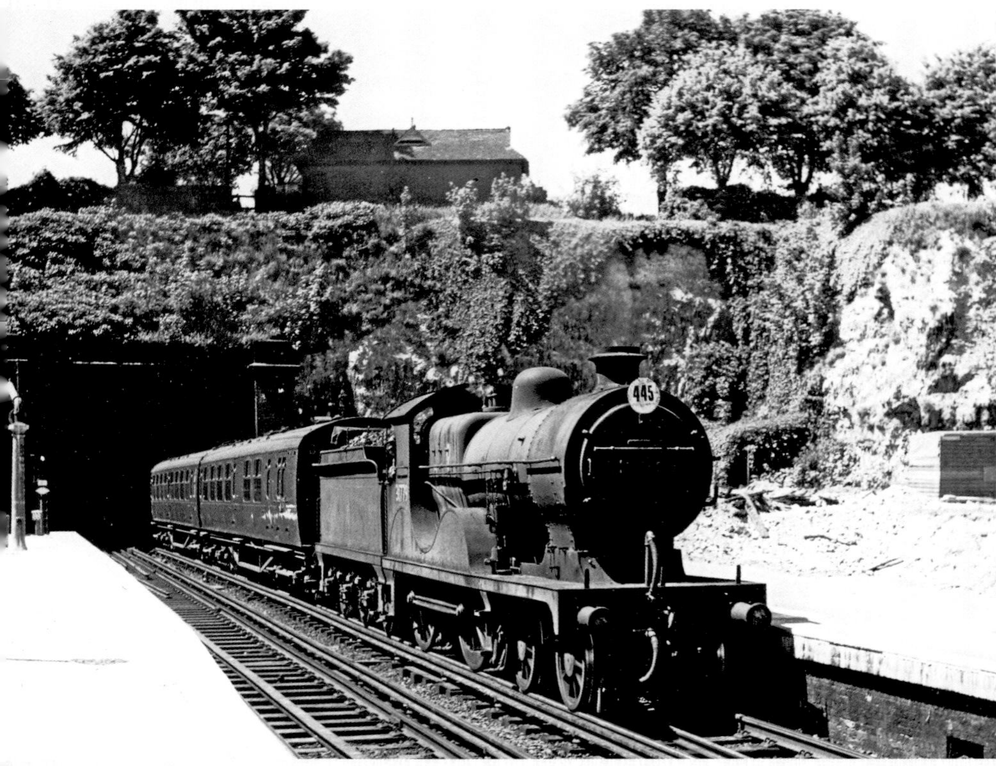

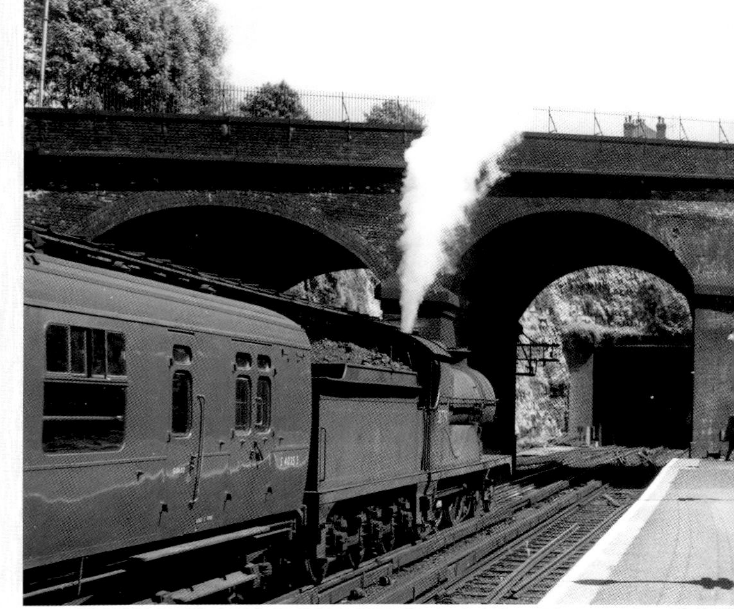

CHATHAM 'L' 4-4-0 No 31779 enters, then leaves Chatham station with a down stopping train on 13 June 1959. The restricted site of the station between Fort Pitt and Chatham tunnels is clearly shown; indeed, it is emphasised by extension of the platforms to accept 12-car electric trains. One wonders whether the building work was completed in time for the start of the full electrified service on 15 June.

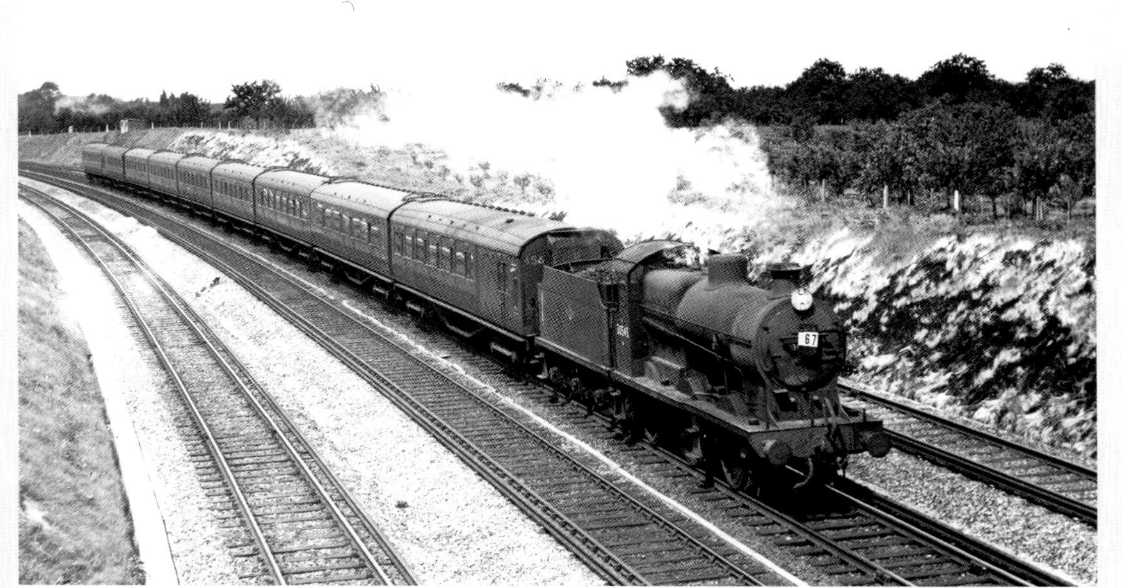

Left: **RAINHAM** 'Q' 0-6-0 No 30545 heads an excursion train for Sheerness-on-Sea along the Kent Coast main line east of Rainham on 18 May 1959. The length from Rainham to Newington was quadrupled as part of the Kent Coast Phase I electrification works.

Below: **GRAVENEY MARSHES** 'Schools' 4-4-0 No 30929 *Malvern* heads an up train from the Kent Coast resorts across Graveney Marshes, east of Faversham, on 18 May 1959. The lads fishing know they've seen it before.

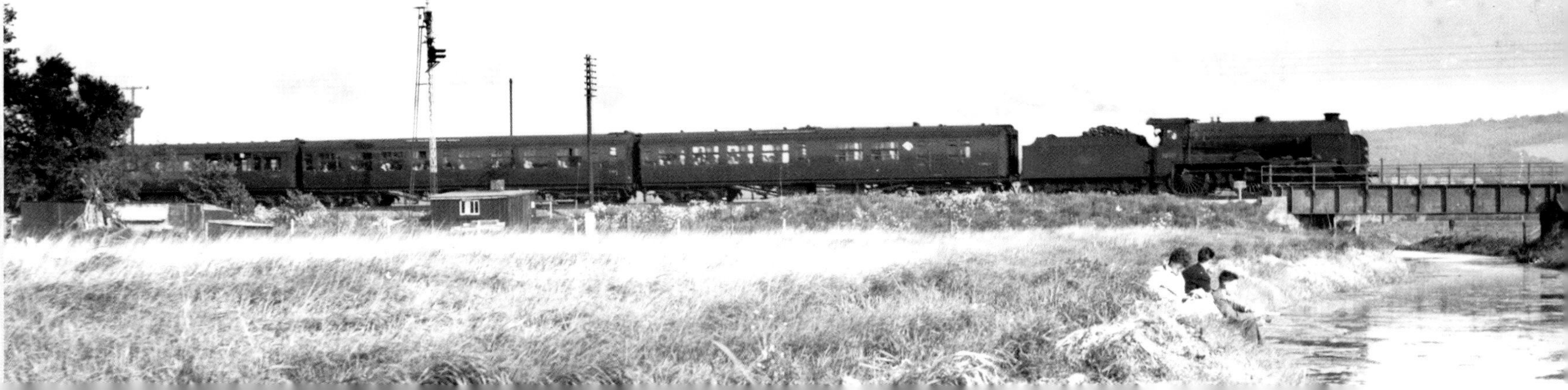

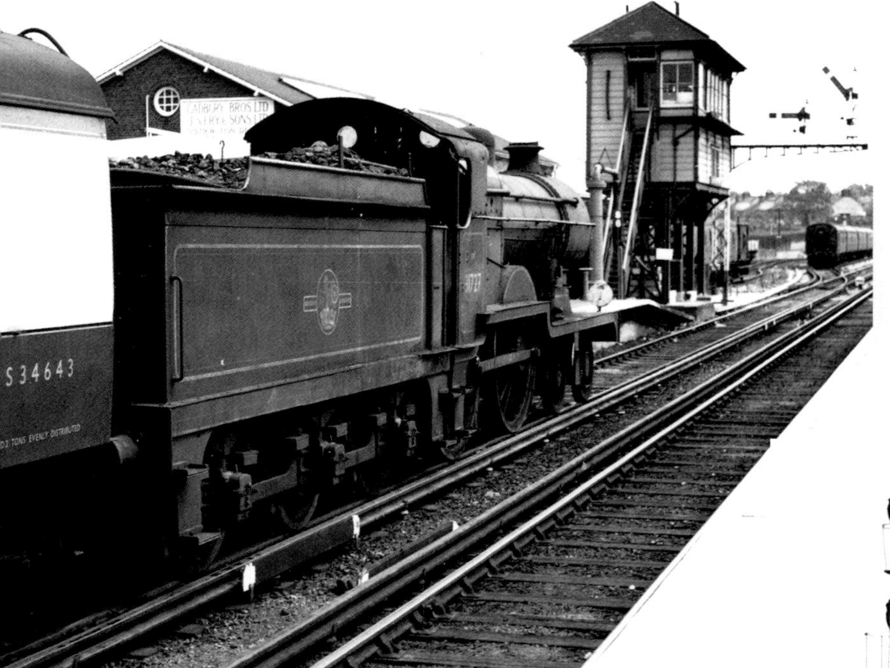

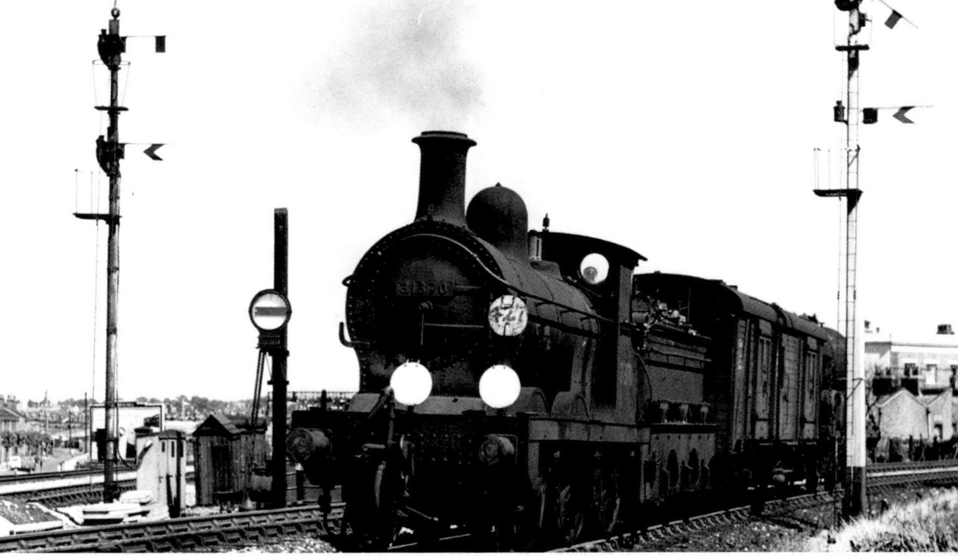

Left: **CANTERBURY EAST** 'D1' 4-4-0 No 31727 stands in Canterbury East station on 30 May 1959 at the head of a stopping train from Faversham to Dover. The signal box and signals had not been renewed.

Right: **LATCHMERE JUNCTION** 'O1' 0-6-0 No 31370 comes round from the 'Brighton' side of Clapham Junction onto the West London Extension line at Latchmere Junction with the Crystal Palace-Kensington Olympia milk empties train – a road trailer – on 27 June 1959.

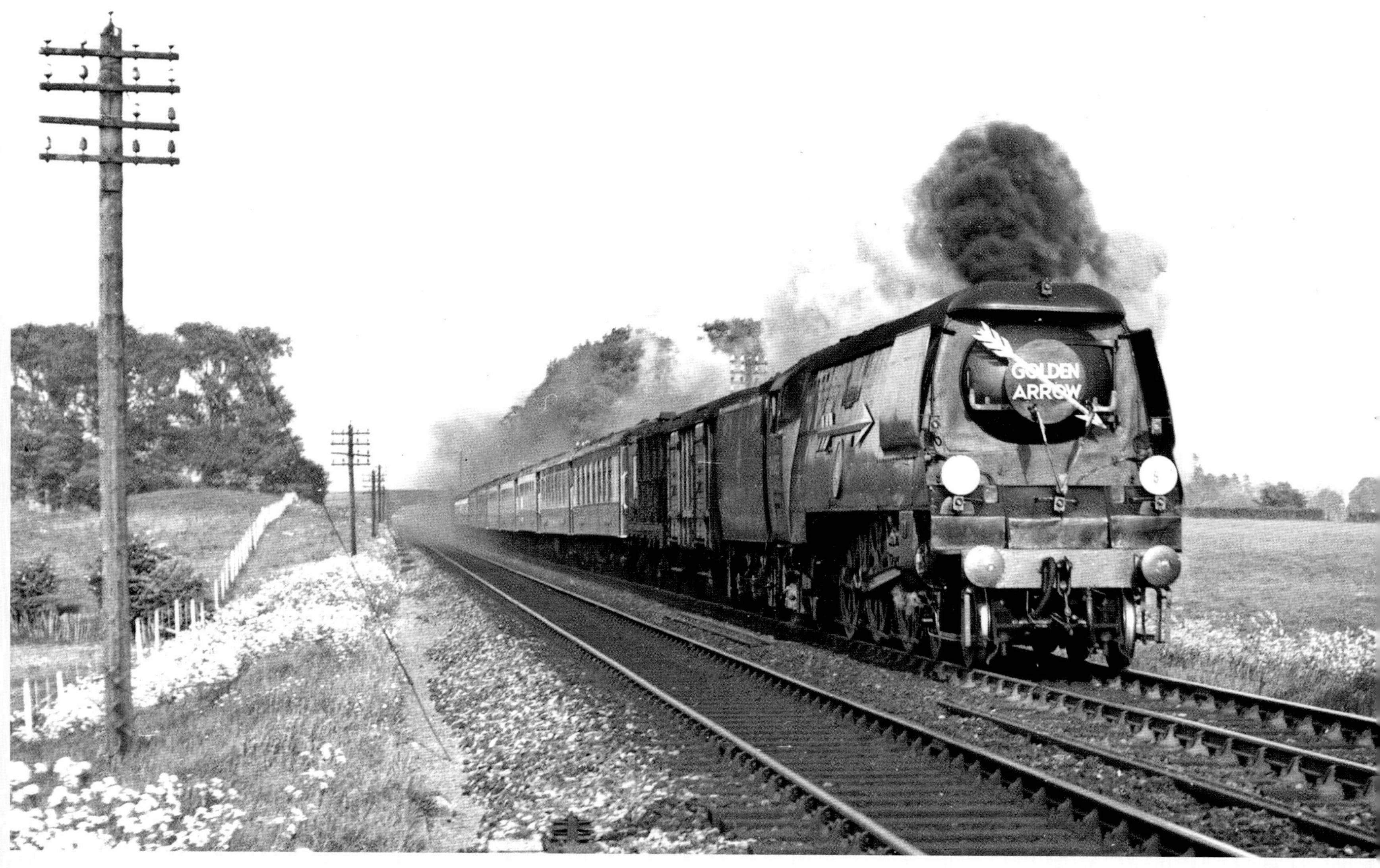

CHART 'Battle of Britain' 4-6-2 No 34085 *501 Squadron* is seen in full cry across the Kentish Weald near Chart signal box (just over 2 miles to the west of Ashford) with the up 'Golden Arrow' on 16 May 1959.

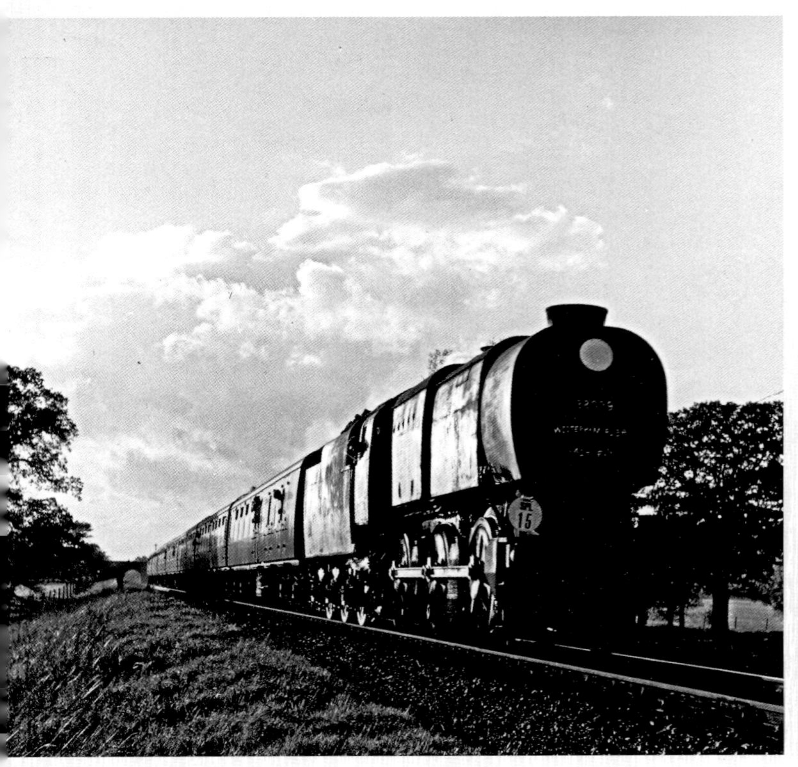

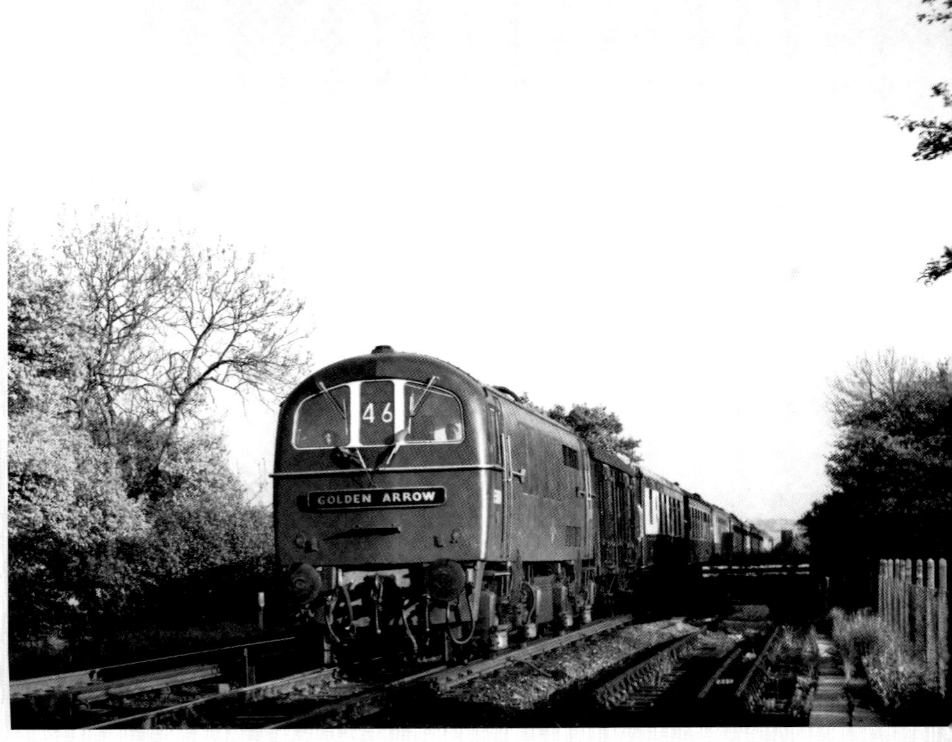

CHEVENING (WESTERHAM BRANCH) 0-6-0 'Q1' No 33029 heads the 4.23pm Westerham-Dunton Green on 28 October 1961 – the last day of service on the branch. The later trains were strengthened, and the 'Q1' and 'D1' No 31739 worked them in place of the usual 'H' 0-4-4 tank.

WEALD An E5XXX electric locomotive nears the site of Weald signal box north of Hildenborough station at the head of the up 'Golden Arrow' on 15 May 1965.

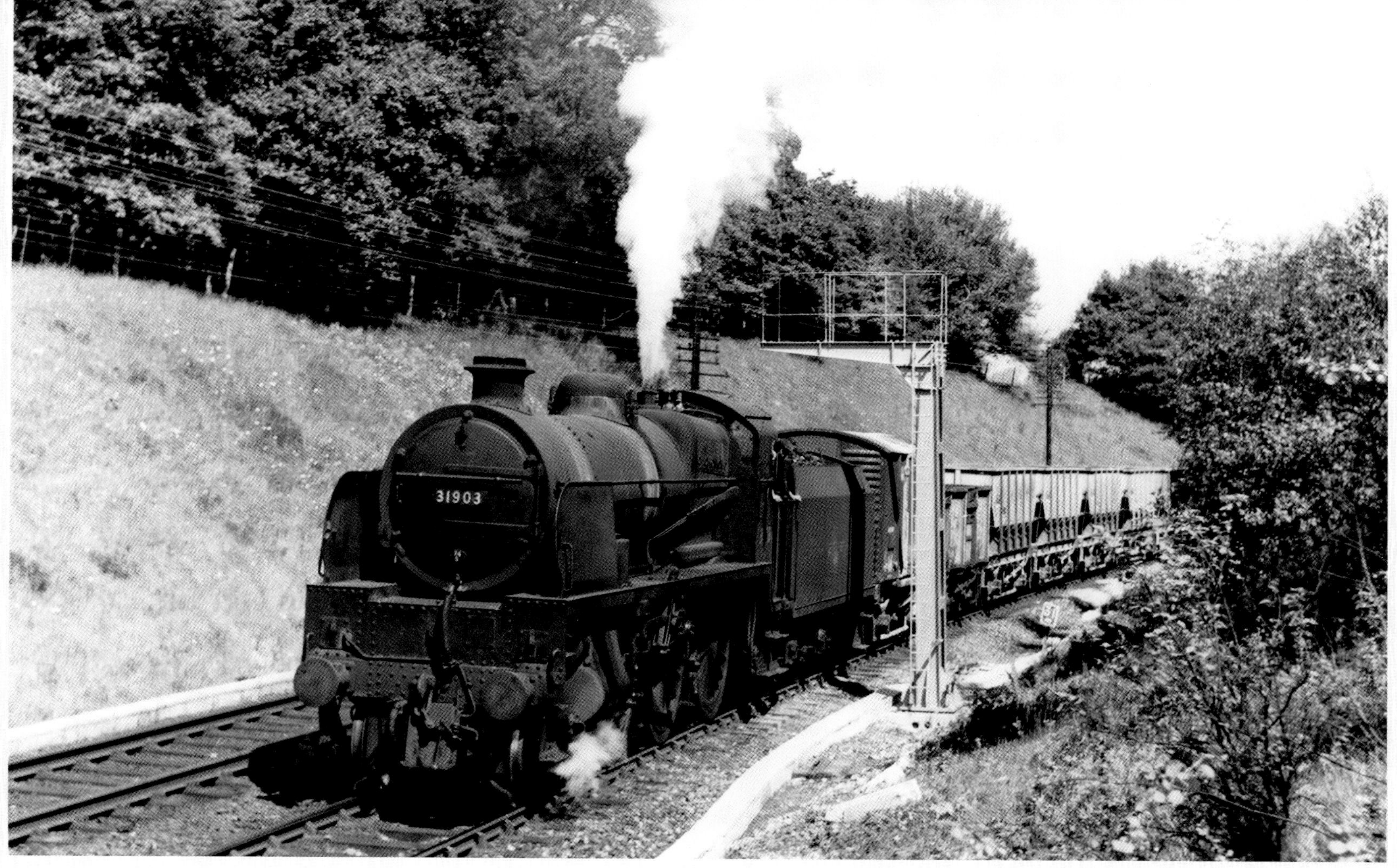

HIGH BROOMS 'U1' 2-6-0 No 31903 heads a train of empty gypsum hopper wagons near High Brooms station on the climb from Tonbridge to Tunbridge Wells on 12 May 1961. The wagons were being taken to the British Gypsum mine at Mountfield, south of Wadhurst, beyond which station the restricted loading gauge permitted the use of three-cylindered Maunsell 'Moguls', but not of two-cylindered. Hence the appearance of a larger-wheeled 'U1' in the absence of a more usual 'N1', rather than the apparently more likely 'N'.

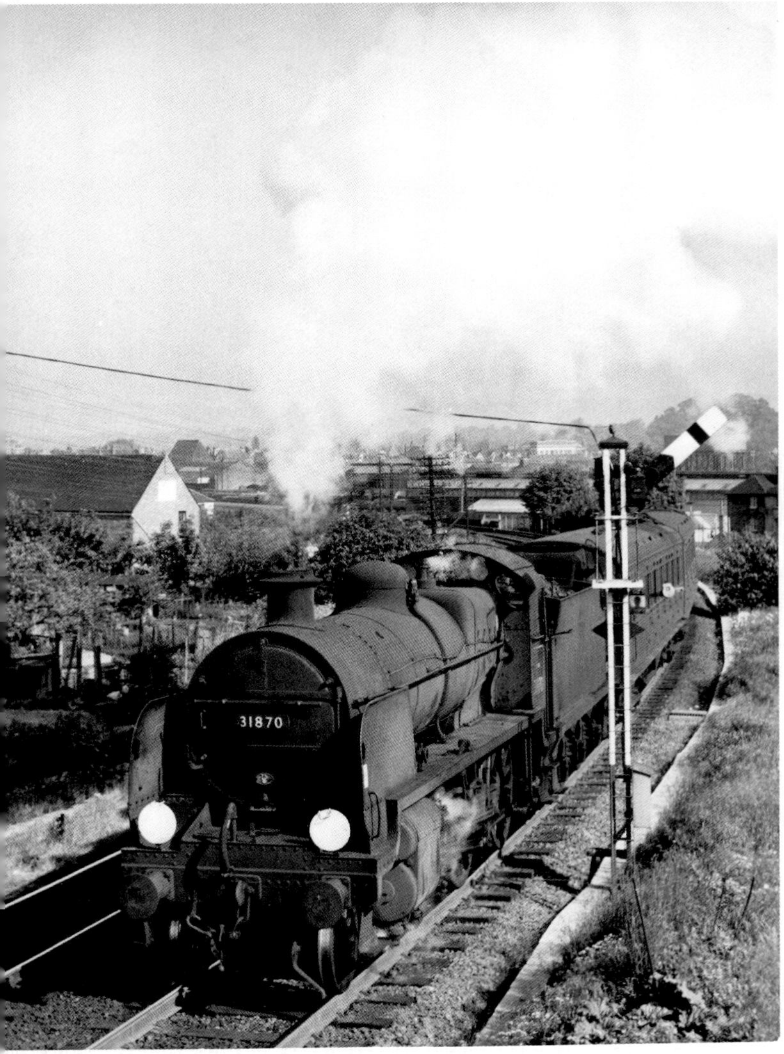

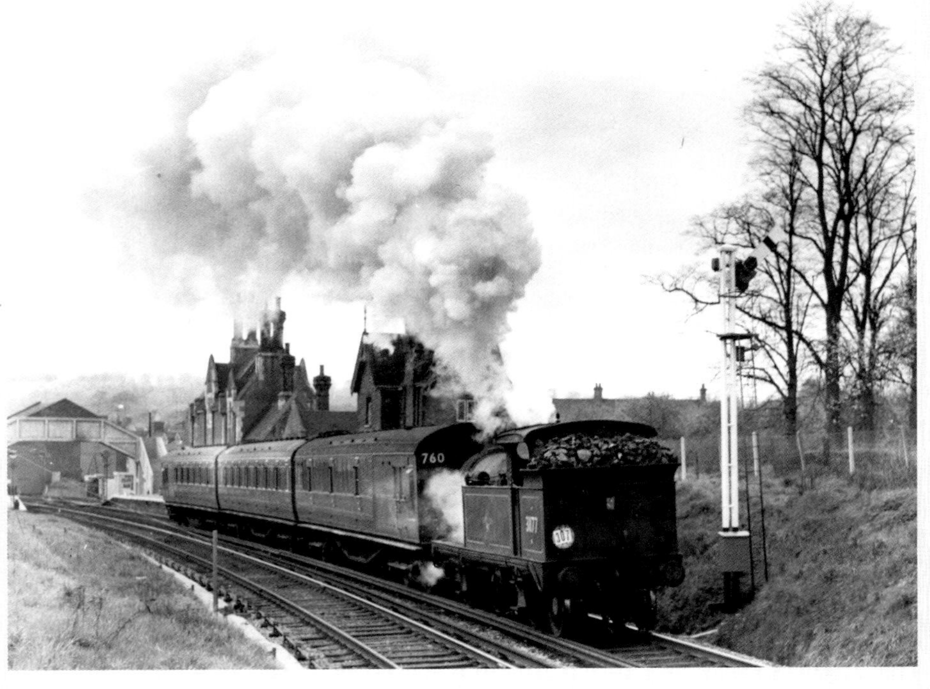

Above: **WATERINGBURY** 'H' 0-4-4T No 31177 makes an energetic restart from Wateringbury with the 2.00pm Sevenoaks-Maidstone West train on 8 April 1961. Preparations for the start of the electrified service in mid-June appear to be well-advanced.

Left: **TONBRIDGE** 'N' 2-6-0 No 31870 climbs the 1 in 47 gradient out of Tonbridge on the line to Hastings with the 9.05am train to Brighton on 12 May 1961. The yard of Tonbridge locomotive depot can be made out in the background.

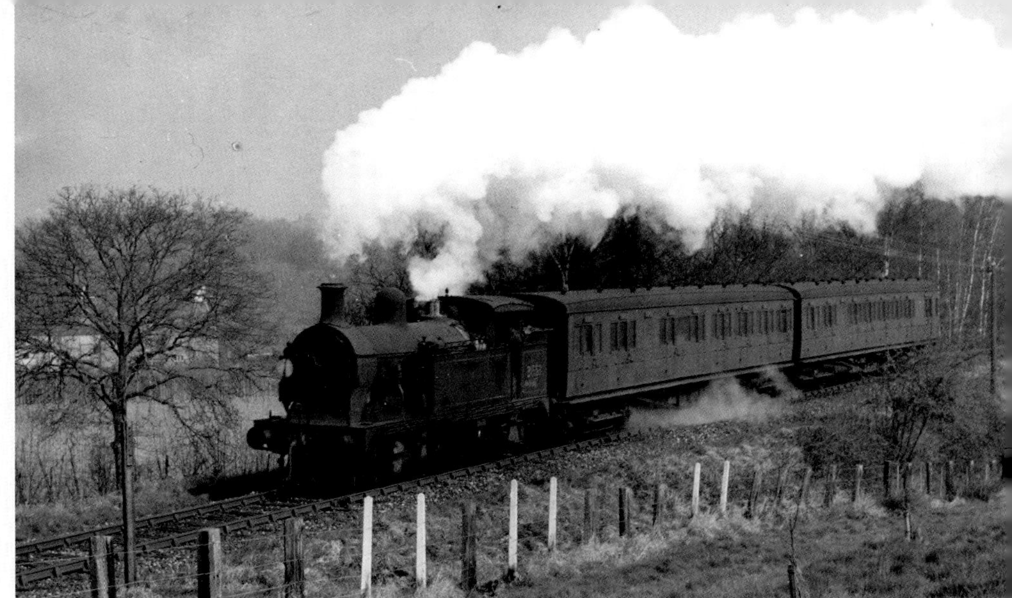

HORSMONDEN 'H' 0-4-4T No 31553 heads a Paddock Wood-Hawkhurst train near Horsmonden on 25 March 1961. An early-morning mist has practically lifted. The branch passenger service will survive only until June.

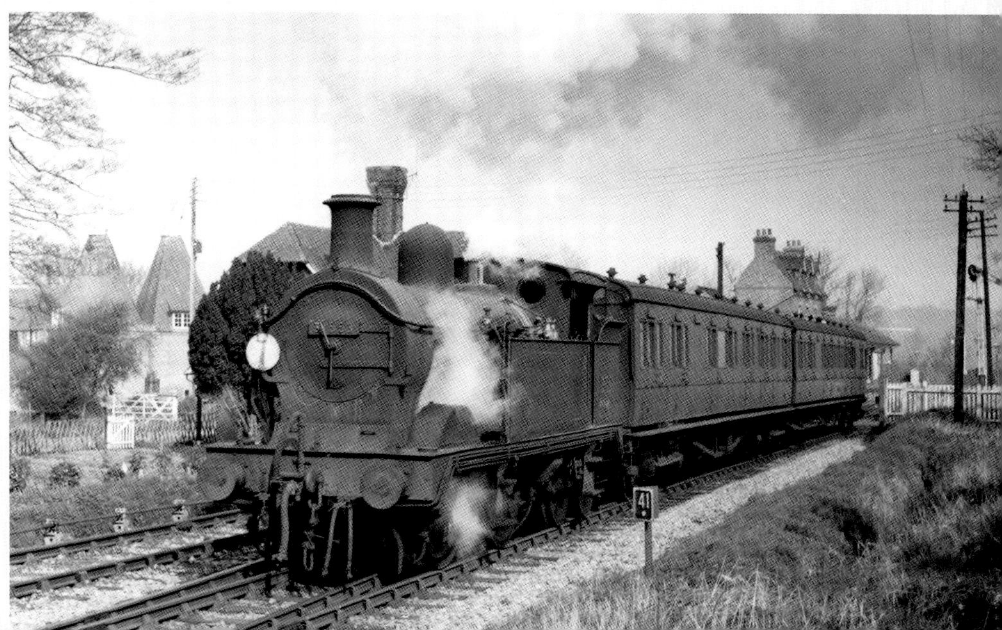

GOUDHURST No 31553 is seen again, this time as it restarts a later train from Goudhurst on 25 March 1961. The unusually tall station building can be seen above the rear coach, and a group of gentrified oast houses is about to disappear behind the locomotive. The quarter milepost shows the distance from Charing Cross.

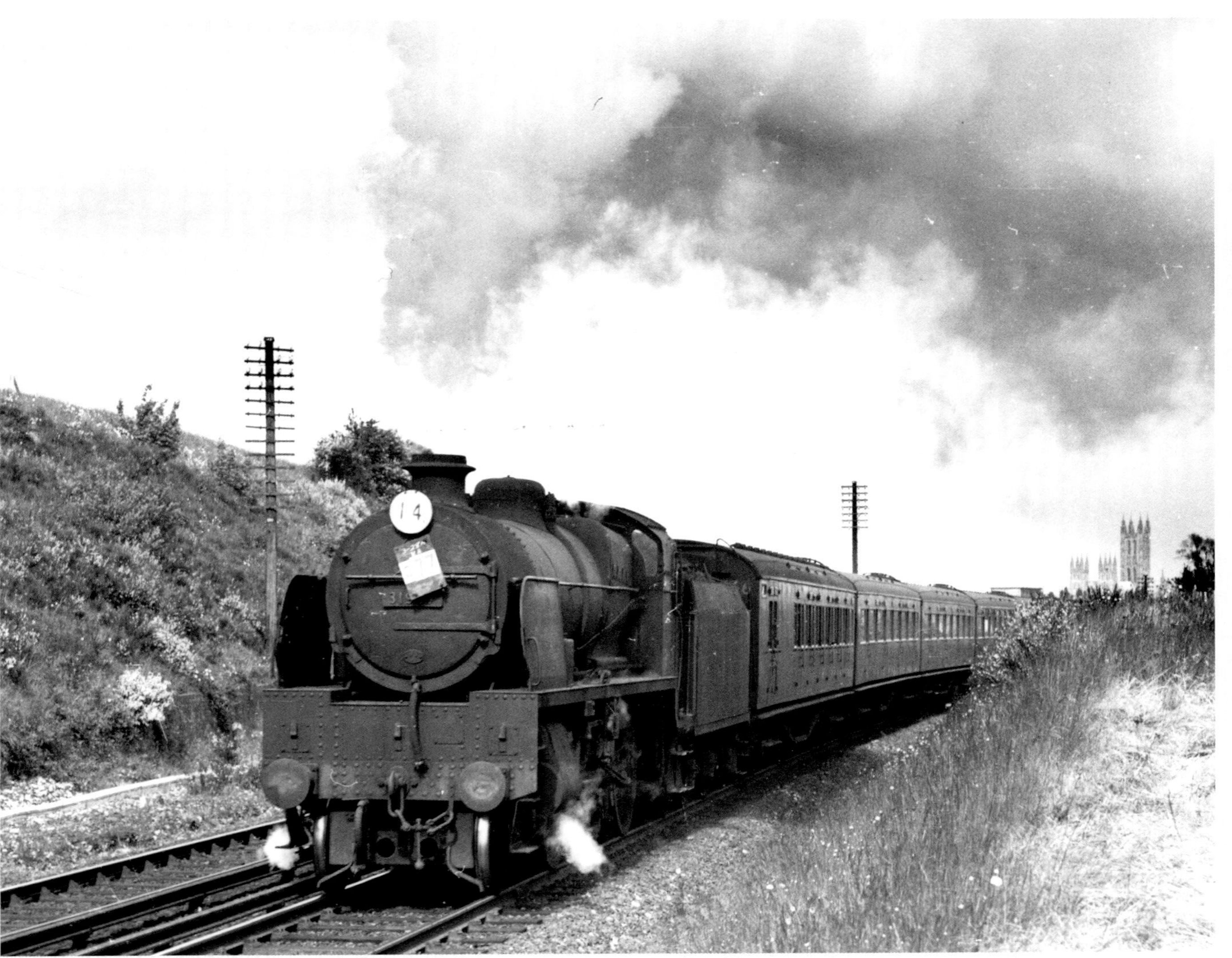

CANTERBURY WEST 'U1' 2-6-0 No 31907 is seen soon after leaving Canterbury West on 18 May 1959 with the 3.28pm train from Ramsgate to Cannon Street. This train ran over the original main line from Tonbridge via Redhill. The towers of Canterbury Cathedral can be seen on the right-hand side.

Right: **FOLKESTONE WARREN** 'N15' 4-6-0 No 30782 *Sir Brian* leads the LCGB 'Kentish Venturer Rail Tour' through Folkestone Warren on 25 February 1962. No 30782 headed the train from London to Ashford via Herne Bay and Dover.

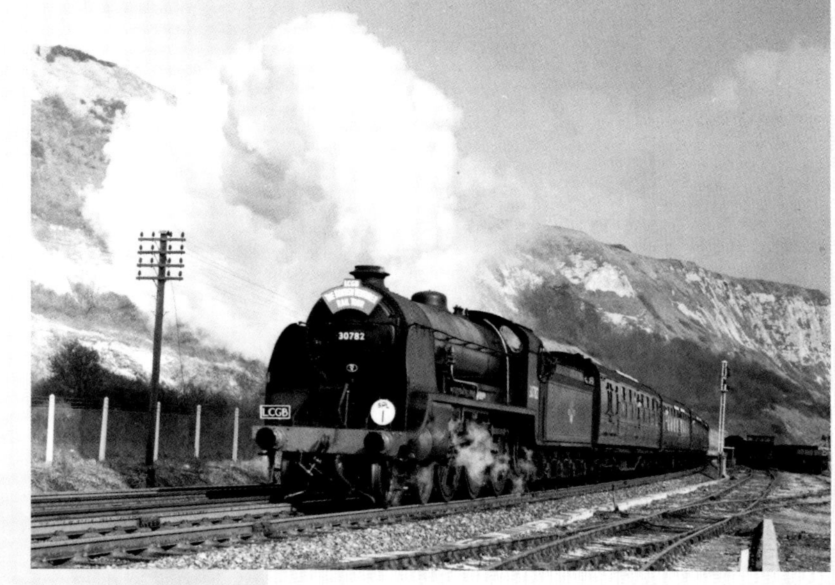

Left: **FOLKESTONE** 'R1' 0-6-0Ts Nos 31340, 31107 and 31174 cross Folkestone harbour and head into the climb to Folkestone Junction on 18 October 1958. At the Junction the train (the up Calais boat train) will be reversed, then leave for London. There was no significance in the relative sizes of the locomotives' dome covers.

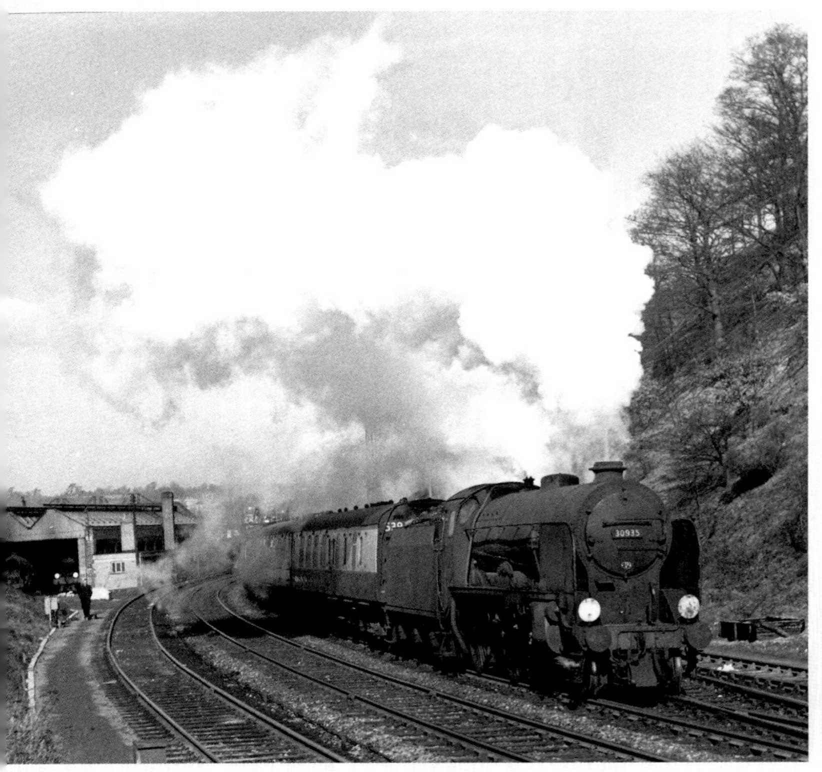

REDHILL 'V' 4-4-0 No 30935 *Sevenoaks* accelerates a Charing Cross-Ramsgate train away from the speed restriction over the junction at Redhill on 28 February 1960. The train had been diverted to the 'old' main line because of engineering works connected with Phase II of the Kent Coast electrification. An 'S15' 4-6-0 and 'D1' 4-4-0 No 31247 can be seen in the locomotive shed on the left.

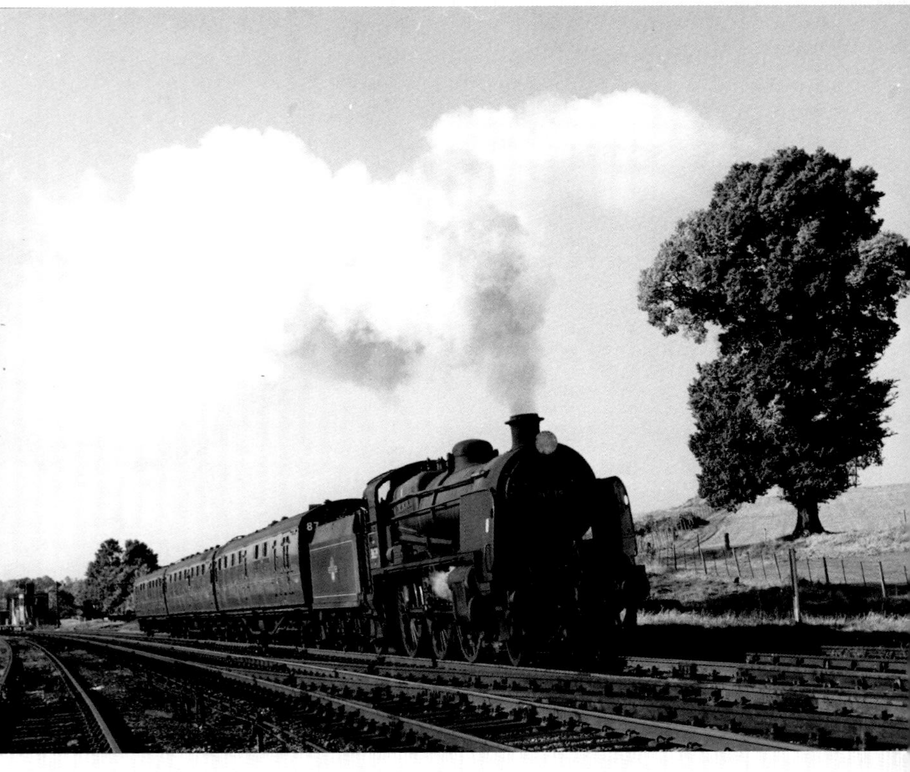

GOMSHALL 'U' 2-6-0 No 31639 leaves Gomshall at the head of the 9.03am Reading-Redhill train on 17 October 1964.

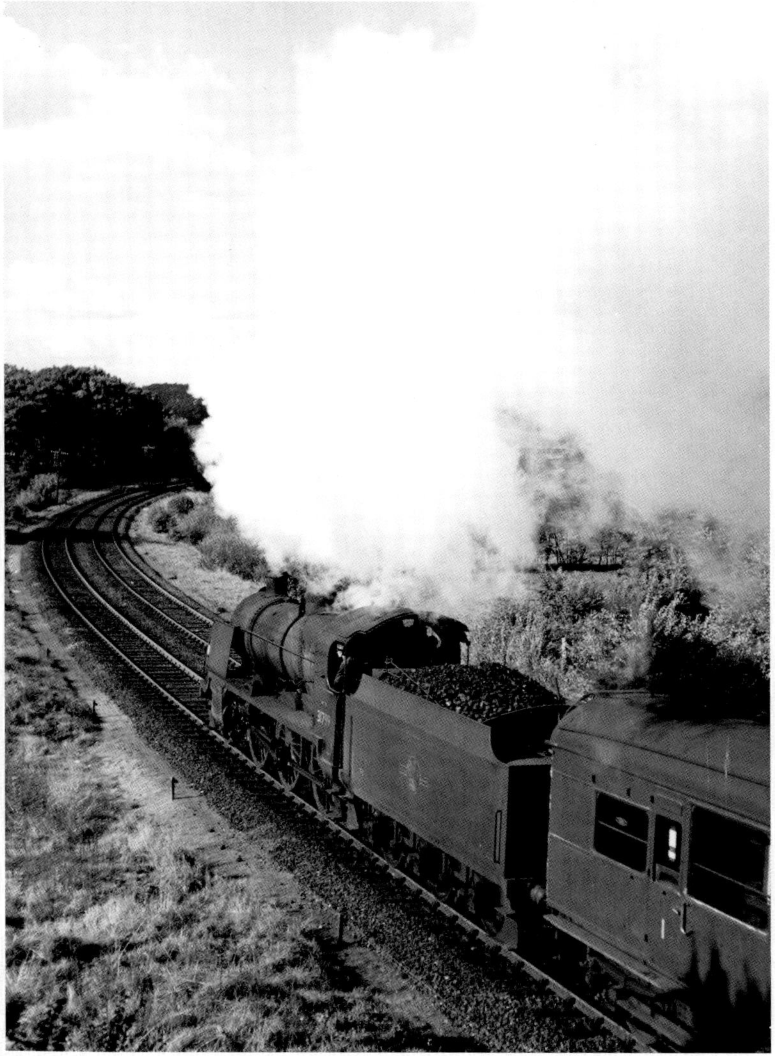

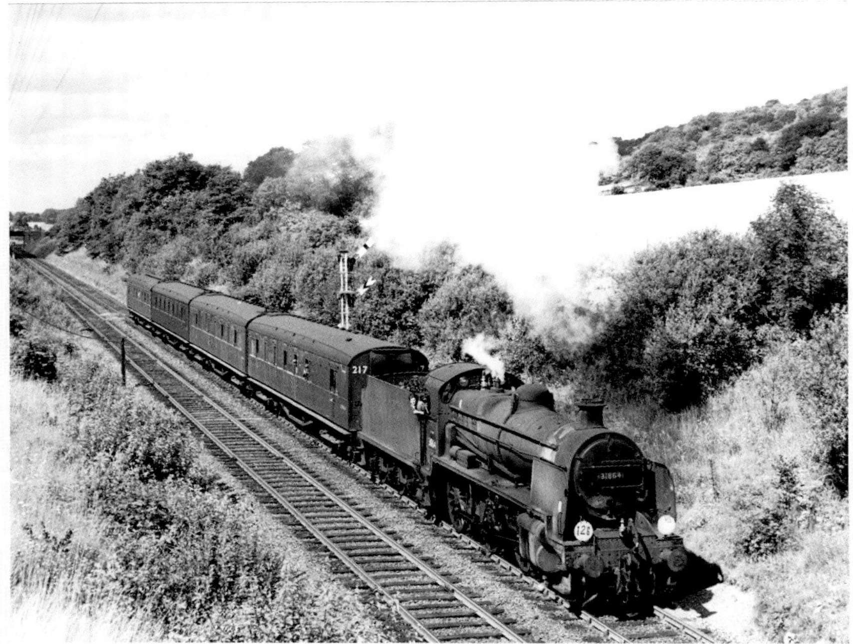

Above: **GOMSHALL** 'N' 2-6-0 No 31864 heads the 9.45am Reading-Redhill train along the foot of the North Downs on 5 August 1962. This photograph was taken about a mile east of Gomshall station.

Left: **SHALFORD** 'U' 2-6-0 No 31799 leaves Shalford with the 12.32pm Redhill-Reading train on 17 October 1964. Half a mile round the curve it will join the Portsmouth Direct line for the passage of Guildford.

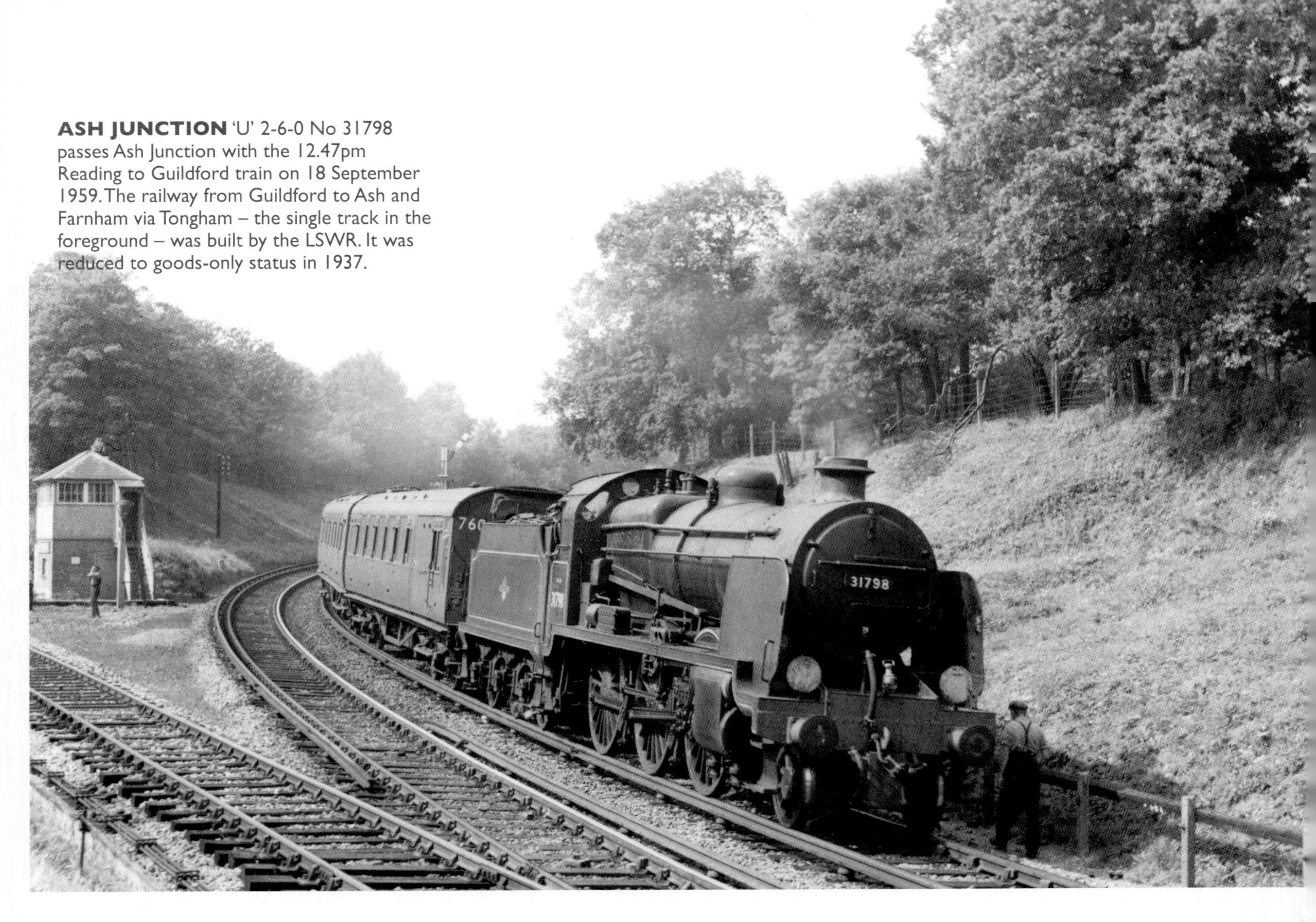

ASH JUNCTION 'U' 2-6-0 No 31798 passes Ash Junction with the 12.47pm Reading to Guildford train on 18 September 1959. The railway from Guildford to Ash and Farnham via Tongham – the single track in the foreground – was built by the LSWR. It was reduced to goods-only status in 1937.

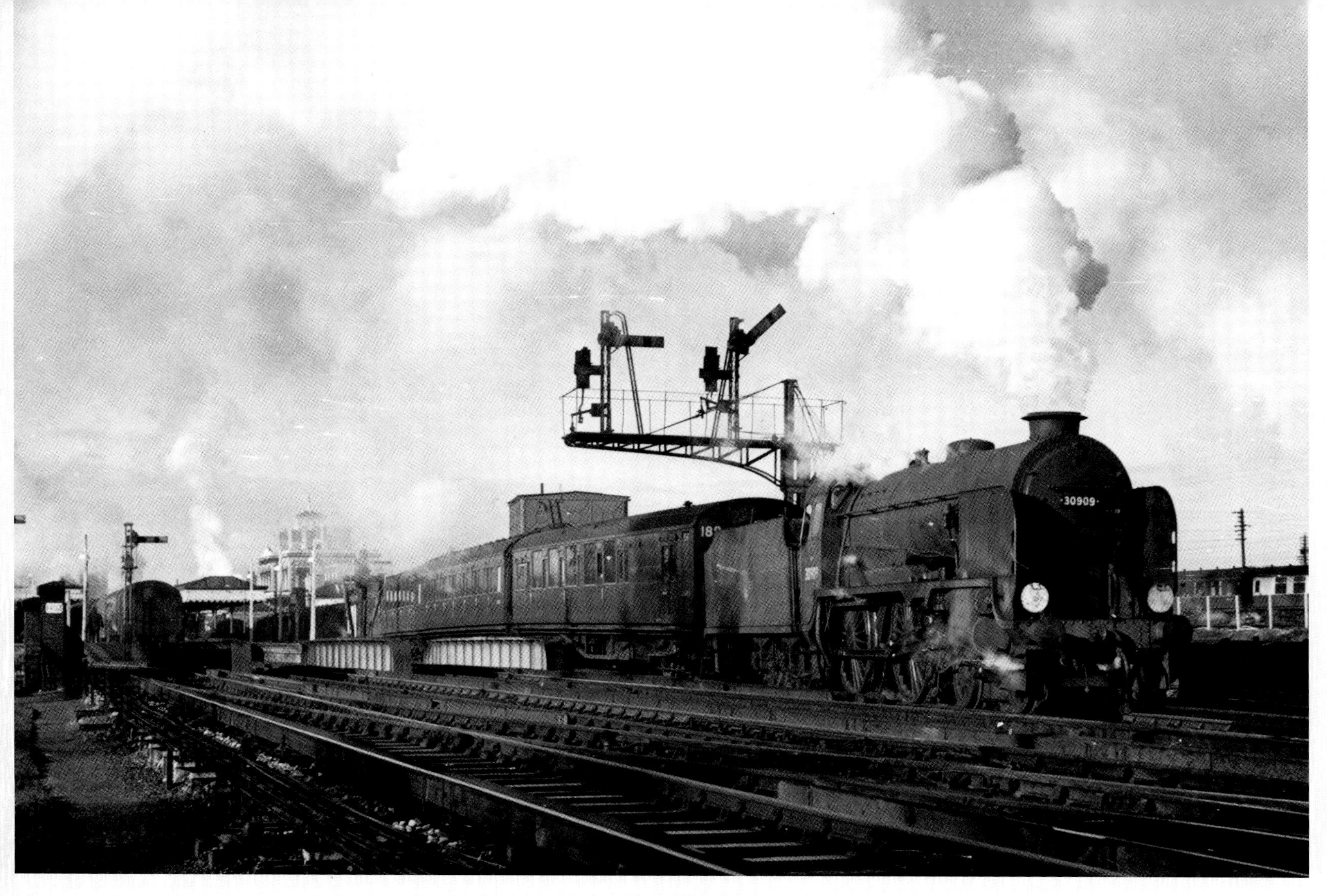

READING SOUTH 'V' 4-4-0 No 30909 *St Pauls* leaves Reading South on 2 January 1959 with the 11.05am train to Redhill.

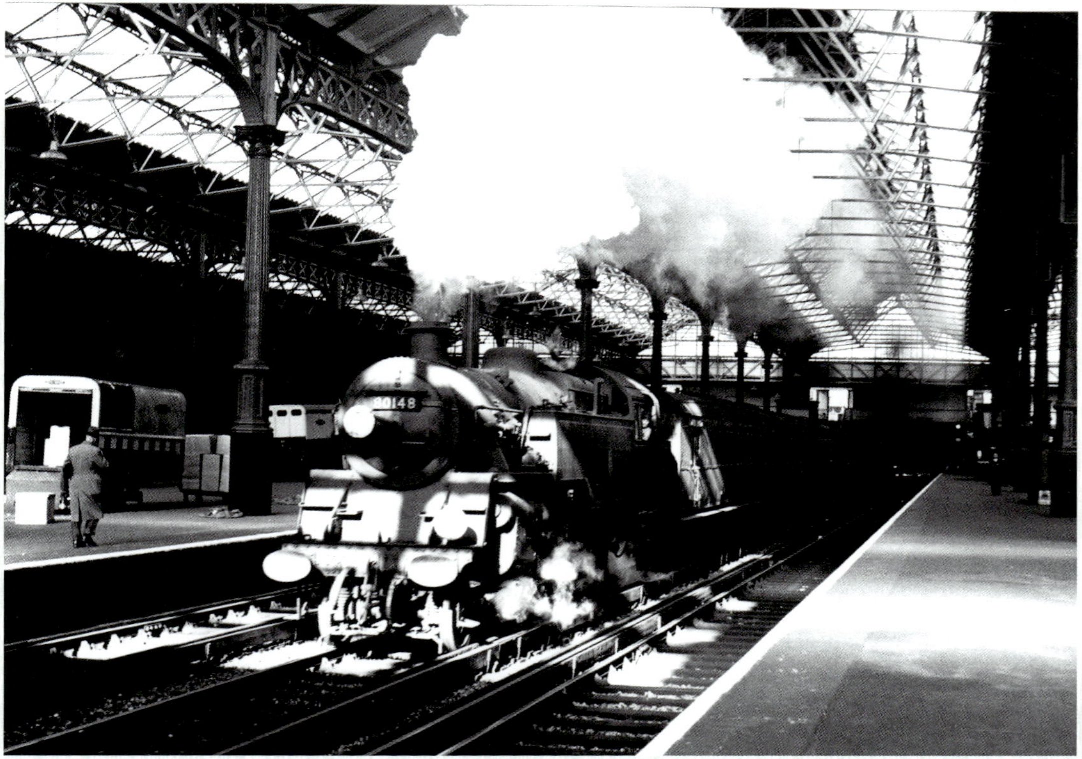

Above: **LONDON VICTORIA** Inside the train shed on the Brighton side of Victoria station, 4MT 2-6-4T No 80148 accelerates the 1.08pm train to Tunbridge Wells West on 31 October 1958. Use of the central 'escape' line permitted two separate trains in the same platform, at the north and south ends respectively.

Below: **GATWICK** 4-4-0 'D' No 31737 canters down the Brighton main line with the Hastings portion of the Birkenhead-South Coast through train in September 1956. The timetable called for an average speed of about 40mph between Redhill and Brighton, which was fortunate as my then camera had a shutter speed of 1/100 second so that the whole train had to be panned.

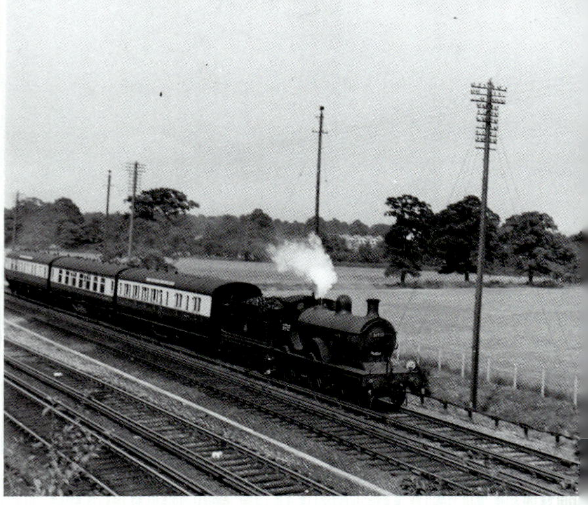

GATWICK AIRPORT (OLD) On a warm July evening 'K' 2-6-0 No 32352 ambles gently home to Three Bridges with a train of material from the day's PWR activities on 31 July 1961. The pre-war Gatwick Airport station, seen in the background, was by this time disused. When built in 1935 it was connected to the then airport terminal by a pedestrian tunnel.

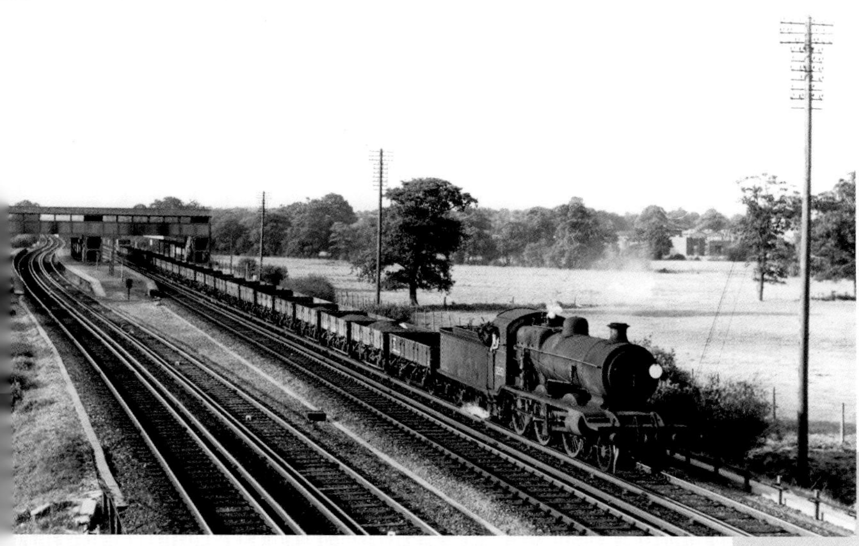

THREE BRIDGES Just before 7.00am, 'H2' 4-4-2 No 32424 *Beachy Head* pulls out of Three Bridges at the head of the 5.32am London Bridge-Brighton fish vans on 25 July 1957. The locomotive was just out of store, and this was a trial run. The new 'Odeon' signal box was the only one on the Southern to reach five bays in length.

BALCOMBE 'U1' 2-6-0 No 31890 passes Balcombe station while hauling the Northampton-Brighton through train on 30 July 1961. The former siding behind the signal box was equipped with catenary during the Second World War in order to test the overhead equipment (for use in marshalling yards) of the Bulleid/Raworth electric locomotives.

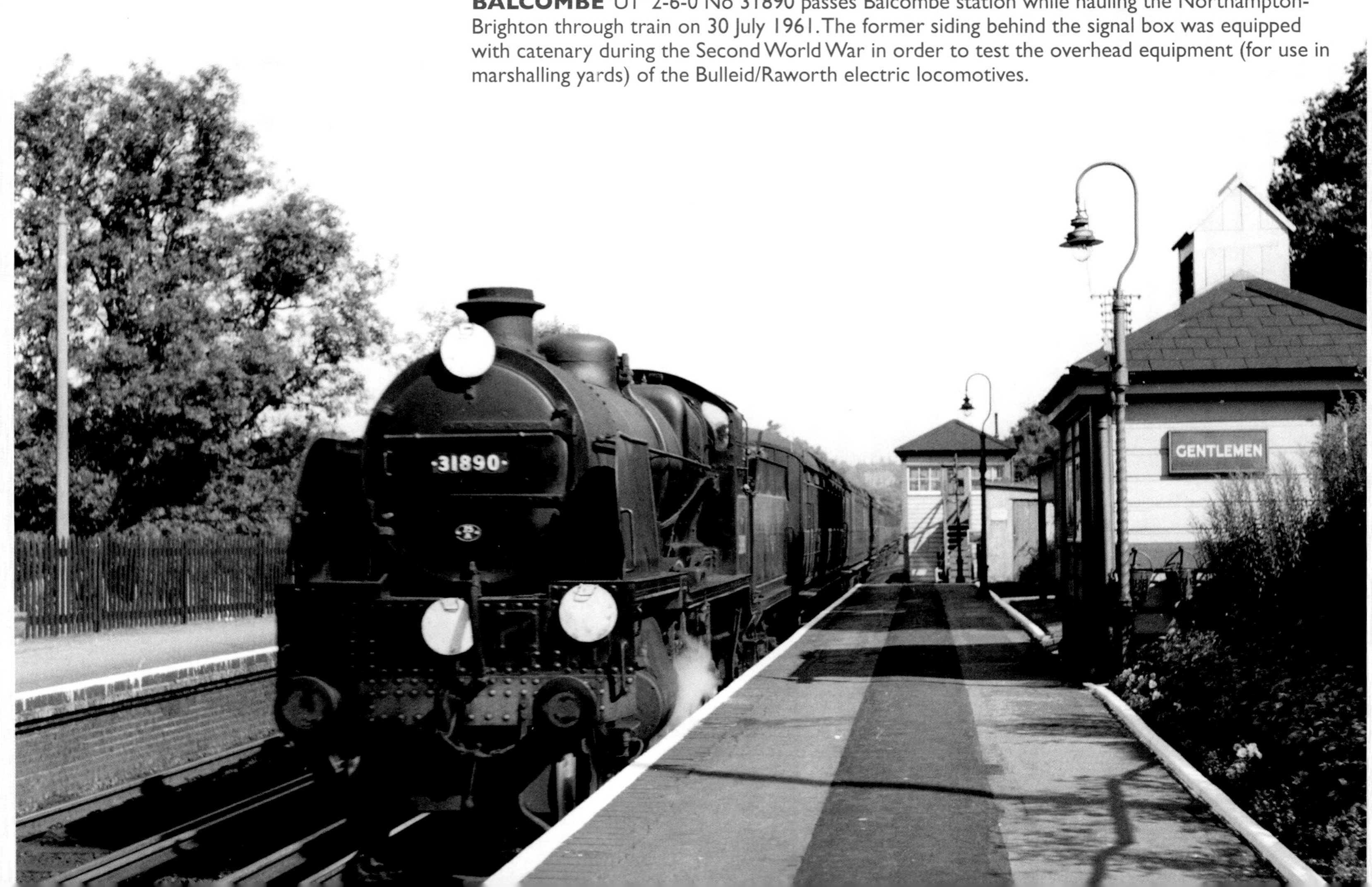

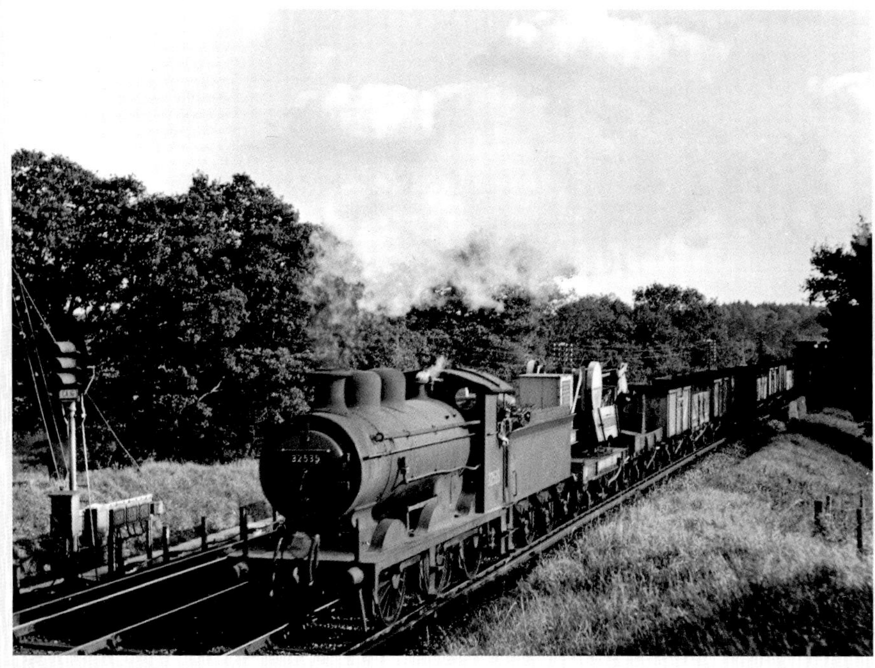

OUSE VALLEY VIADUCT 'C2X' 0-6-0 No 32535 comes off the viaduct (two of the north-end pavilions can be seen above the rear of the train) with the 5.02pm Haywards Heath-Three Bridges goods train on 26 September 1958.

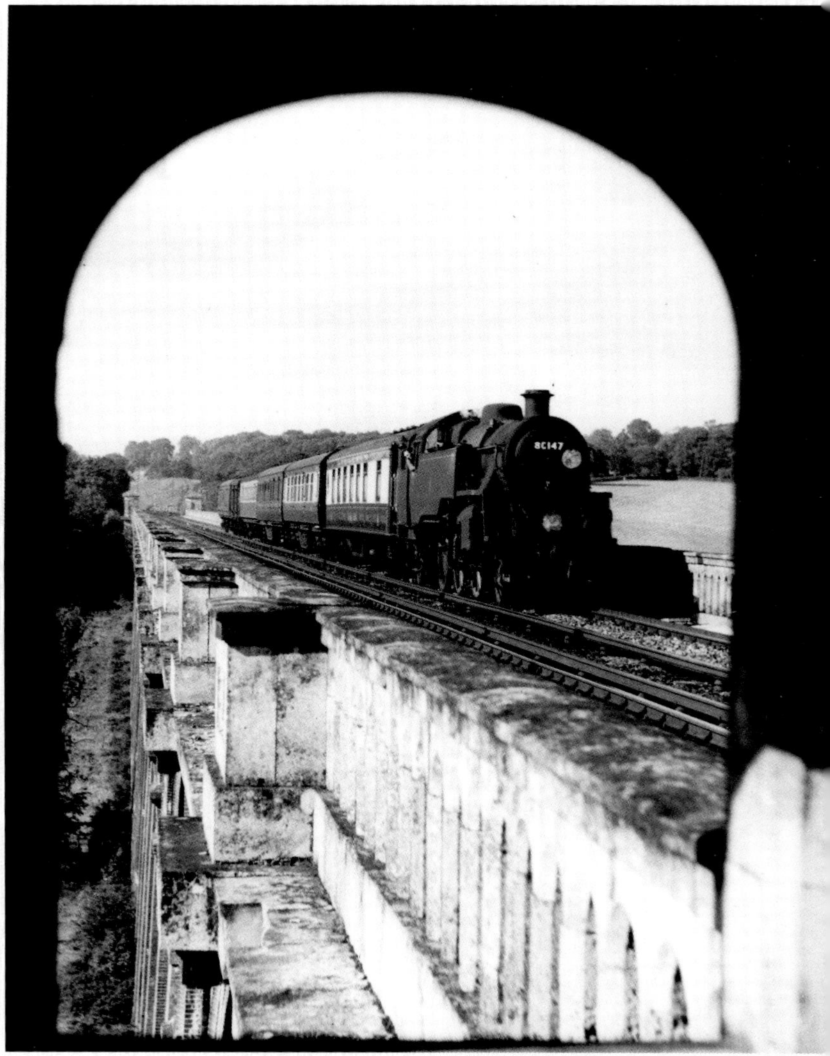

OUSE VALLEY VIADUCT The 1.02pm London Bridge-Brighton afternoon van train, with empty coaching stock (ECS) for Preston Park and Lancing Works, crosses the viaduct on 24 September 1958. The locomotive, 4MT 2-6-4T No 80147 is coasting, as was normal. Probably the Copyhold Junction distant signal at the north end of the viaduct was 'on'.

Right: **OUSE VALLEY VIADUCT** 'T9' 4-4-0 restored as LSWR No 120 heads a Bluebell Railway excursion across the viaduct on 21 October 1962. The 'T9' worked the train to and from Haywards Heath, from where a pair of Bluebell locomotives headed it to Horsted Keynes, and back again after a trip to Sheffield Park.

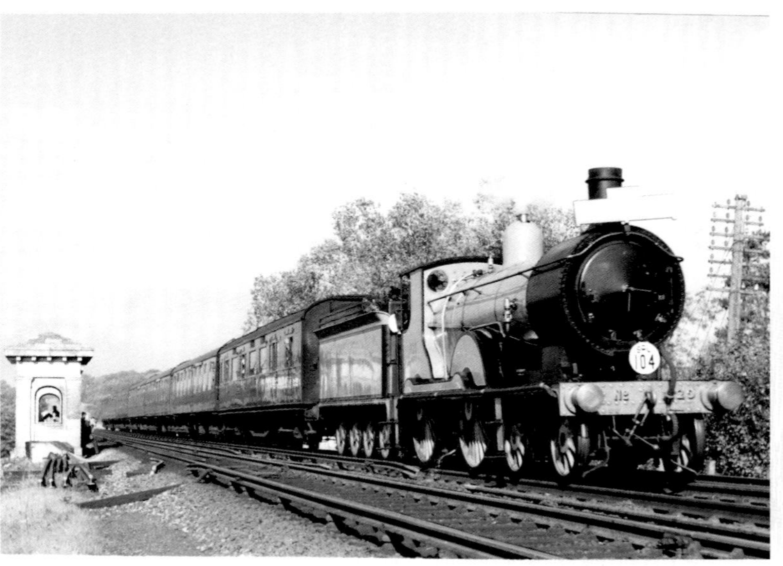

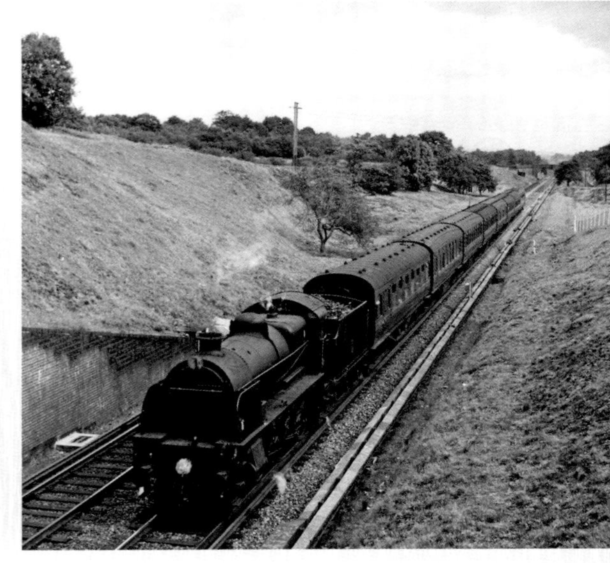

Right: **OUSE VALLEY VIADUCT** The 3.00pm Victoria-Brighton 'Brighton Belle' comes off the viaduct on 6 October 1958.

Top right: **CLAYTON TUNNEL** 'N1' 2-6-0 No 31876 nears Clayton Tunnel with the Birmingham New Street-Hastings through train on 30 July 1961.

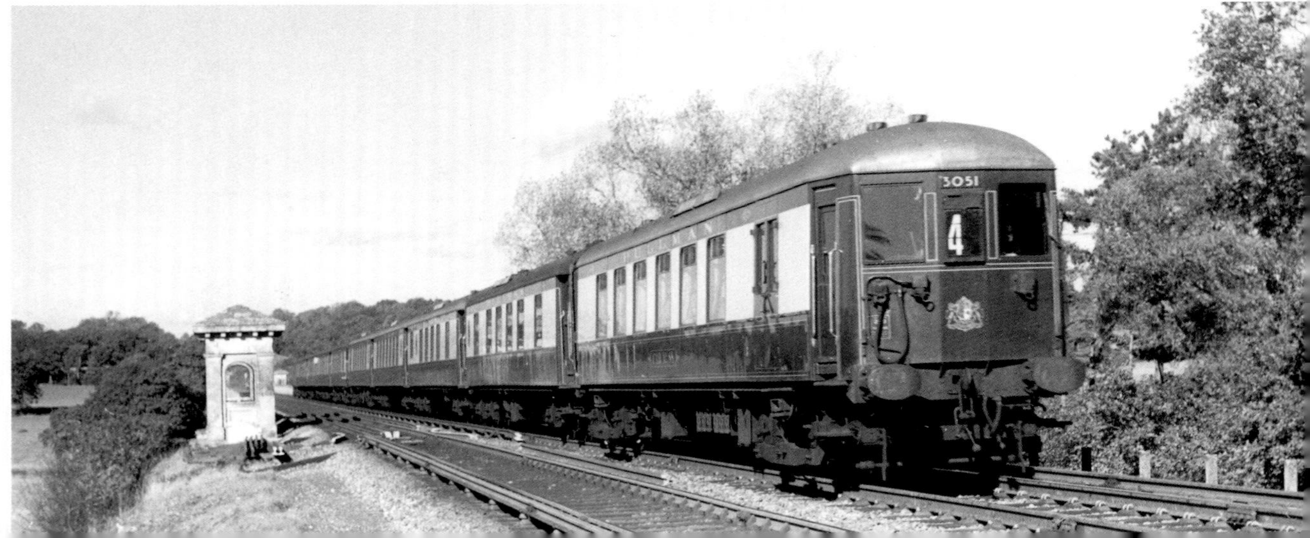

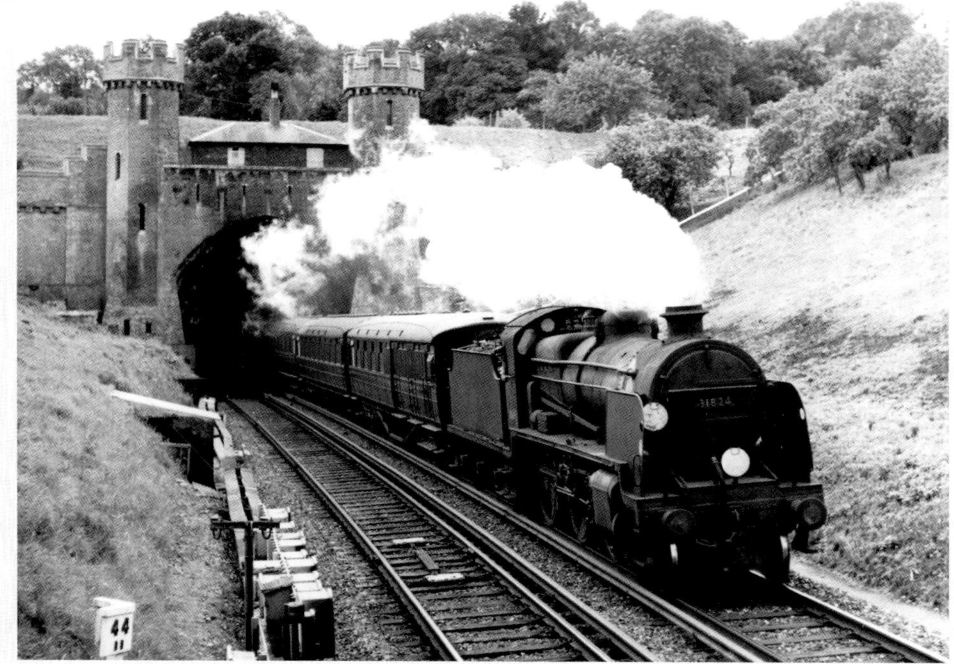

CLAYTON TUNNEL 'N' 2-6-0 No 31824 emerges from the tunnel at the head of a train of Eastern Region ECS on 30 July 1961. The cottage above the entrance was clearly inhabited, as it still is.

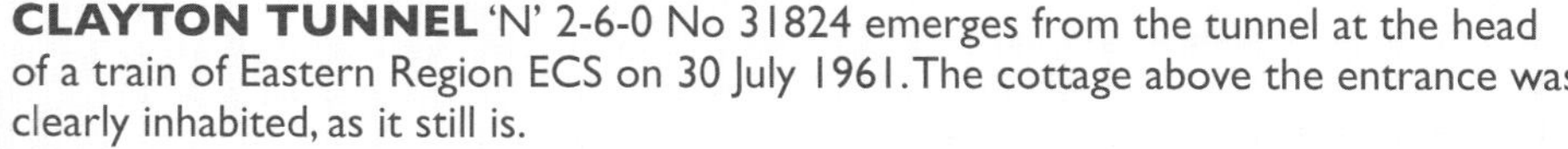

THREE BRIDGES It's 10.08am on Sunday 26 May 1963, and 'H' 0-4-4T No 31263 (now preserved on the Bluebell Railway) erupts from the tunnel-like overall roof of its bay with the train to East Grinstead. The bay and its roof dated back to the opening of the branch line in 1855. The building on the right masks the original station entrance of 1840, which was moved to its present position in 1908 as part of the incomplete rebuilding and realignment of the station.

THREE BRIDGES On a Sunday evening in January 1961 'H' 0-4-4T No 31005 stands in the East Grinstead bay – Platform 6 – at Three Bridges waiting for departure. The platform had been lengthened for the 1933 electrification, so that its other face onto the Down Main would accommodate 12-car trains.

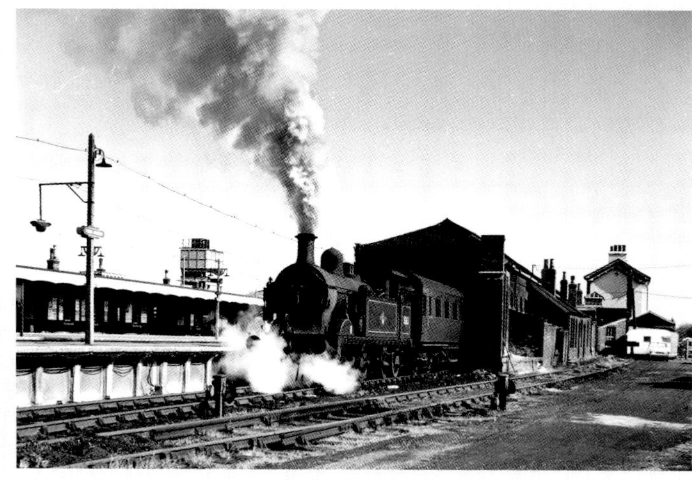

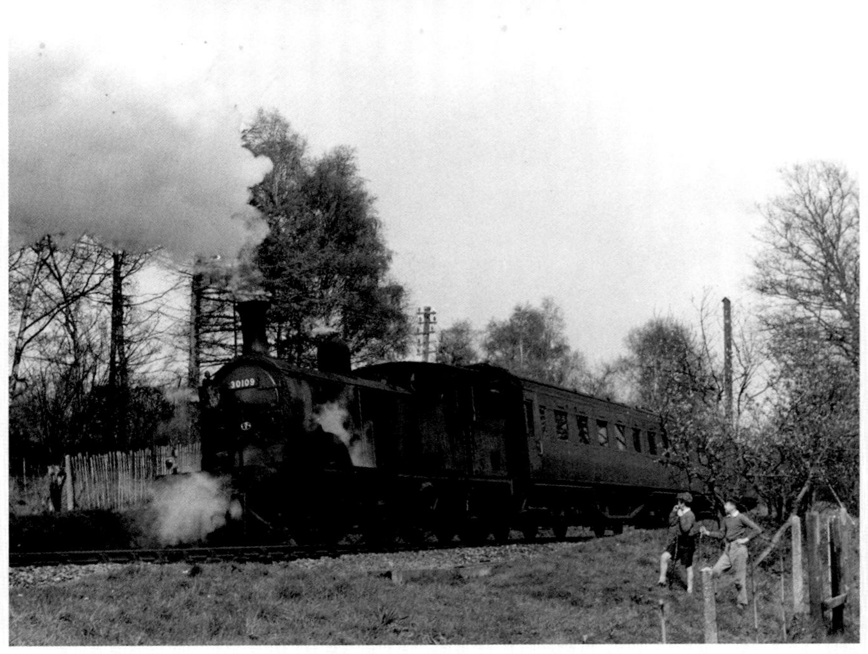

THREE BRIDGES On 5 February 1960 'M7' 0-4-4T No 30109 propels the 2.51pm to East Grinstead up the 1 in 88 gradient out of Three Bridges and past a couple of appreciative lads.

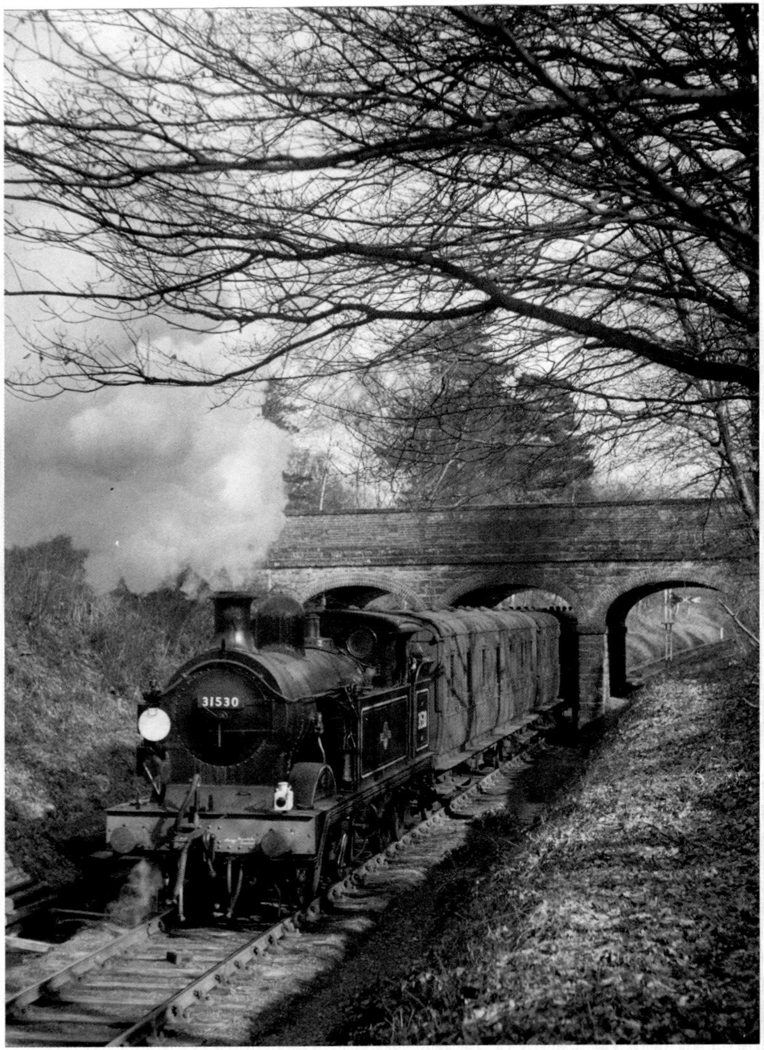

THREE BRIDGES The 1.08pm Three Bridges-East Grinstead train is propelled through the cutting at Worth, 1 mile on its way, by 'H' 0-4-4T No 31530 on 21 February 1960.

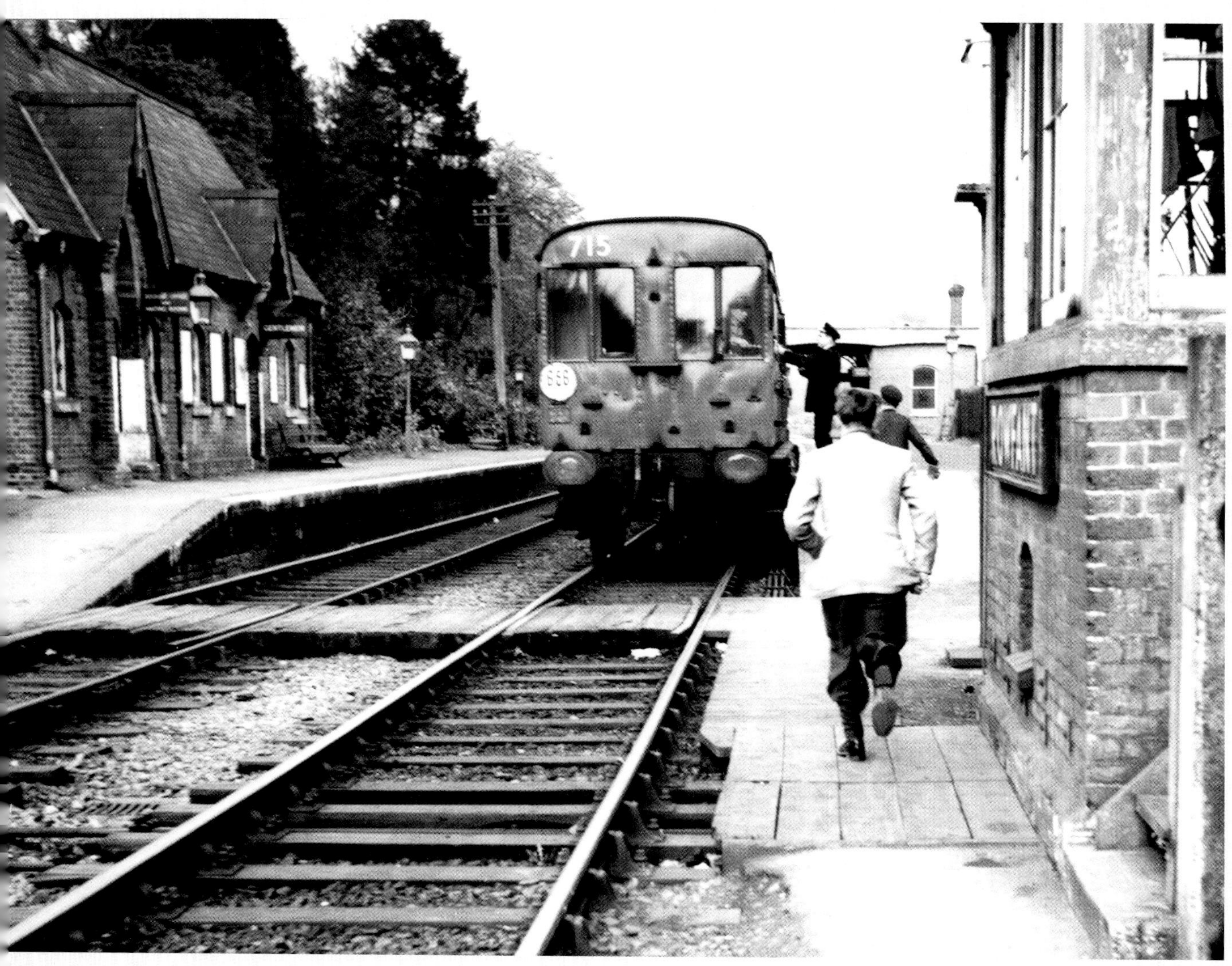

ROWFANT Activity as the 4.27pm East Grinstead-Three Bridges calls there on 12 April 1957. A latecomer, having dumped his bicycle, runs to board the train. The porter-signalman carries a heavy package to the guard's van, while the guard and driver have a discussion as the staff for the section to Three Bridges is handed over.

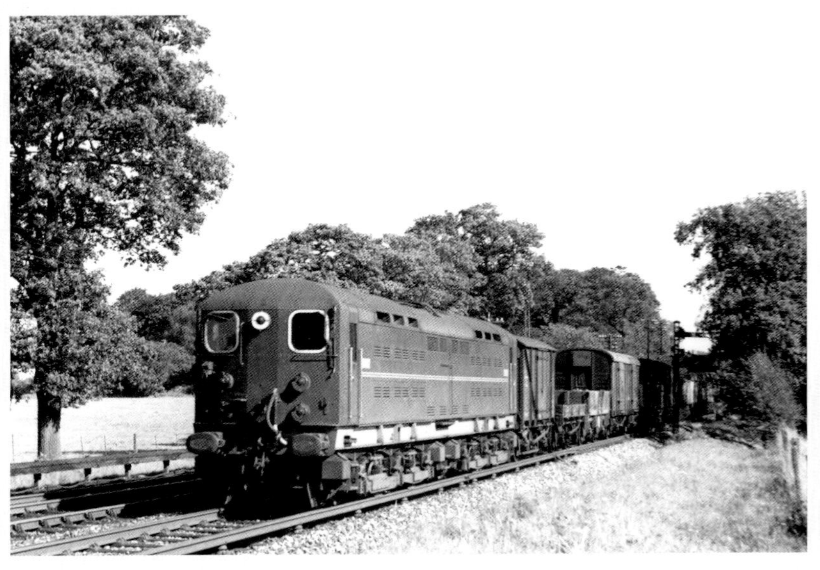

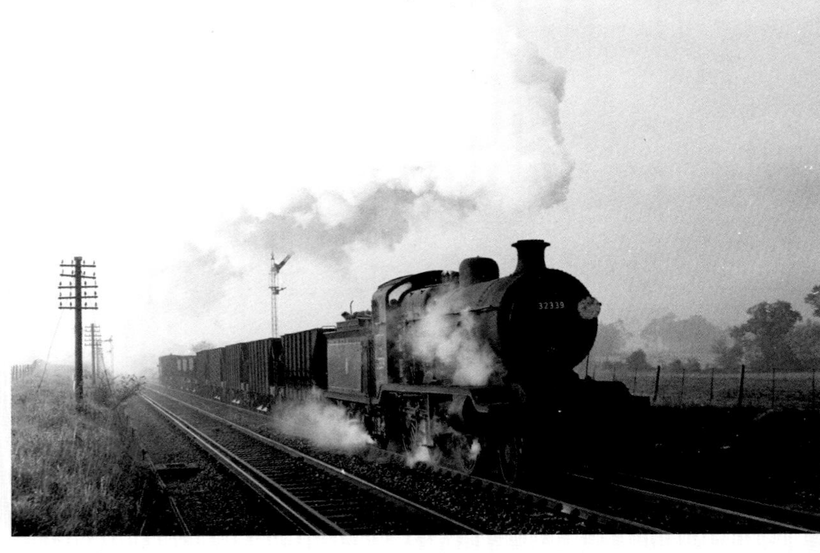

Above: **THREE BRIDGES** Bulleid/Raworth electric locomotive No 20002 passes the distant signal for Crawley level crossing at the head of the 1.19pm Three Bridges-Chichester goods train on 26 September 1958.

Above right: **FAYGATE** 'K' 2-6-0 No 32339 approaches Faygate with the 5.30am Salisbury-Three Bridges ballast train on a misty 14 November 1958.

Right: **CHRIST'S HOSPITAL** A Reading South-Brighton excursion train runs through the Guildford branch platforms at Christ's Hospital station on 6 June 1960. As was by then customary, it is headed by an 0-6-0 'Q1', in this case No 33039. It will continue to Horsham, the next station, where a turnover locomotive, probably a 'K' 2-6-0, will be provided to take the train to Brighton via Steyning.

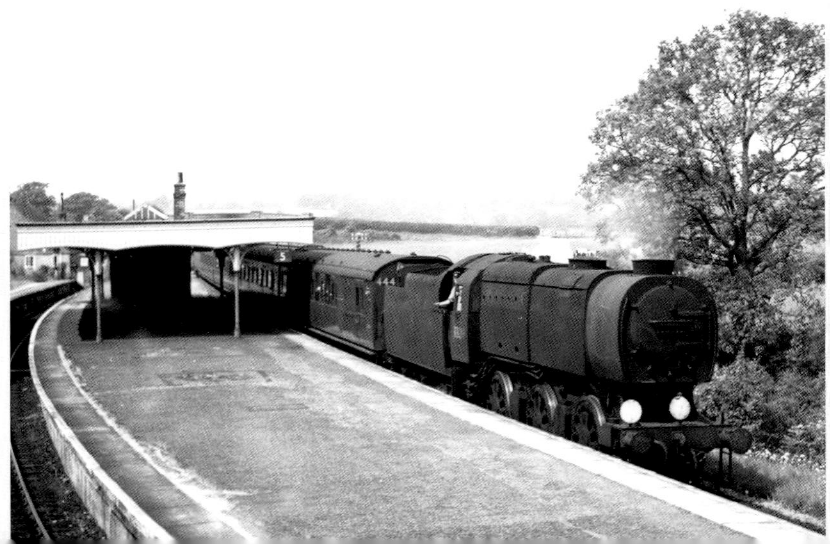

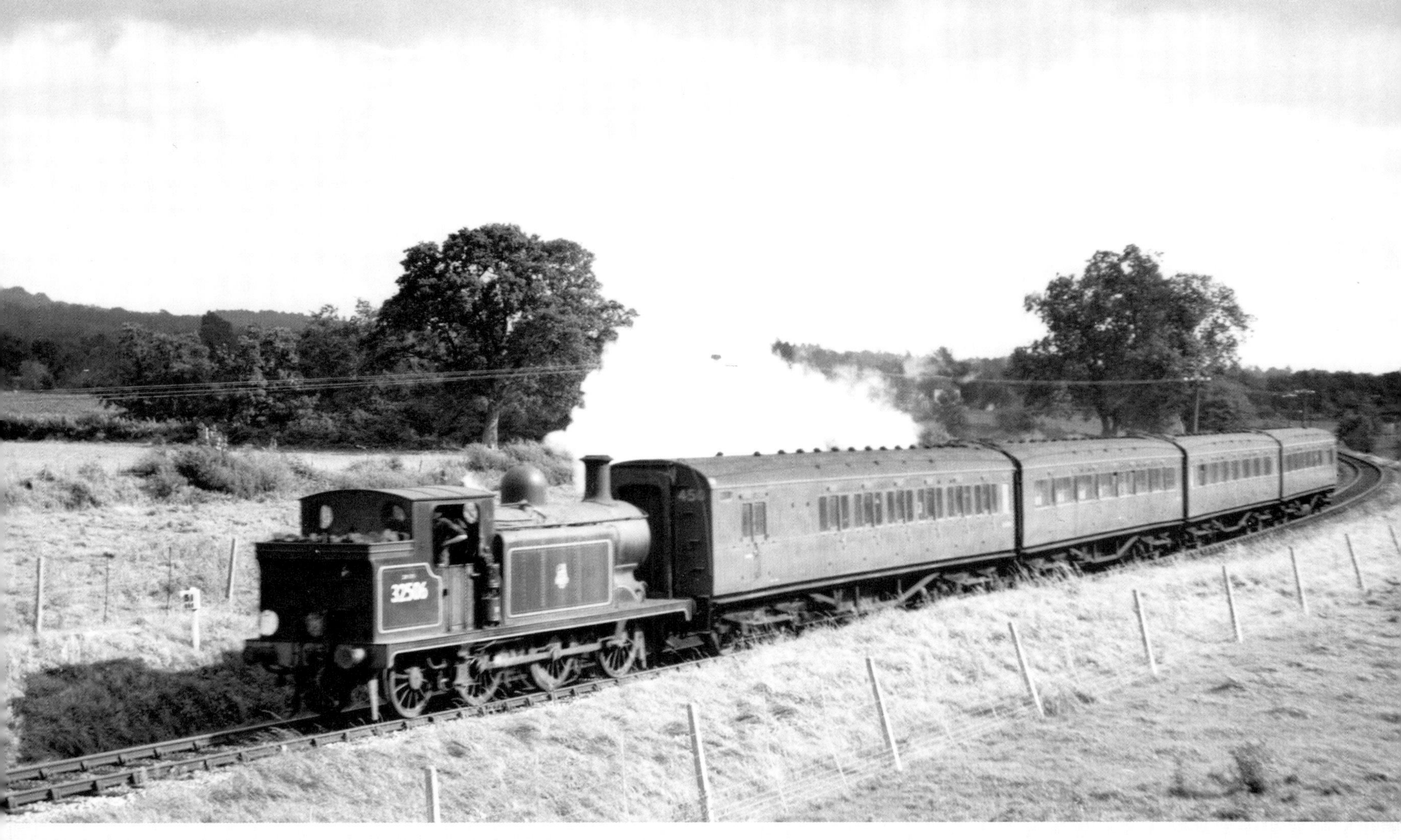

CRANLEIGH Headed by 'E4' 0-6-2T No 32506, the 1.38pm (SO) Cranleigh-Guildford train was photographed near Cranleigh on 4 October 1958. I was en route to photograph a 'T9' on the Portsmouth Direct line.

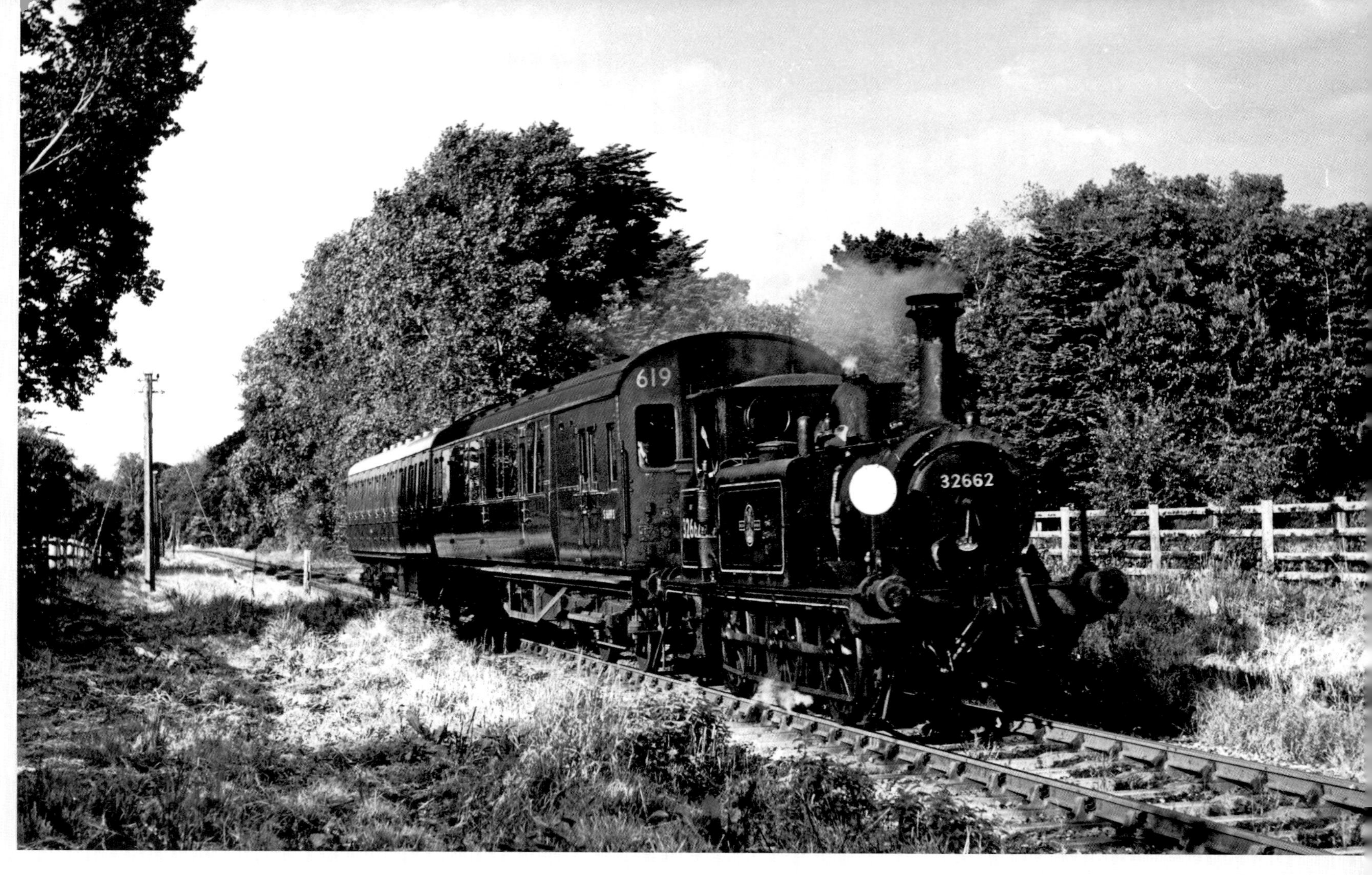

LANGSTON 'A1X' 0-6-0T No 32662 nears Langston and the bridge to Hayling Island on 18 August 1963. Over weekends in the summer so many trains ran on the branch that I didn't bother to record the time of any.

Left: **LANGSTON** On 30 March 1963 'A1X' 0-6-0T No 32661 pulls away from Langston with the 3.35pm train from Havant. There was plenty of time for full note-taking in the winter timetable!

Below: **FORD** The LCGB's 'South Coast Limited Rail Tour' is brought through Ford station on 24 June 1962 by 'K' 2-6-0 No 32353, which has shut off steam for the slack over Ford bridge across the River Arun, and is working the Bognor Regis to Haywards Heath via Hove leg of the journey. Since 1962 the loop platform has been removed, the goods yard behind the station has become an industrial park, the semaphores are now colour lights, and the crossing gates lifting barriers.

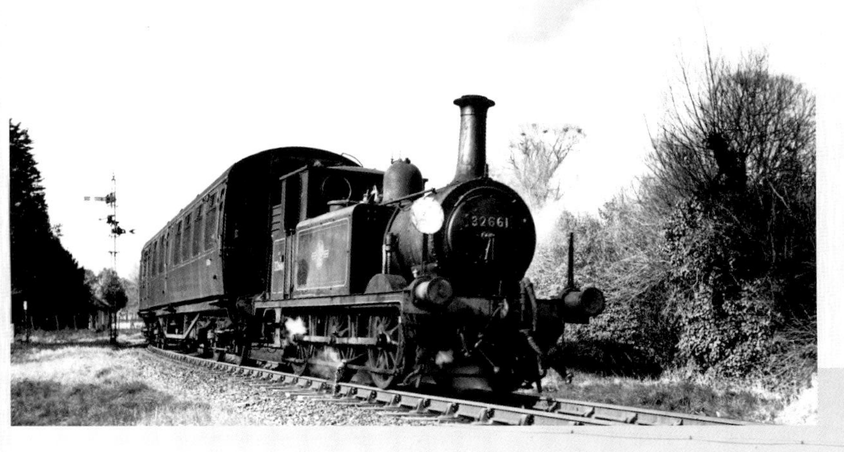

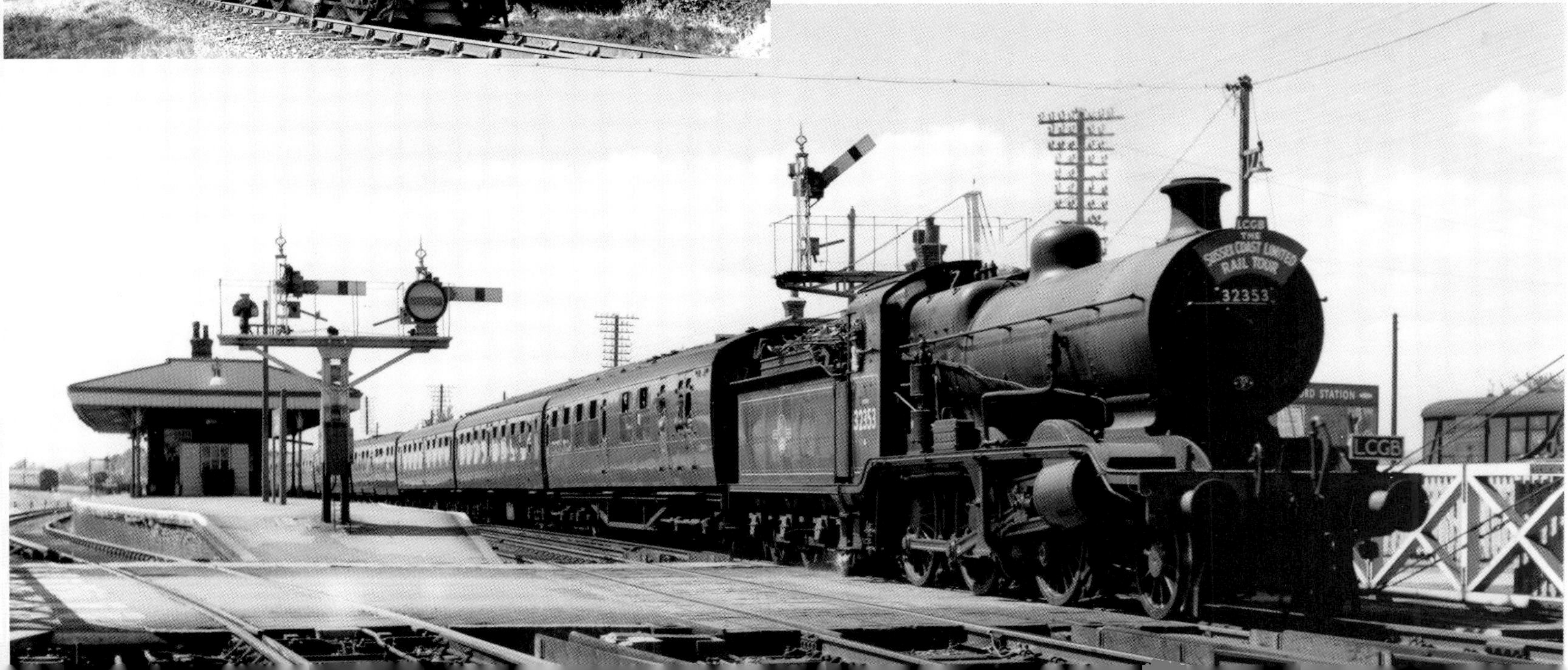

Right: **BRIGHTON** In a flurry of smoke and steam, 'L' 4-4-0 No 31777 draws the through train from Bournemouth into Brighton station on 17 April 1957; it had been checked outside by signal. Dimly visible through the smoke are two 2-6-4Ts in Brighton shed yard.

Below: **BRIGHTON** After working its last public train on 13 April 1958, 'H2' 4-4-2 No 32424 *Beachy Head* runs as a light engine into Brighton London Road station on its way from Newhaven to the shed. Through Ditchling Road Tunnel can be glimpsed the signal box at Kemp Town Junction.

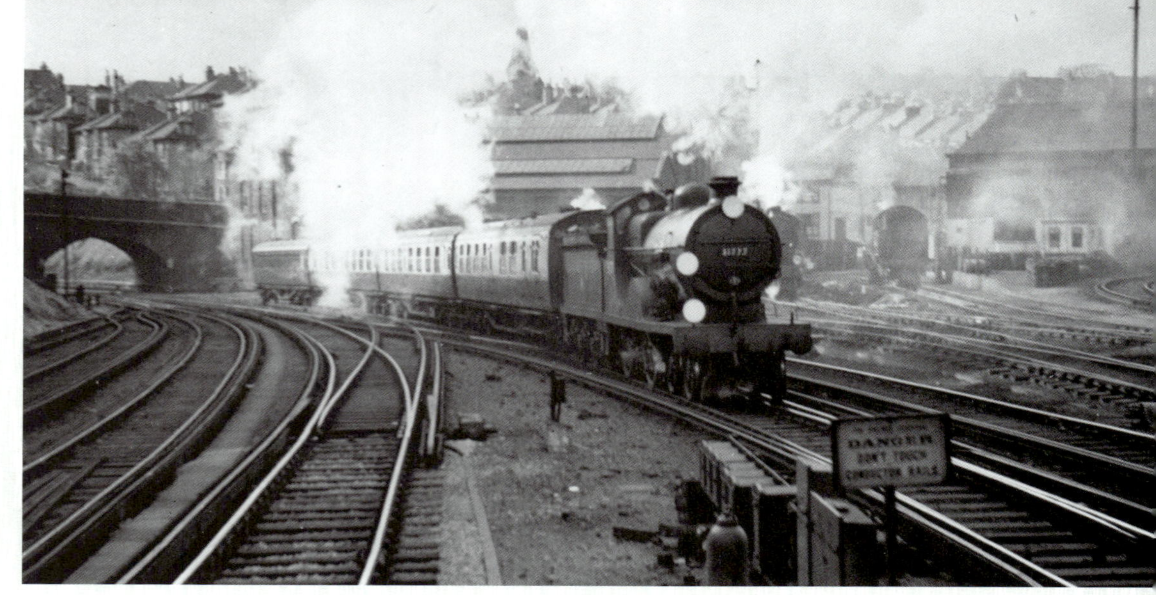

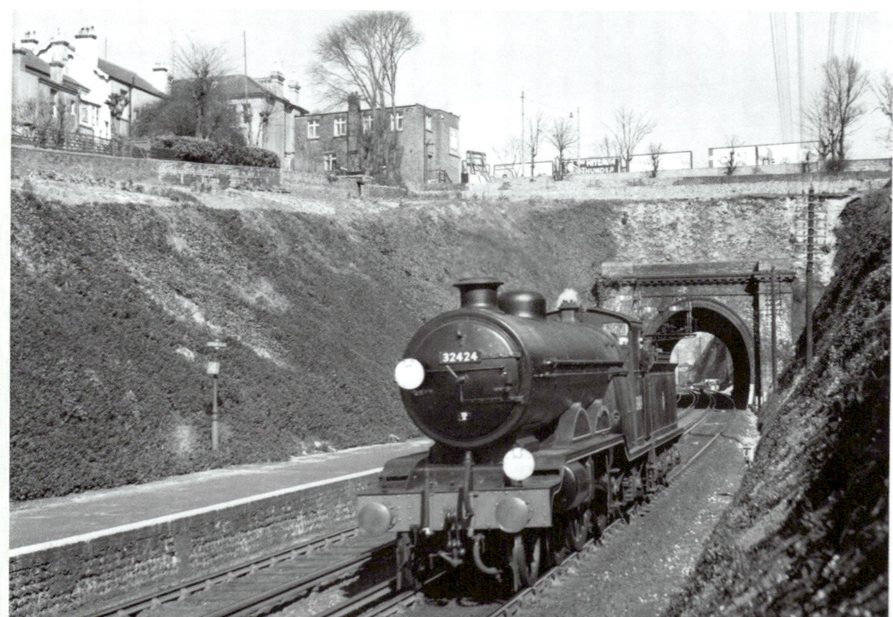

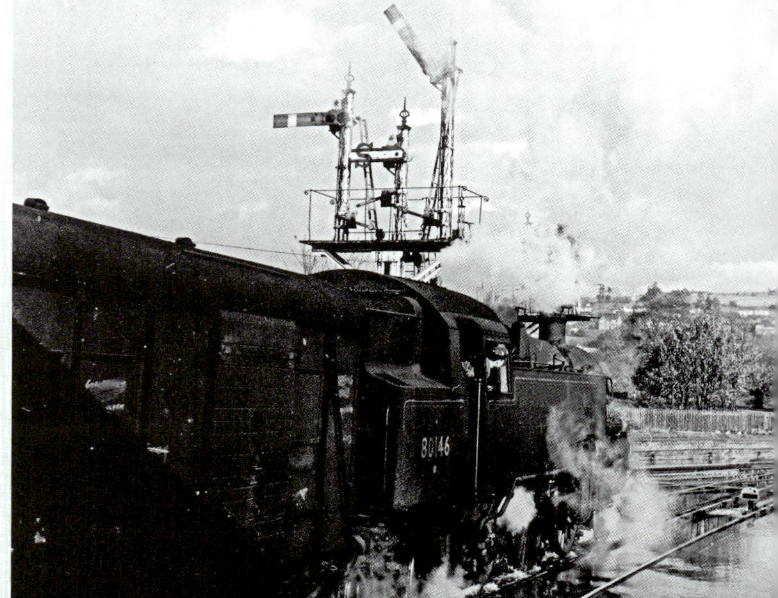

Right: **LEWES** Headed by 'K' 2-6-0 No 32346, the Leicester-Hastings (SO) through train approaches Southerham Junction on 14 June 1958. The town of Lewes spreads itself across the background.

Left: **LEWES** On 5 November 1960 4MT 2-6-4T No 80146 leaves Lewes station. Parts of the town and much of the surrounding country had been flooded so the 'juice rail' had to be switched off. A half-hourly-interval steam service was run between Brighton and Eastbourne until the waters had subsided.

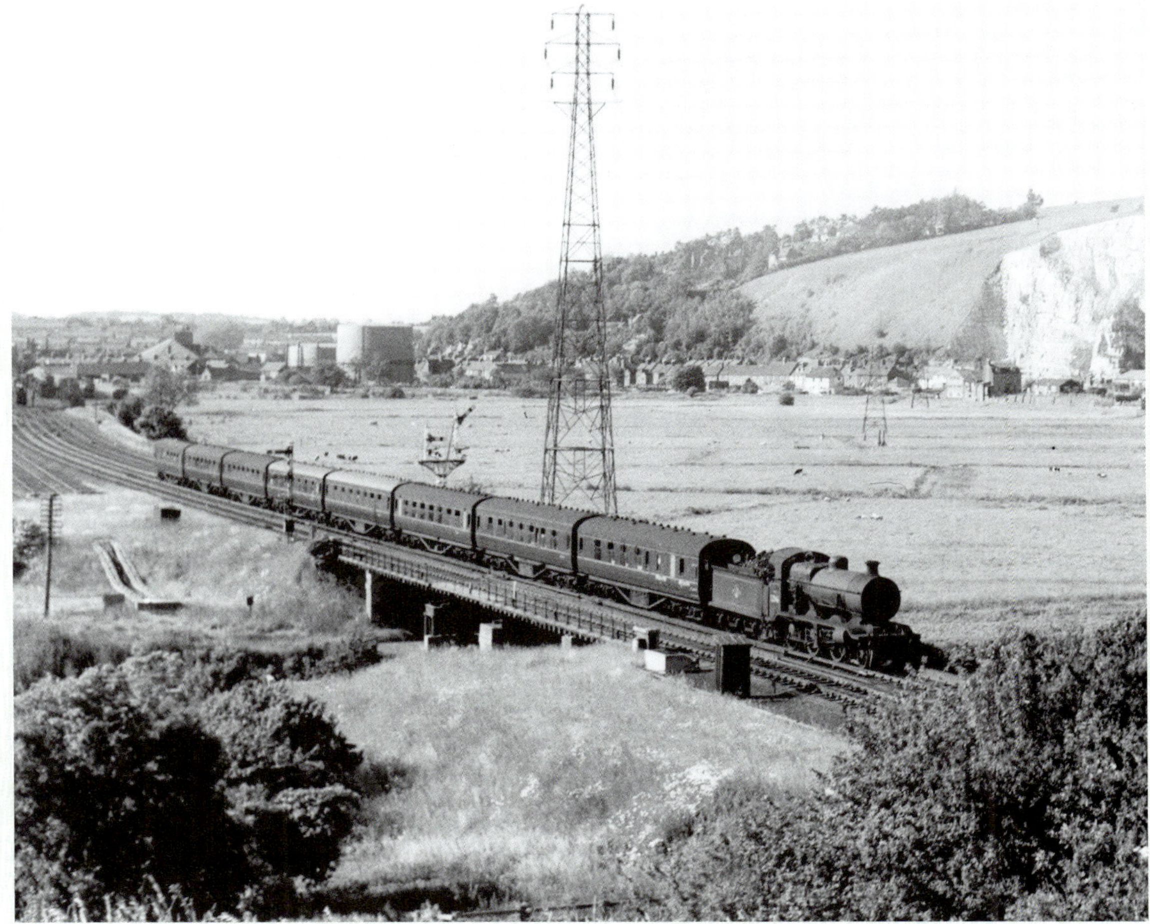

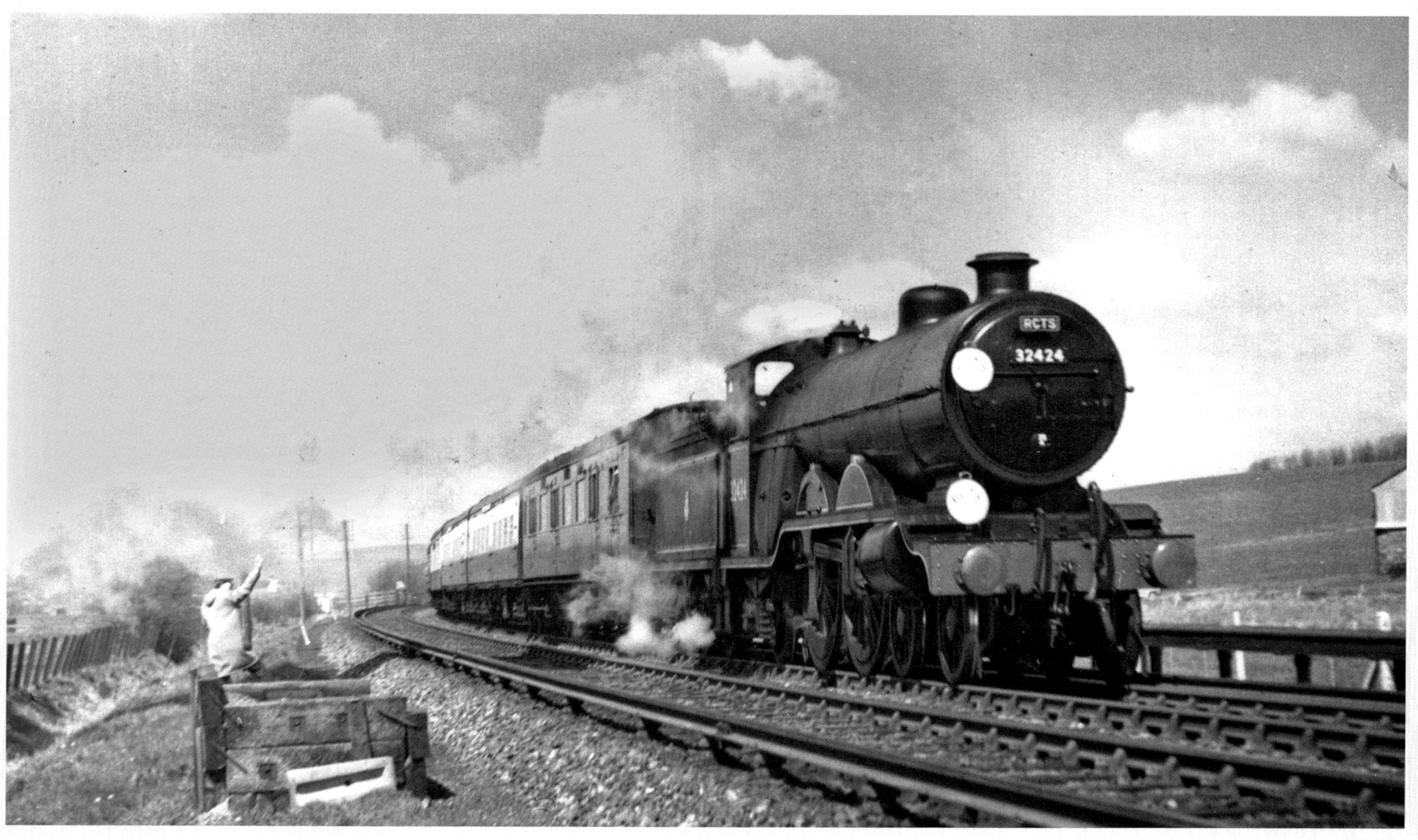

NEWHAVEN On 13 April 1958, on her last run in public service, 'H2' 4-4-2 No 32424 *Beachy Head* romps down the branch to Newhaven with the RCTS's 'Sussex Coast Limited' special train from London Victoria.

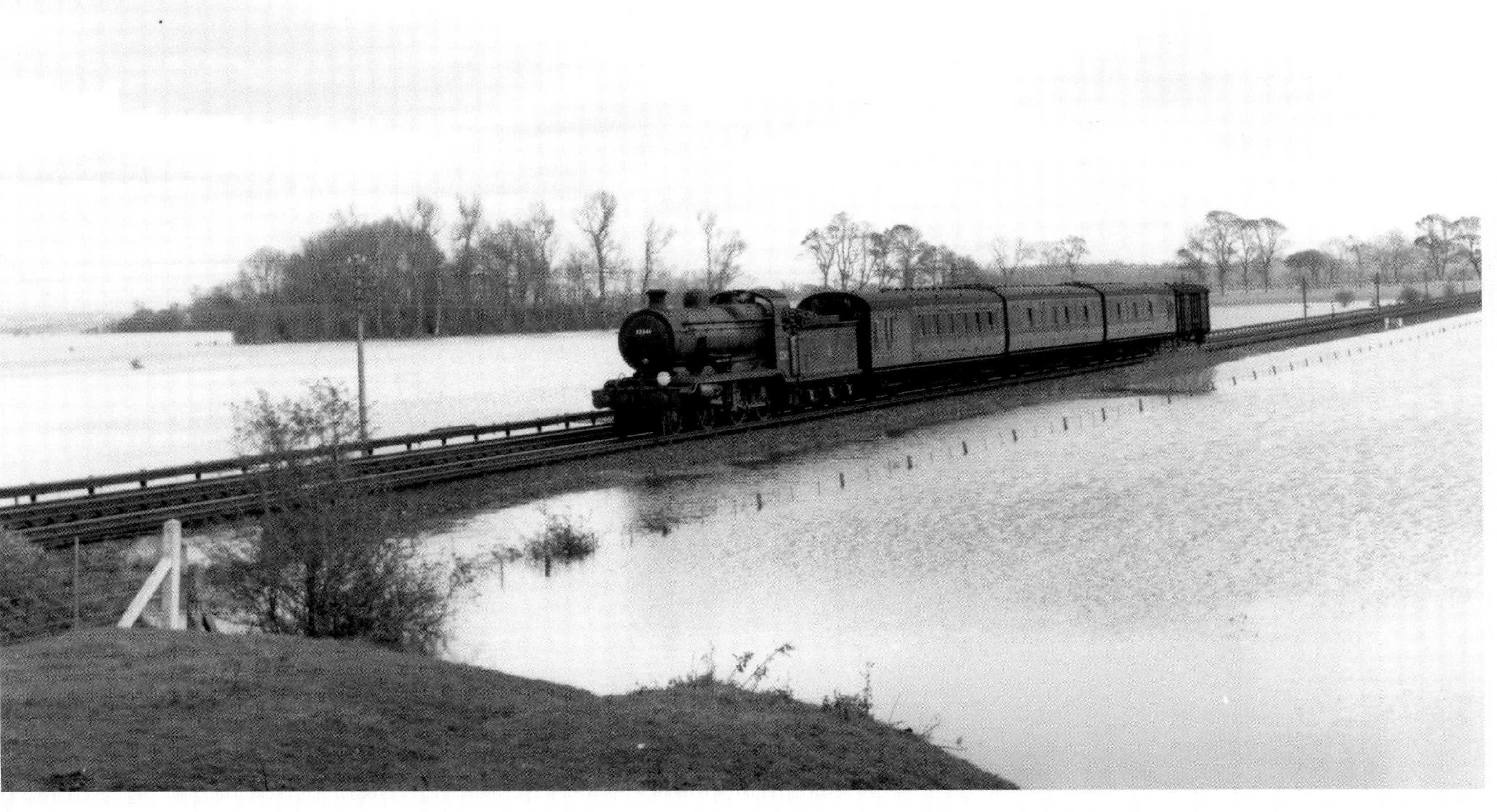

GLYNDE During the Lewes floods emergency service, 'K' 2-6-0 No 32341 approaches Glynde with an Eastbourne-Brighton train on 5 November 1960. The extent of the floods can be judged from this scene – they had been draining for 48 hours.

Left: **WARLINGHAM** 4MT 2-6-4T No 80031 crosses Warlingham Viaduct and the chalk pit at the head of the 9.08am Victoria-Tunbridge Wells West train on 3 October 1959. This was a Saturday and the dust from the workings was temporarily abated.

Below: **EAST GRINSTEAD** At St Margaret's Junction, about half a mile north of the station, Fairburn 4MT 2-6-4T No 42082 leads the 2.08pm Victoria-Tunbridge Wells West train onto the spur line to the High Level station and the line to Groombridge on 24 October 1958. The junction was named after the adjacent convent of St Margaret of Antioch.

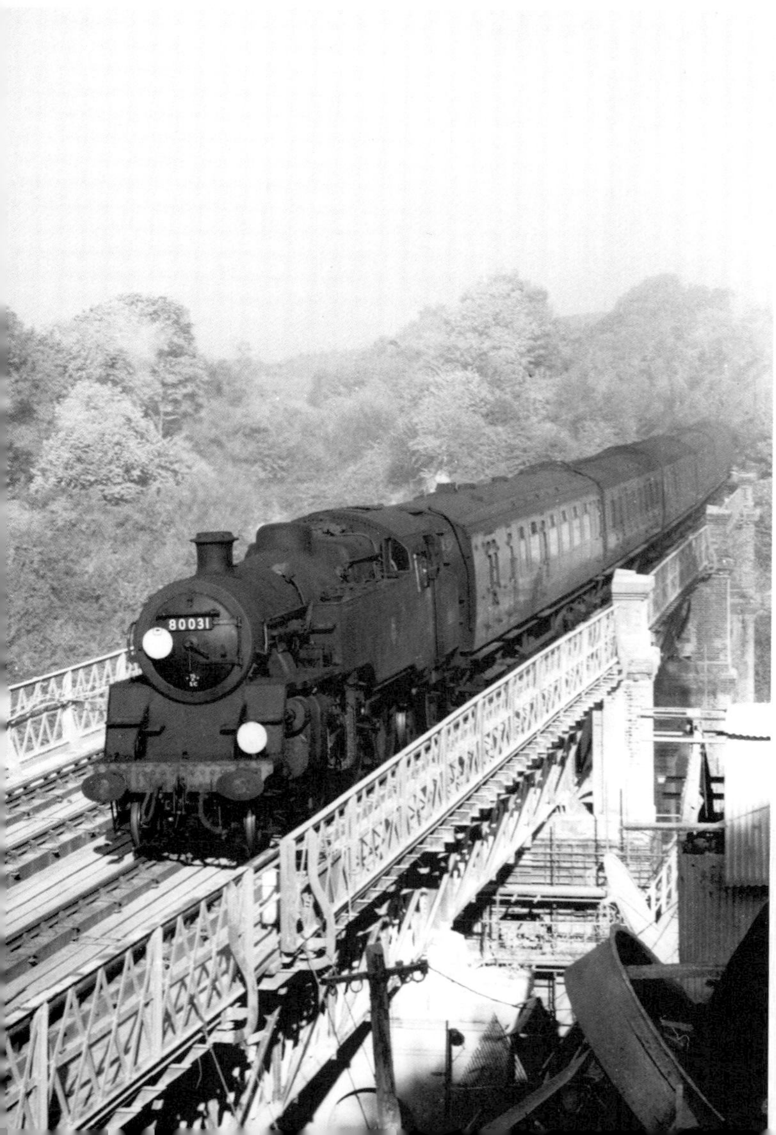

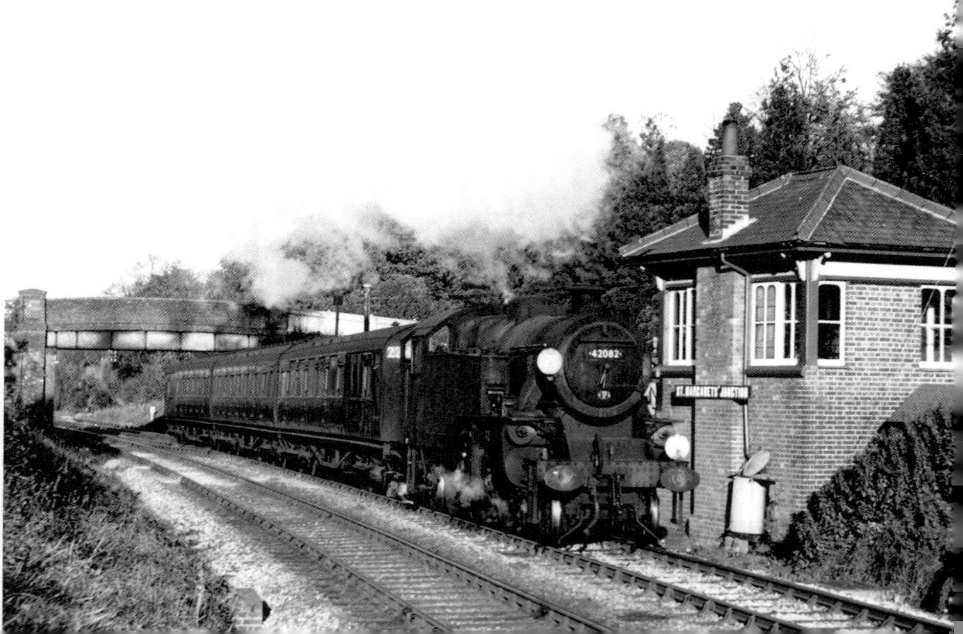

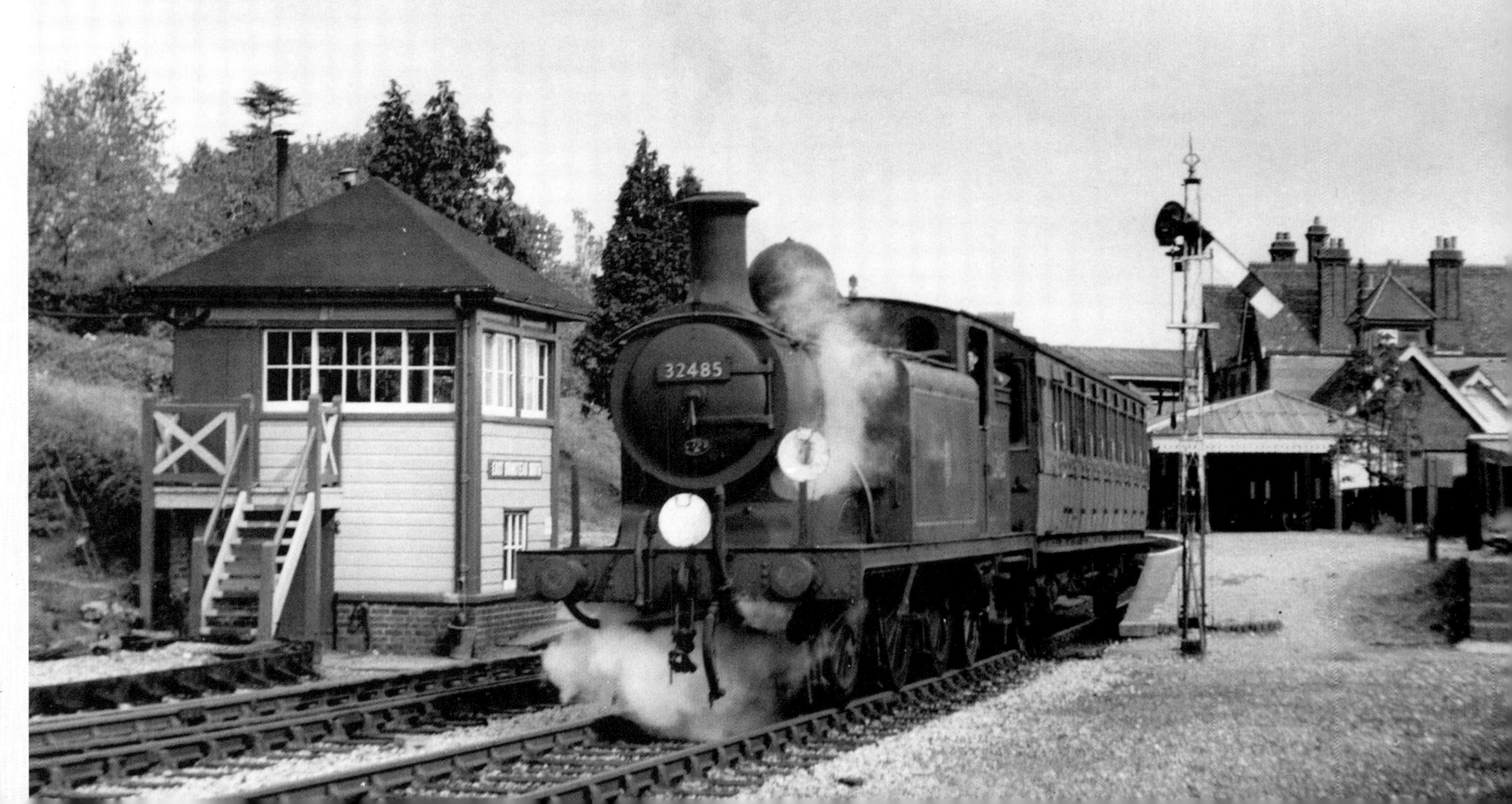

EAST GRINSTEAD As part of the 'sulky' service, run because BR was legally obliged to reopen the line, 'E4' 0-6-2T No 32485 leaves the Low Level station with the 12.28pm to Lewes on 26 September 1957. This is the site of today's station, but the High Level station, shown here in the background, has all been swept away.

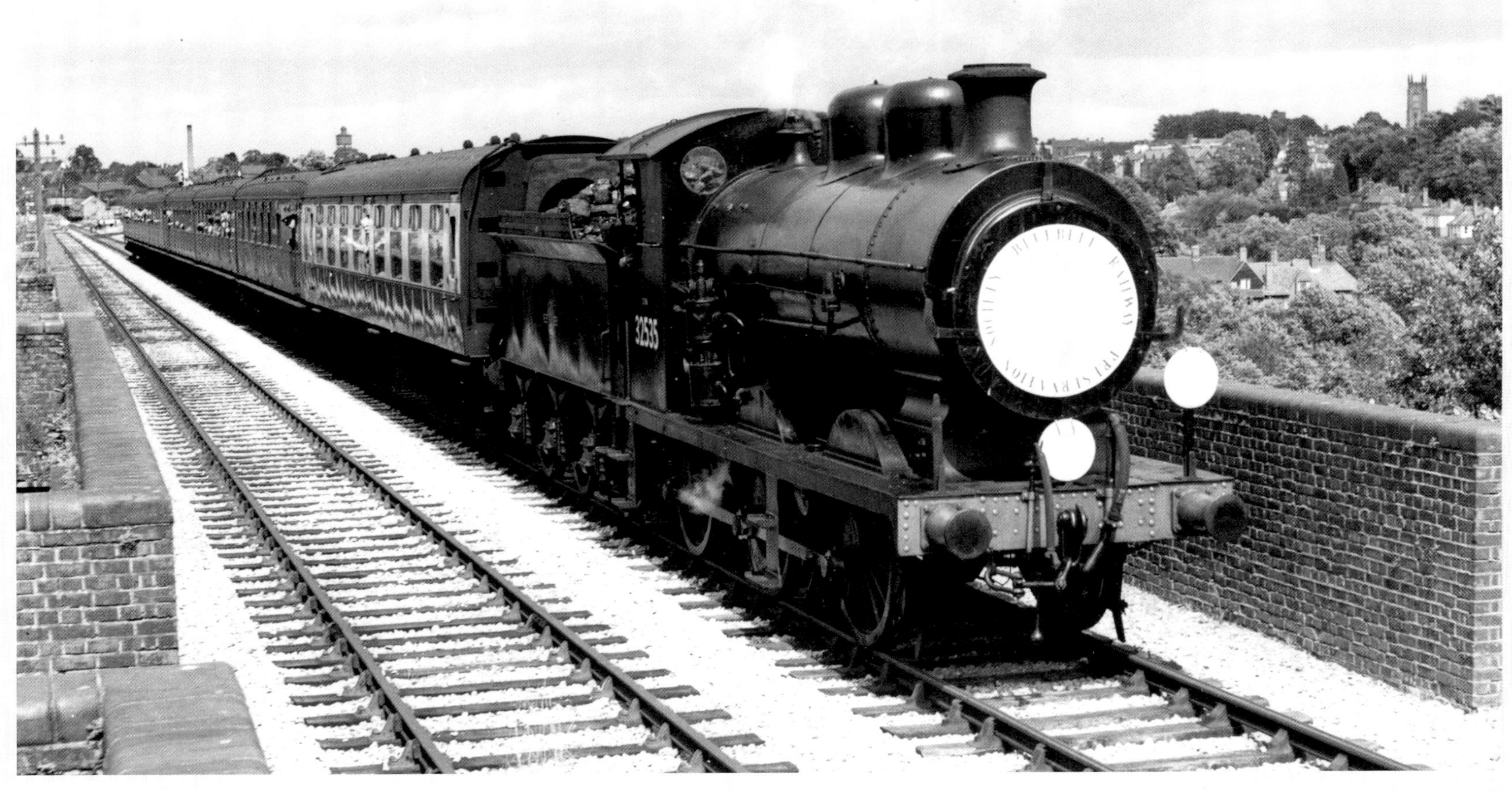

EAST GRINSTEAD A Bluebell Railway special train, drawn by 0-6-0 'C2X' No 32535, crosses the Imberhorne Viaduct on 12 July 1959. The line had been closed finally 15 months earlier, and a line of surplus wagons, parked on the Up line, obliged me to stand on the parapet. The tower of St Swithun's church is on the right.

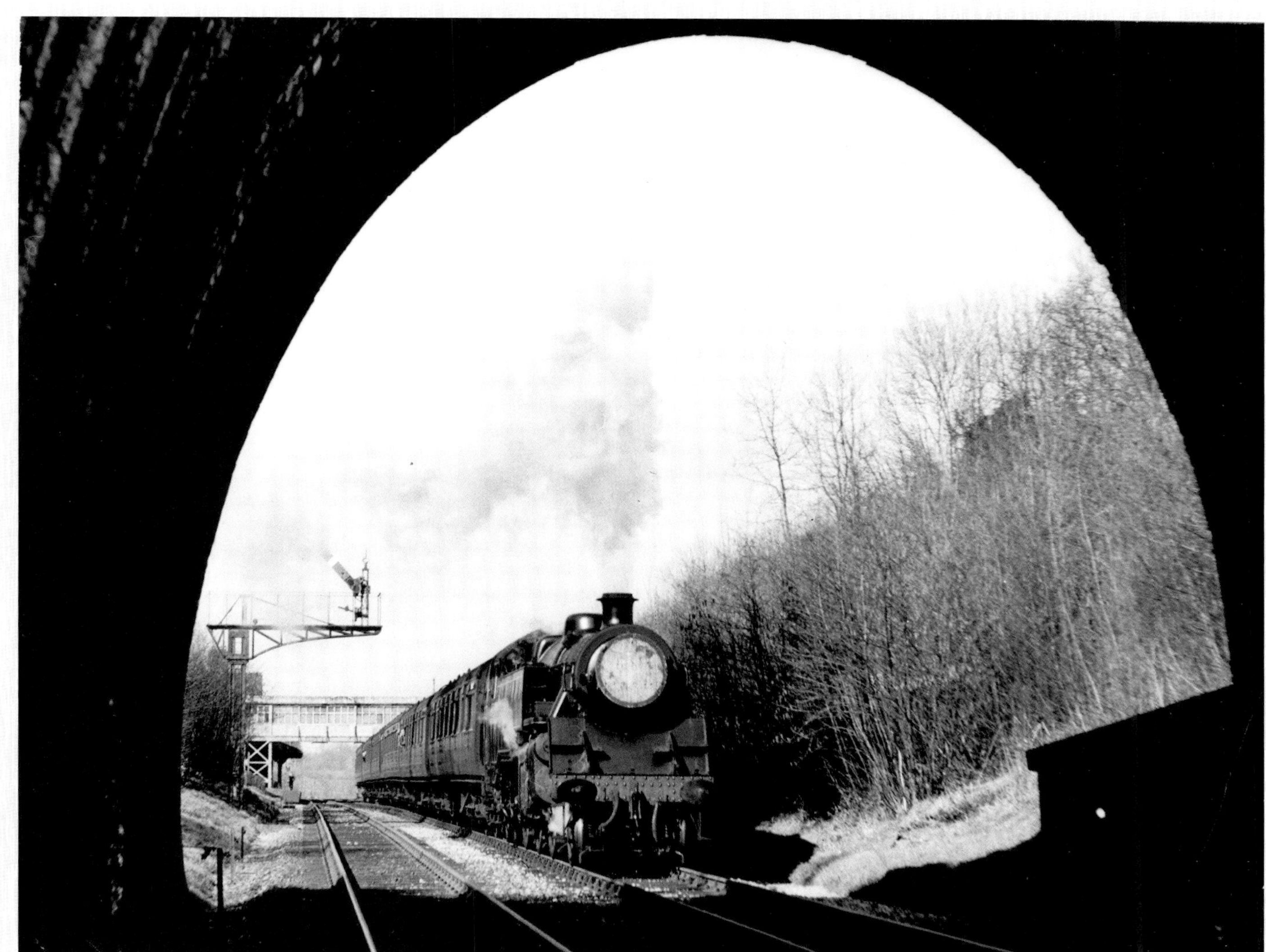

WEST HOATHLY 4MT 2-6-4T No 80154, the last locomotive built at Brighton Works, approaches Sharpthorne Tunnel with the penultimate southbound train of the 'sulky' service – the 2.28pm from East Grinstead to Lewes – on 16 March 1958. After an earlier cold spell there were still large icicles hanging from the tunnel lining.

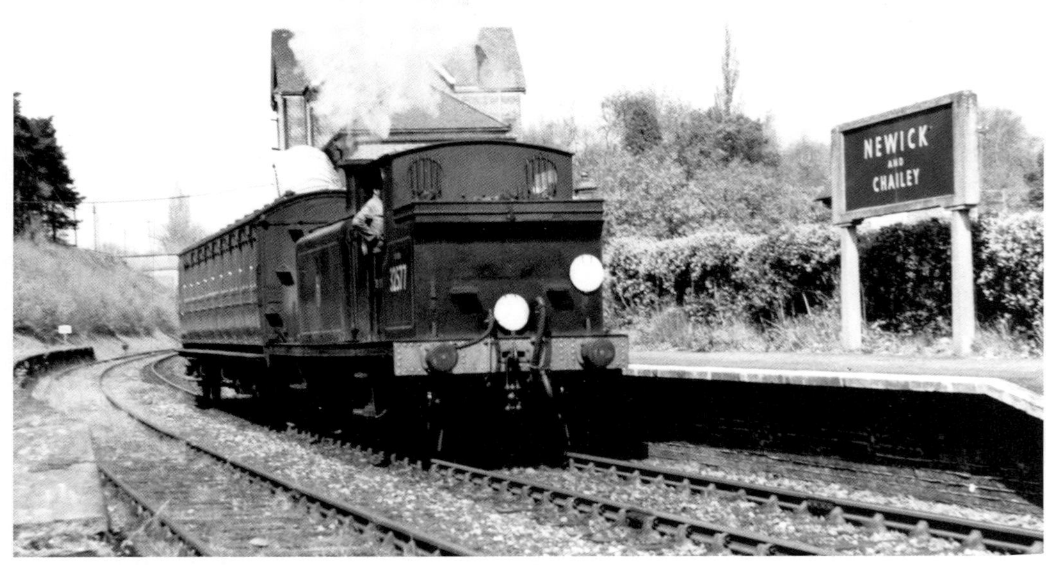

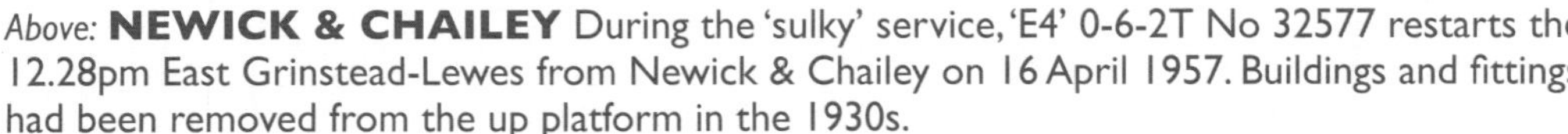

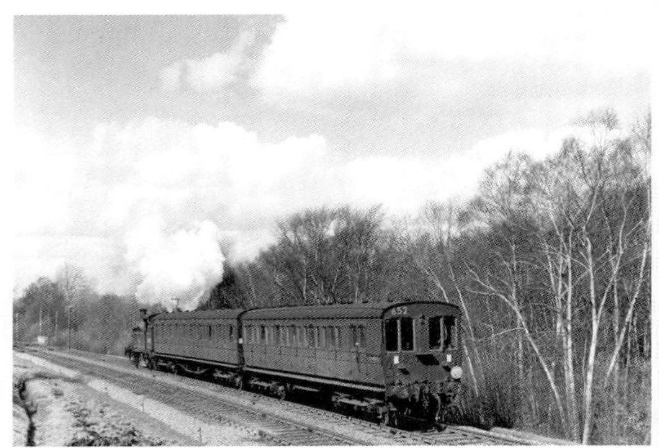

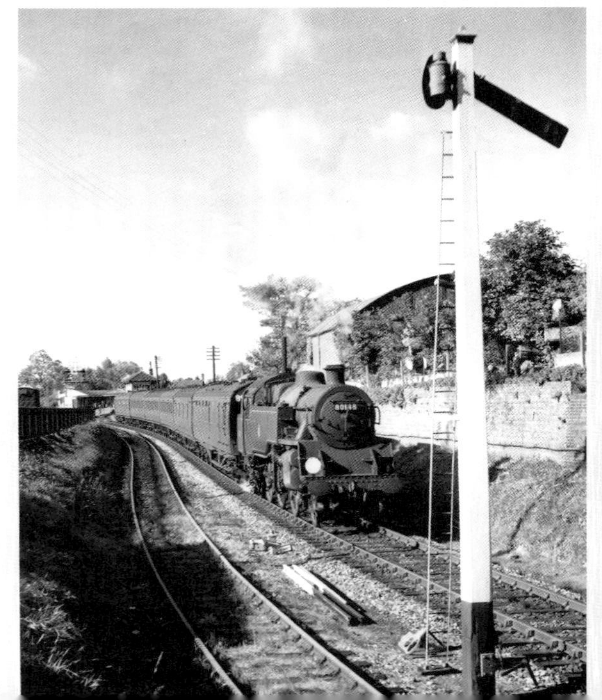

Above: **NEWICK & CHAILEY** During the 'sulky' service, 'E4' 0-6-2T No 32577 restarts the 12.28pm East Grinstead-Lewes from Newick & Chailey on 16 April 1957. Buildings and fittings had been removed from the up platform in the 1930s.

Above right: **HEVER** Set No 652 is propelled away from Hever by 'H' 0-4-4T No 31278 while forming the 2.04pm Oxted-Tunbridge Wells West train on 31 March 1962. The control coach is ex-LSWR, while the trailer is ex-SECR, hence the different profiles.

Right: **EAST GRINSTEAD** 4MT 2-6-4T No 80148 pulls away from the High Level station with the 9.08am Victoria-Tunbridge Wells West on 16 October 1958. The advanced starter signal and post are still ex-LBSCR equipment.

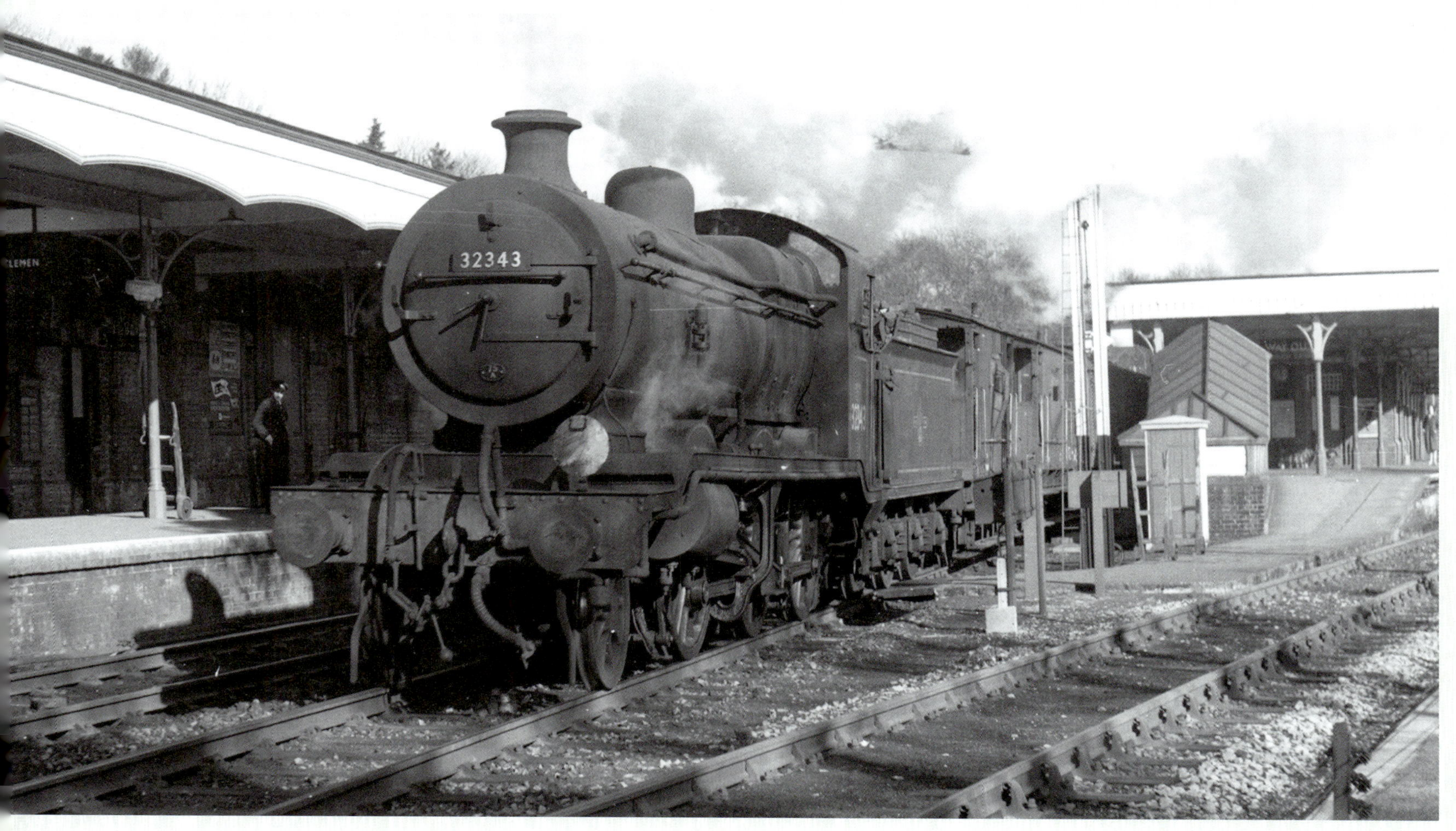

GROOMBRIDGE The Tunbridge Wells West-Brighton goods train trundles through Groombridge station at about noon on 16 February 1960, headed by 'K' 2-6-0 No 32343. This was a regular working for a 'K'.

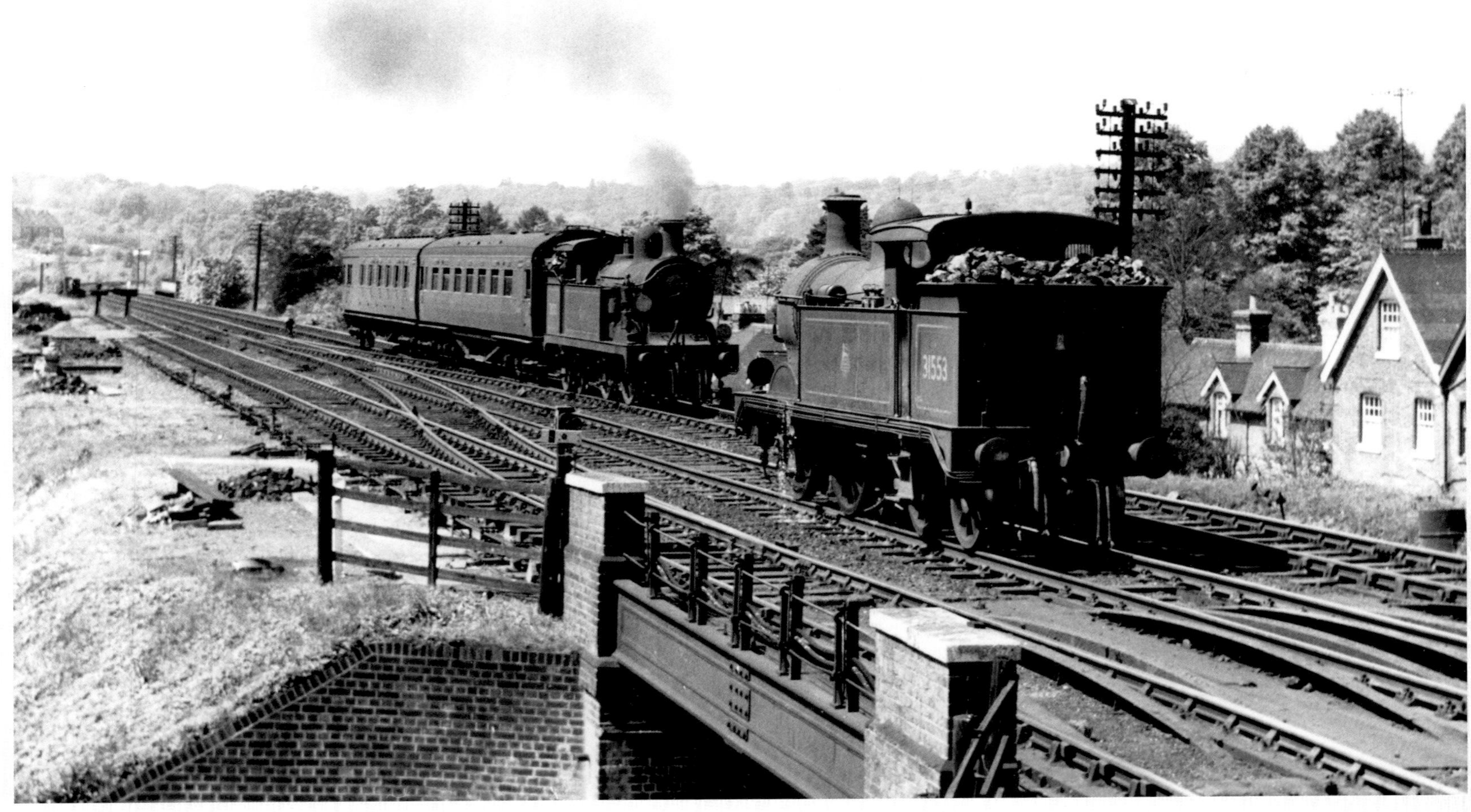

TUNBRIDGE WELLS WEST A train from Oxted via Edenbridge Town approaches the station on 13 May 1961. It is headed by 'H' 0-4-4T No 31522, which is about to be relieved by sister loco No 31553.

Bluebell Railway

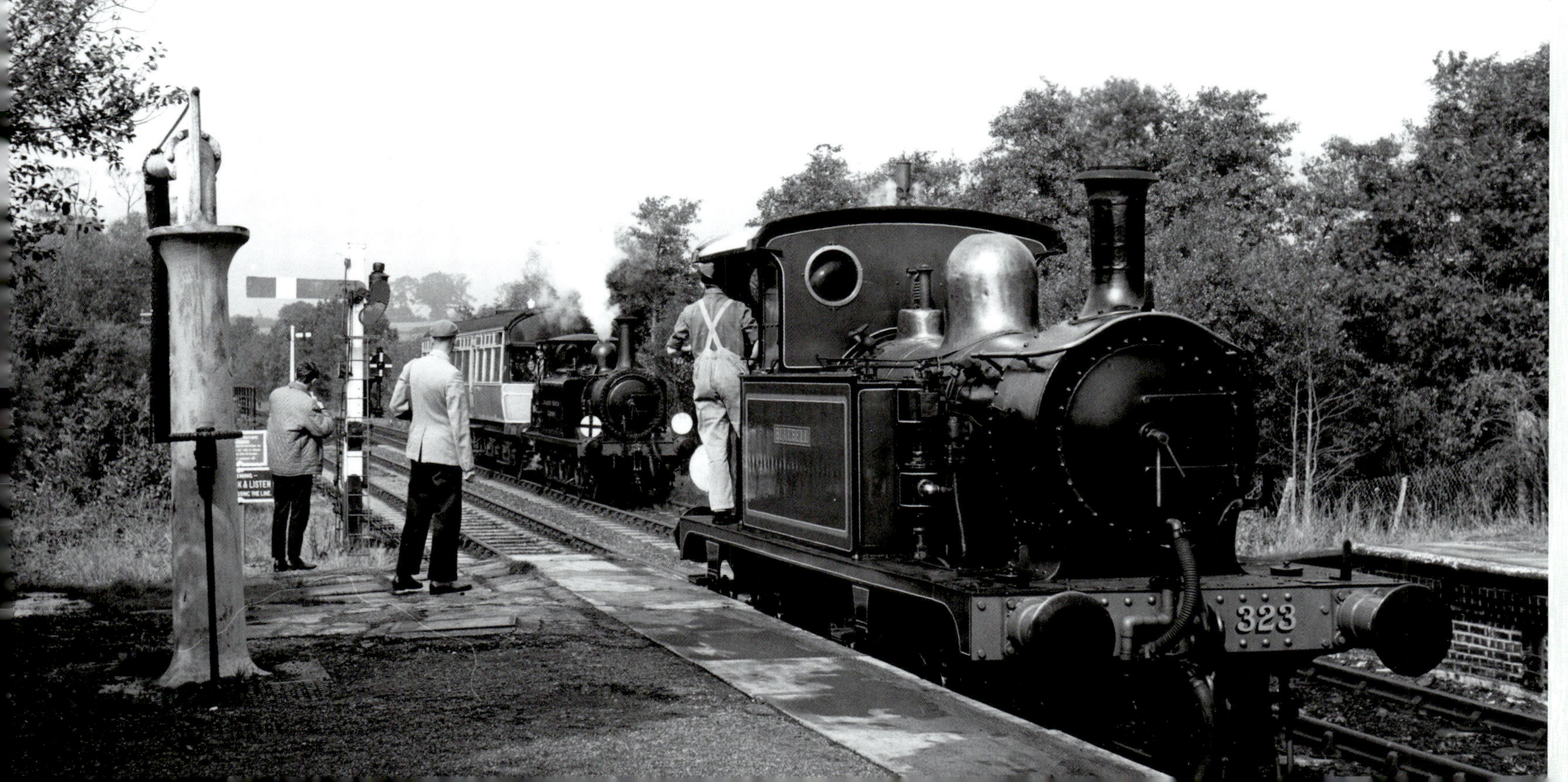

SHEFFIELD PARK Ex-SECR 'P' 0-6-0T No 323 stands at the platform, waiting to take over the train, the ex-LNWR observation car, from ex-LBSCR 'A1X' 0-6-0T No 72 *Fenchurch*, which is approaching on 17 September 1967 with the 2.25pm departure from Horsted Keynes.

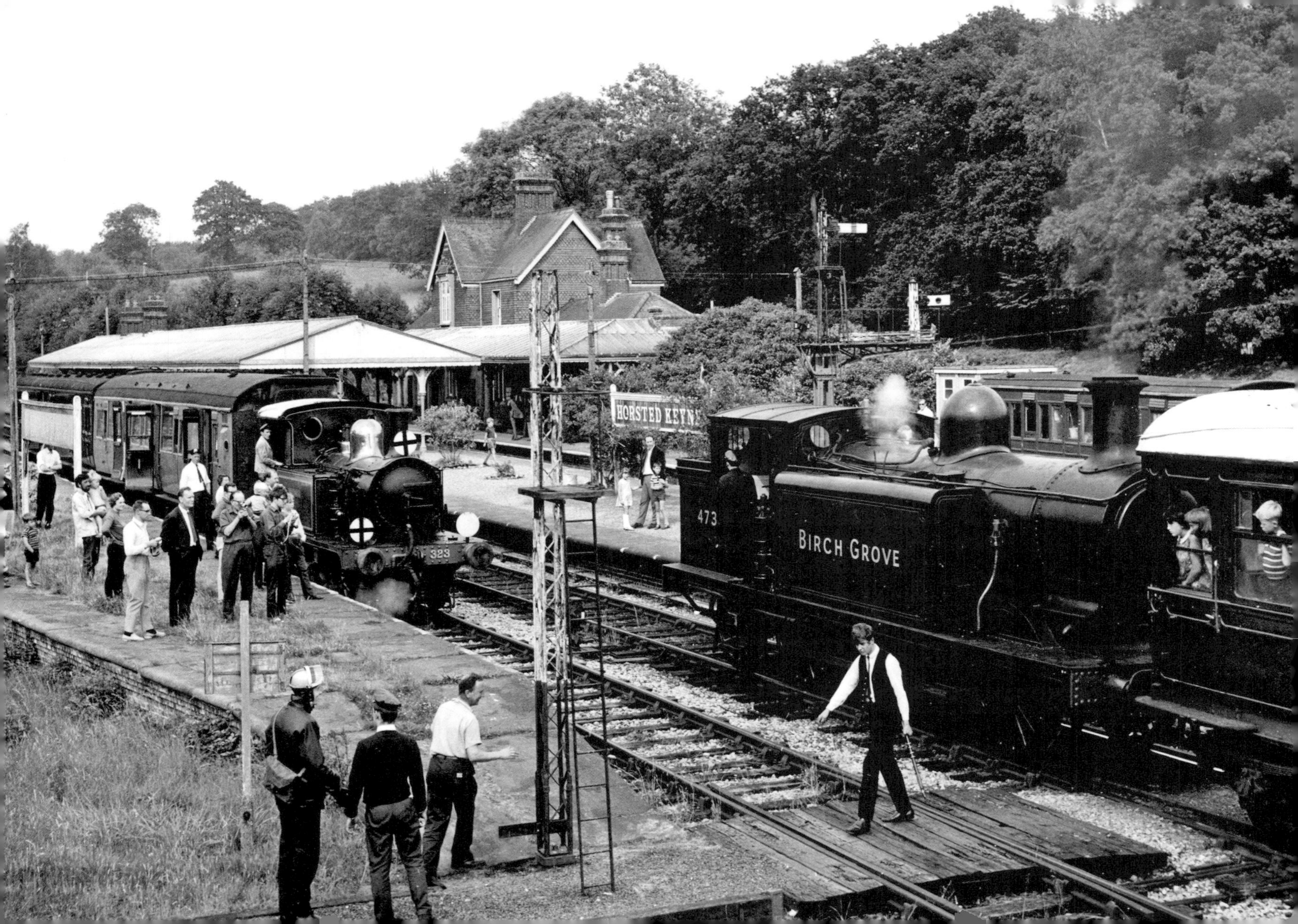

HORSTED KEYNE
473
BIRCH GROVE
323

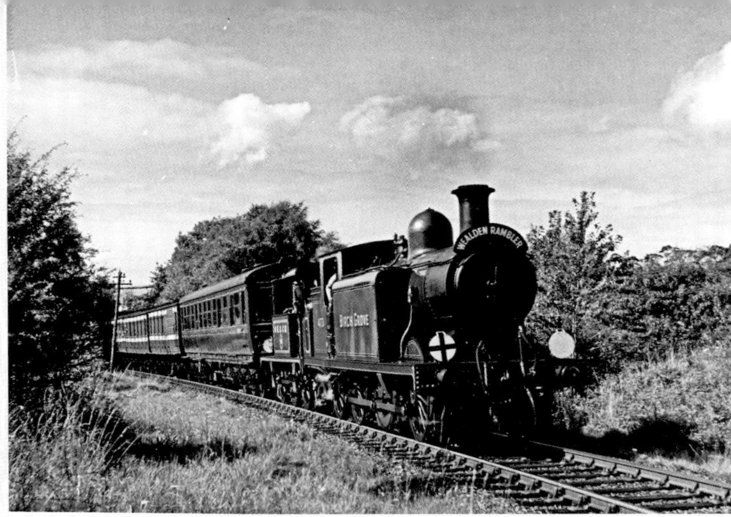

Above: **ROCK CUTTING** Ex-LBSCR 'E4' 0-6-2T No 473 *Birch Grove* pilots ex-SECR 'P' 0-6-0T No 27 near Rock Cutting, about 1¾ miles south of Horsted Keynes, with a working of the 'Wealden Rambler' on 15 August 1965. This special train was distinguished by the presence in its consist of the ex-LBSCR directors' saloon, the leading vehicle in the train, which was used as a refreshment car.

Left: **HORSTED KEYNES** *Birch Grove* is seen again rolling into Horsted Keynes, where ex-SECR 'P' 0-6-0T No 323 waits to leave for Sheffield Park on 21 July 1968. The signalman has collected the single-line staff from the fireman of the 'E4' and is returning to his cabin.

Right: **WATER WORKS** Ex-LSWR '0415' 4-4-2T No 488 nears the water works, 1 mile south of Horsted Keynes, with a train from Sheffield Park on 23 May 1965. In the preceding winter the lineside telephone wires had been stolen. The line was worked by use of the public network, and this shot became possible until the wires were restrung. The underbridge has since been demolished.

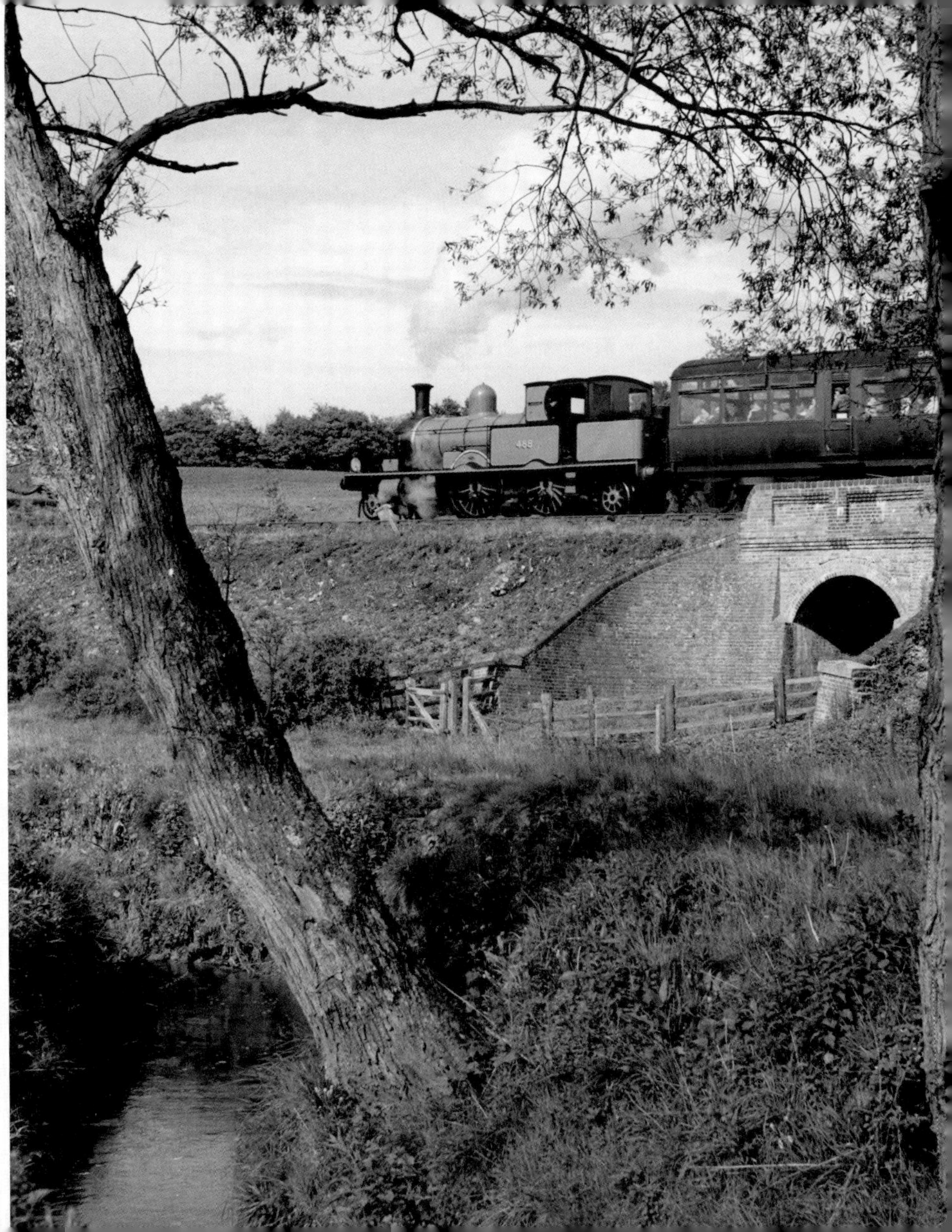

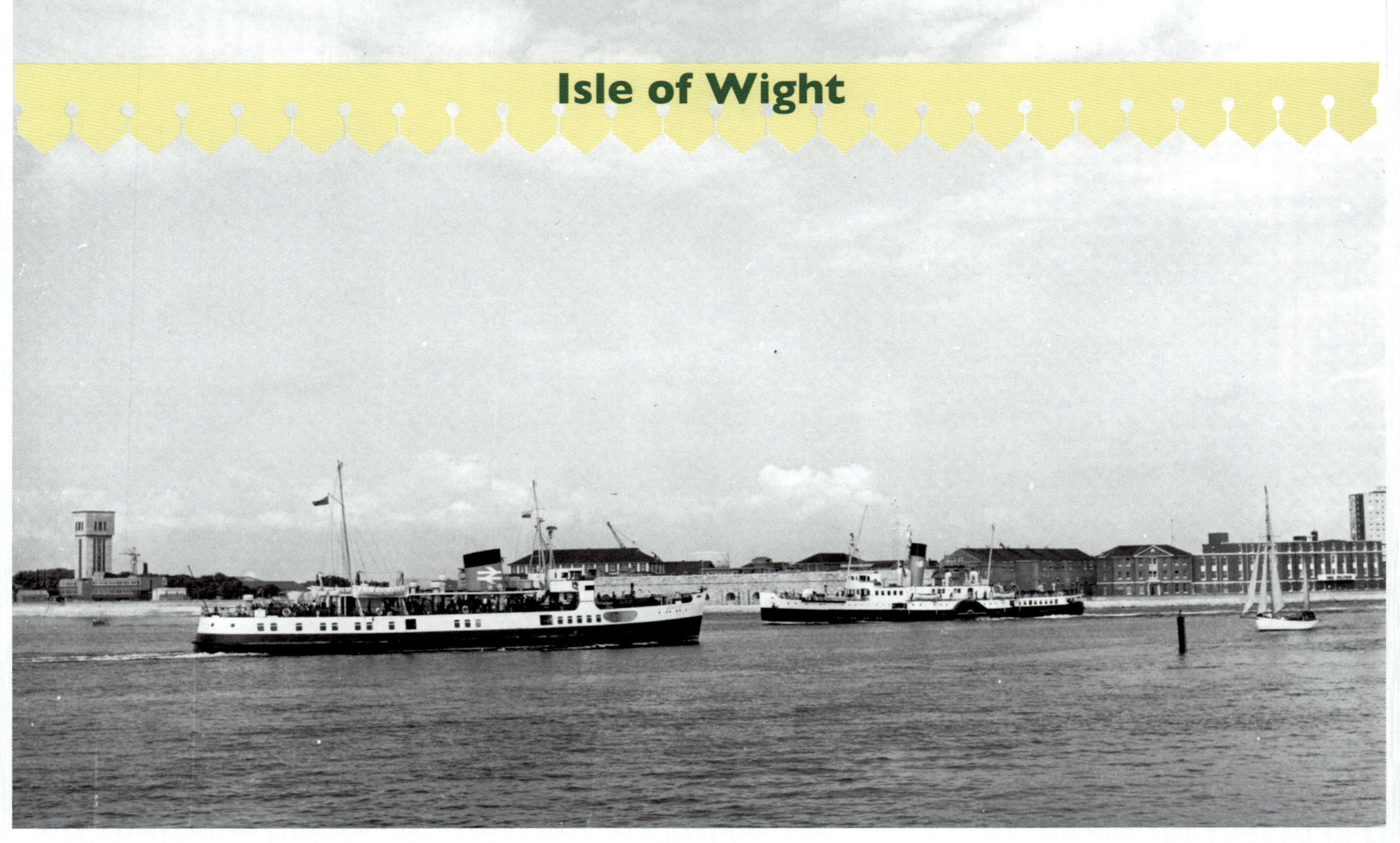

PORTSMOUTH A crossing shot at sea! Two generations of Portsmouth-Ryde ferries meet in the mouth of Portsmouth Harbour; the post-war *MV Brading* arrives as one of the 1930s paddle steamers heads for Ryde on 27 June 1965. Both vessels have been painted in Rail Blue.

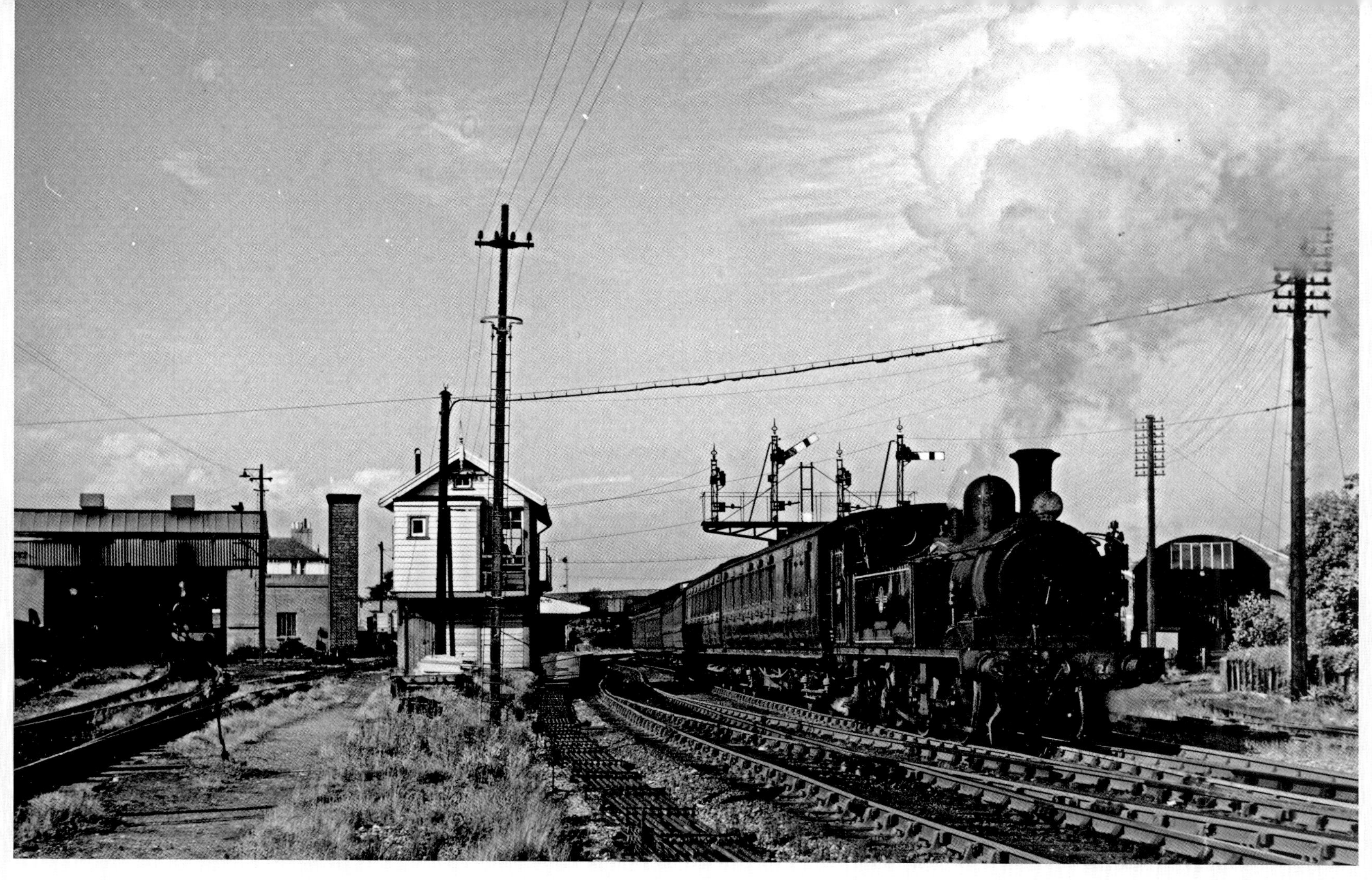

RYDE ST JOHN'S ROAD 'O2' 0-4-4T No W21 *Sandown* leaves Ryde St John's Road station with the 5.42pm Ryde Pier Head-Ventnor on 26 June 1965. Two other 'O2s' can be dimly seen, but not identified, in the running shed on the left, while part of Ryde Works can be seen beyond No W21 on the right.

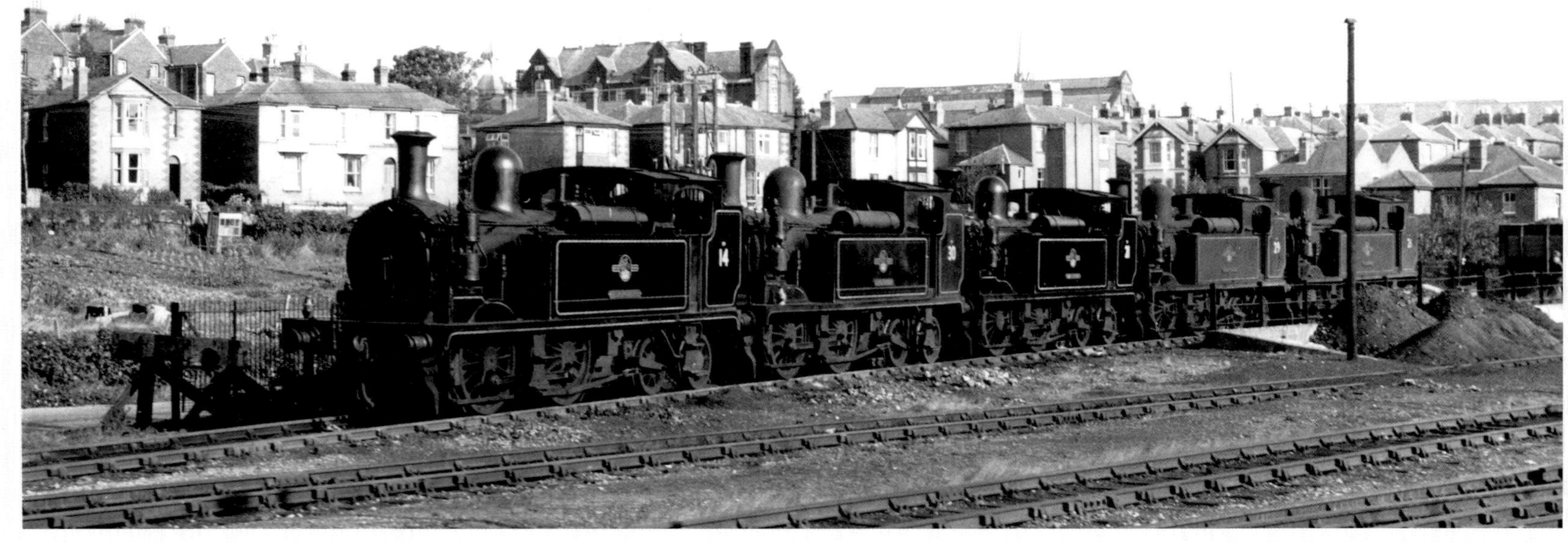

RYDE ST JOHN'S ROAD At Ryde St John's Road shed on 16 September 1961 there was a line of 'O2s' out of steam: Nos W14 *Fishbourne*, W30 *Shorwell*, W21 *Sandown*, W29 *Alverstone* and W26 *Whitwell*.

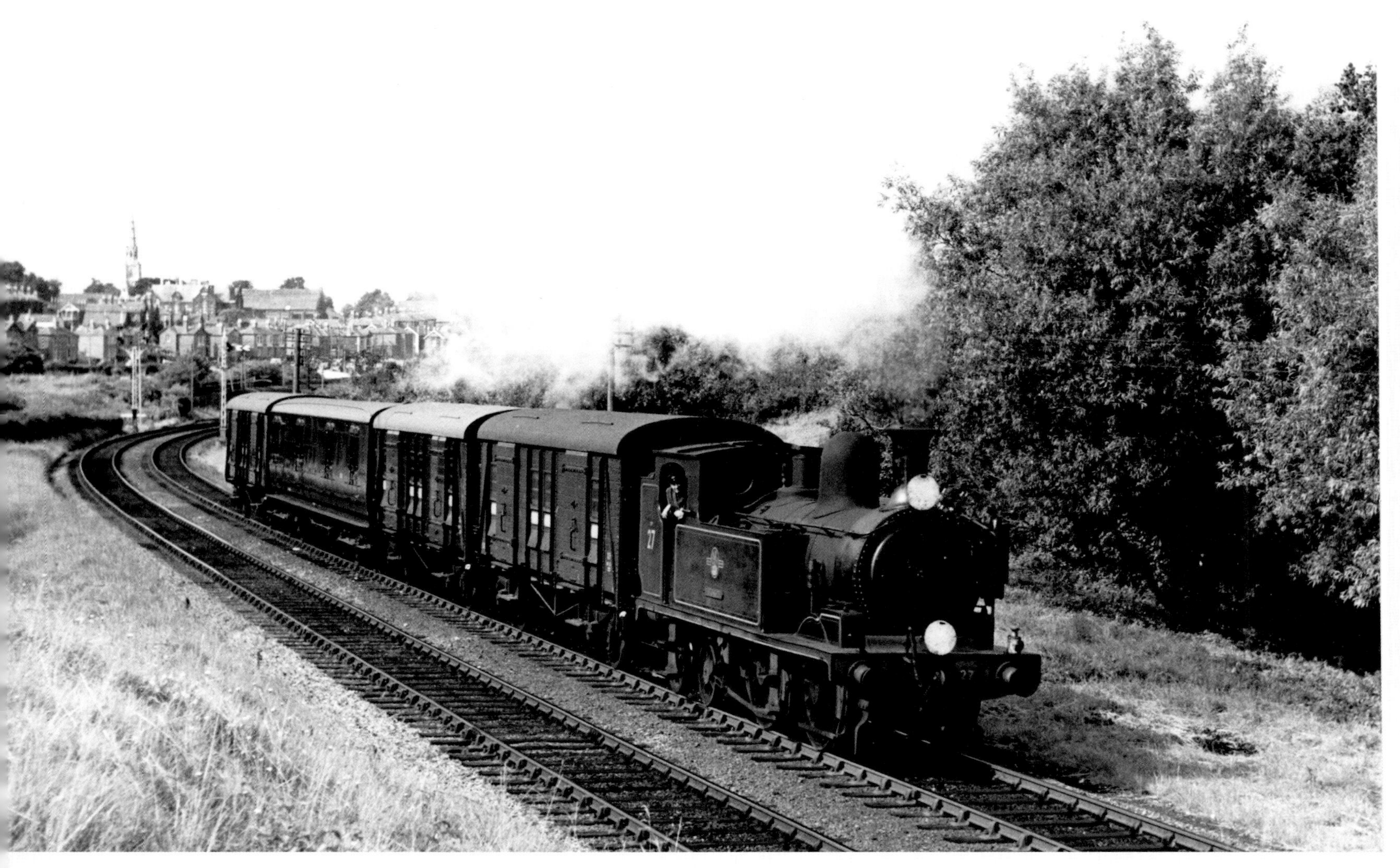

RYDE ST JOHN'S ROAD Just round the curve on the way to Smallbrook Junction and Sandown, 'O2' 0-4-4T No W27 *Merstone* heads away from Ryde with the 5.10pm vans train on 7 July 1963.

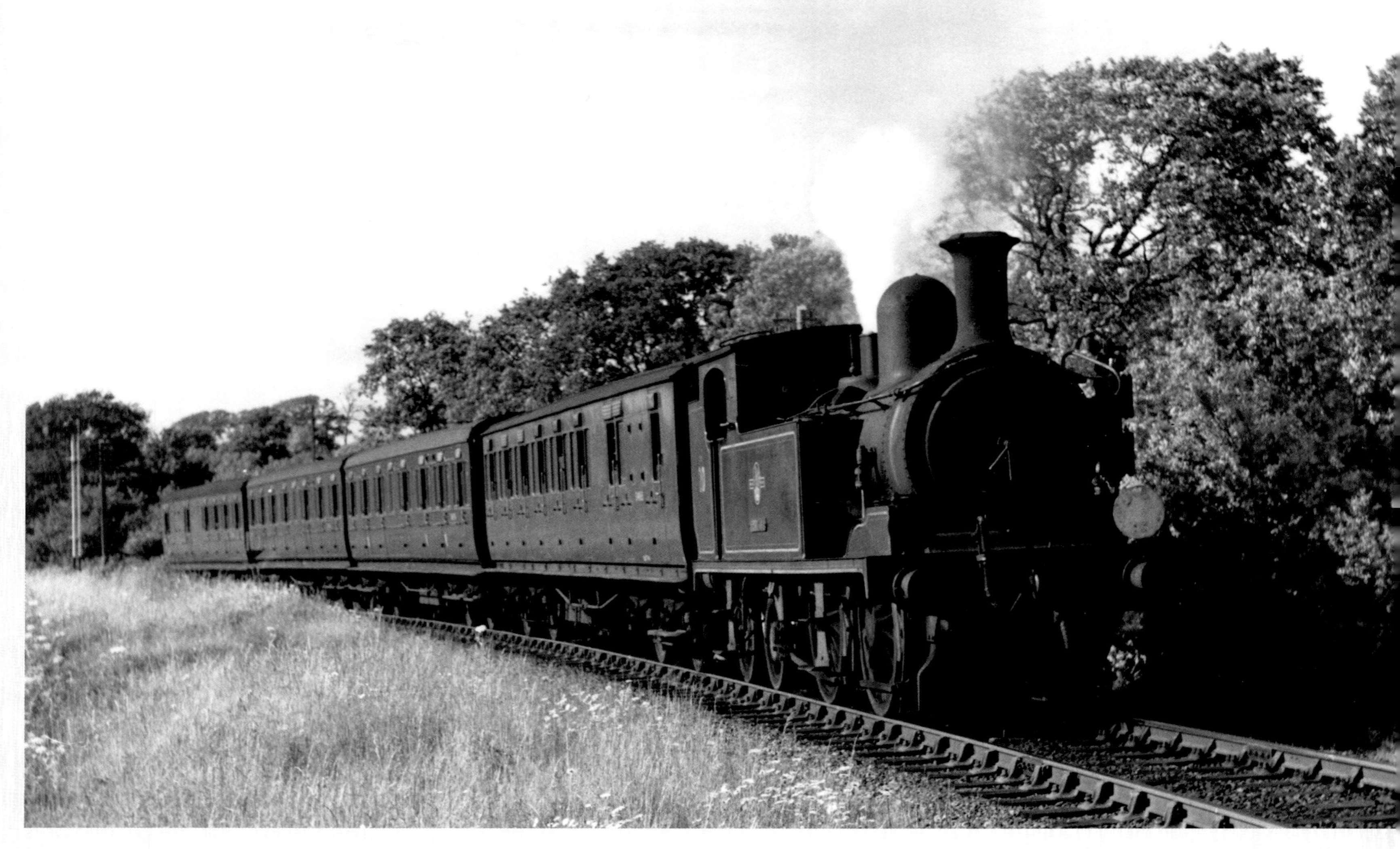

SMALLBROOK JUNCTION 'O2' 0-4-4T No W20 *Shanklin* rounds the curve from Smallbrook Junction with the line to Ventnor, at the head of the 5.35pm from Ryde Pier Head to Cowes on 16 June 1962.

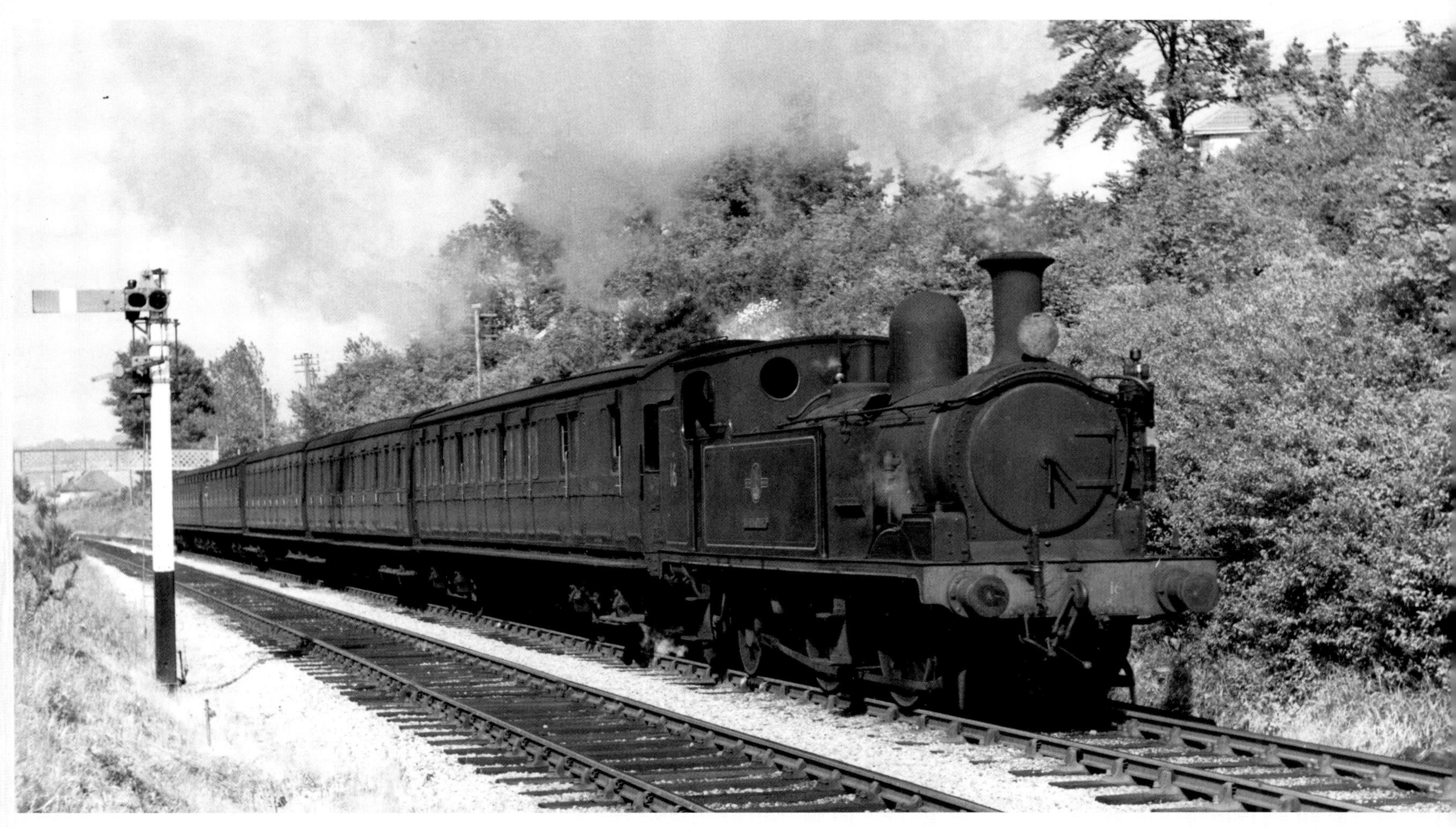

SANDOWN 'O2' 0-4-4T No W16 *Ventnor* nears Sandown with a train of empty stock on the double-tracked stretch from Brading on 17 June 1962.

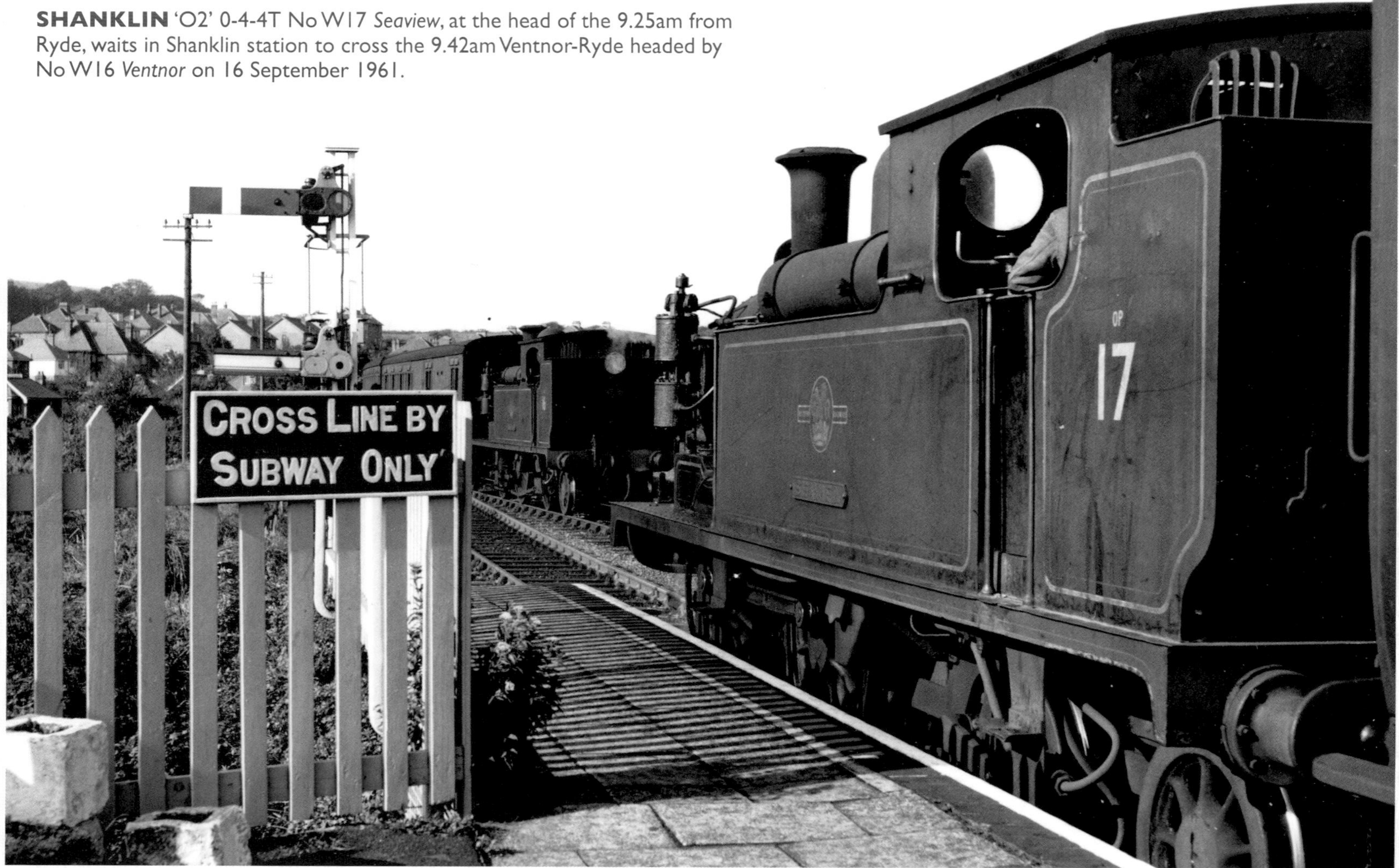

SHANKLIN 'O2' 0-4-4T No W17 *Seaview*, at the head of the 9.25am from Ryde, waits in Shanklin station to cross the 9.42am Ventnor-Ryde headed by No W16 *Ventnor* on 16 September 1961.

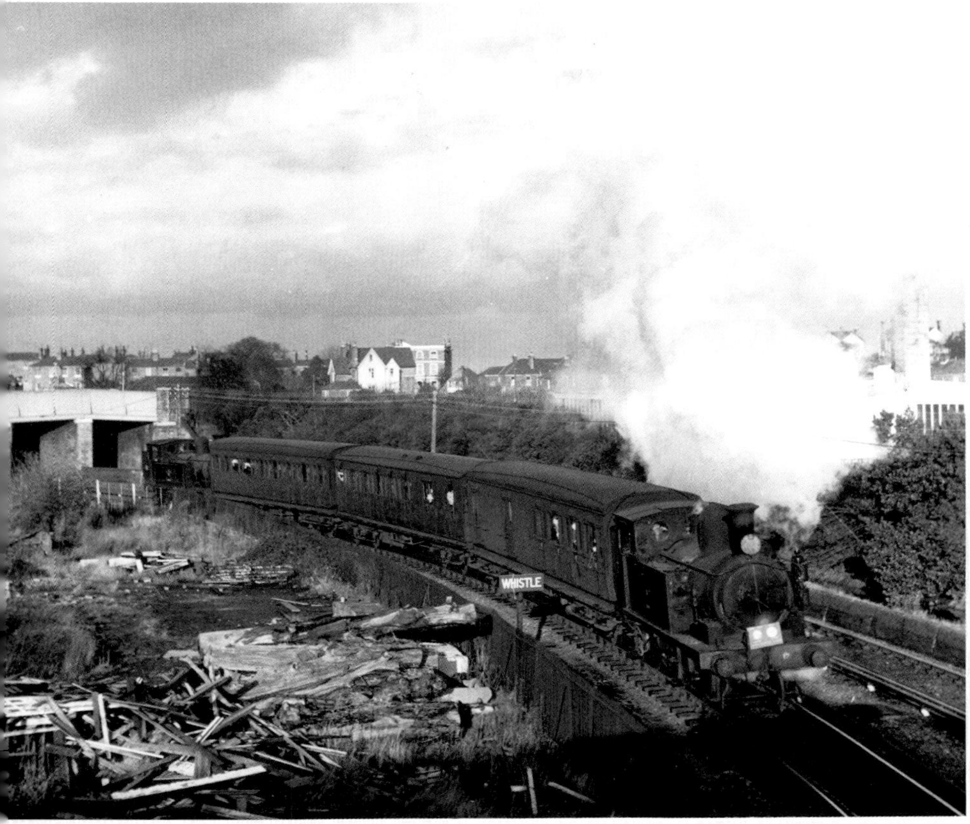

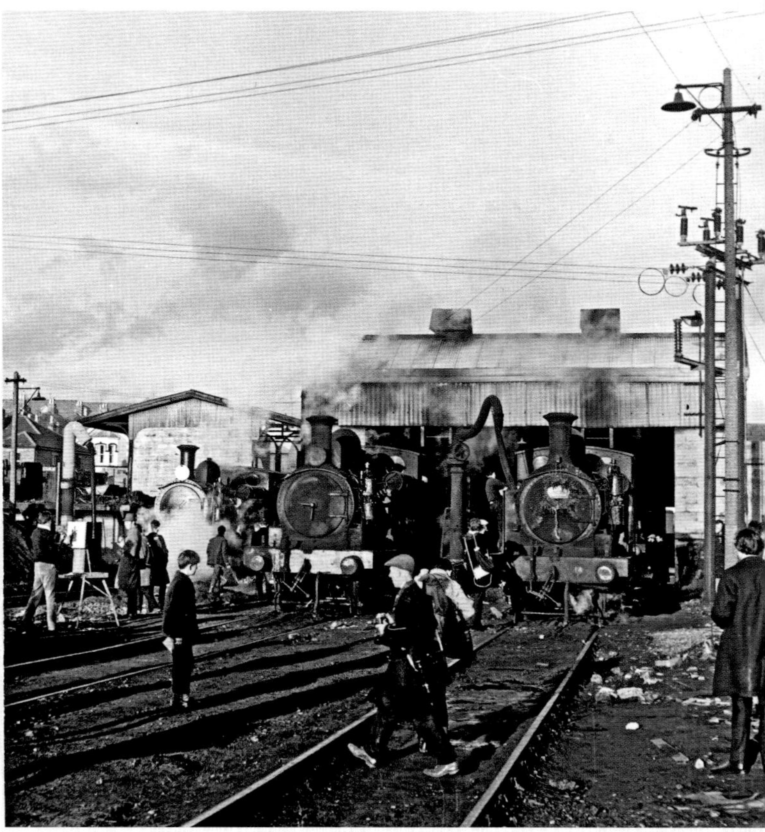

RYDE ST JOHN'S ROAD On 31 December 1966, the last day of the steam service, 'O2' 0-4-4T No W17 *Seaview* nears Ryde St John's Road with a train for Shanklin. No W16 *Ventnor* is attached to the rear of the train. For the last 3½ months of the steam service, up trains terminated at Ryde Esplanade, where locomotives could not run round. A turn-over locomotive was therefore attached to the rear of each train at St John's Road on the up journey, then worked the train to Shanklin and back.

RYDE ST JOHN'S ROAD It was open house at Ryde shed on the last day of the steam service. Seen here from the left are David Shepherd painting, then 'O2' 0-4-4Ts Nos W31 *Chale*, W27 *Merstone* and W14 *Fishbourne*, and spectators everywhere! A memorable ending to 1966.

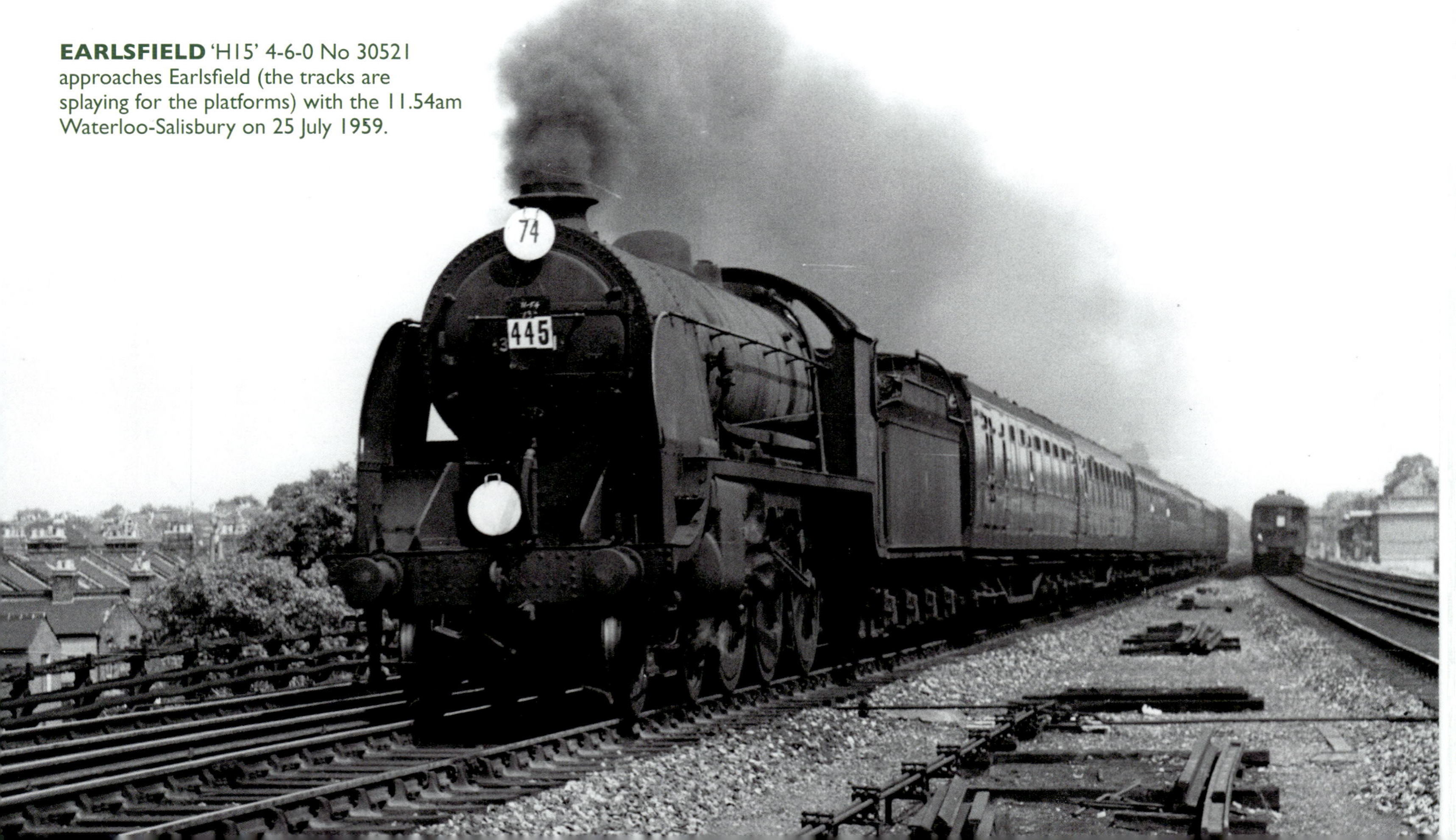

EARLSFIELD 'H15' 4-6-0 No 30521 approaches Earlsfield (the tracks are splaying for the platforms) with the 11.54am Waterloo-Salisbury on 25 July 1959.

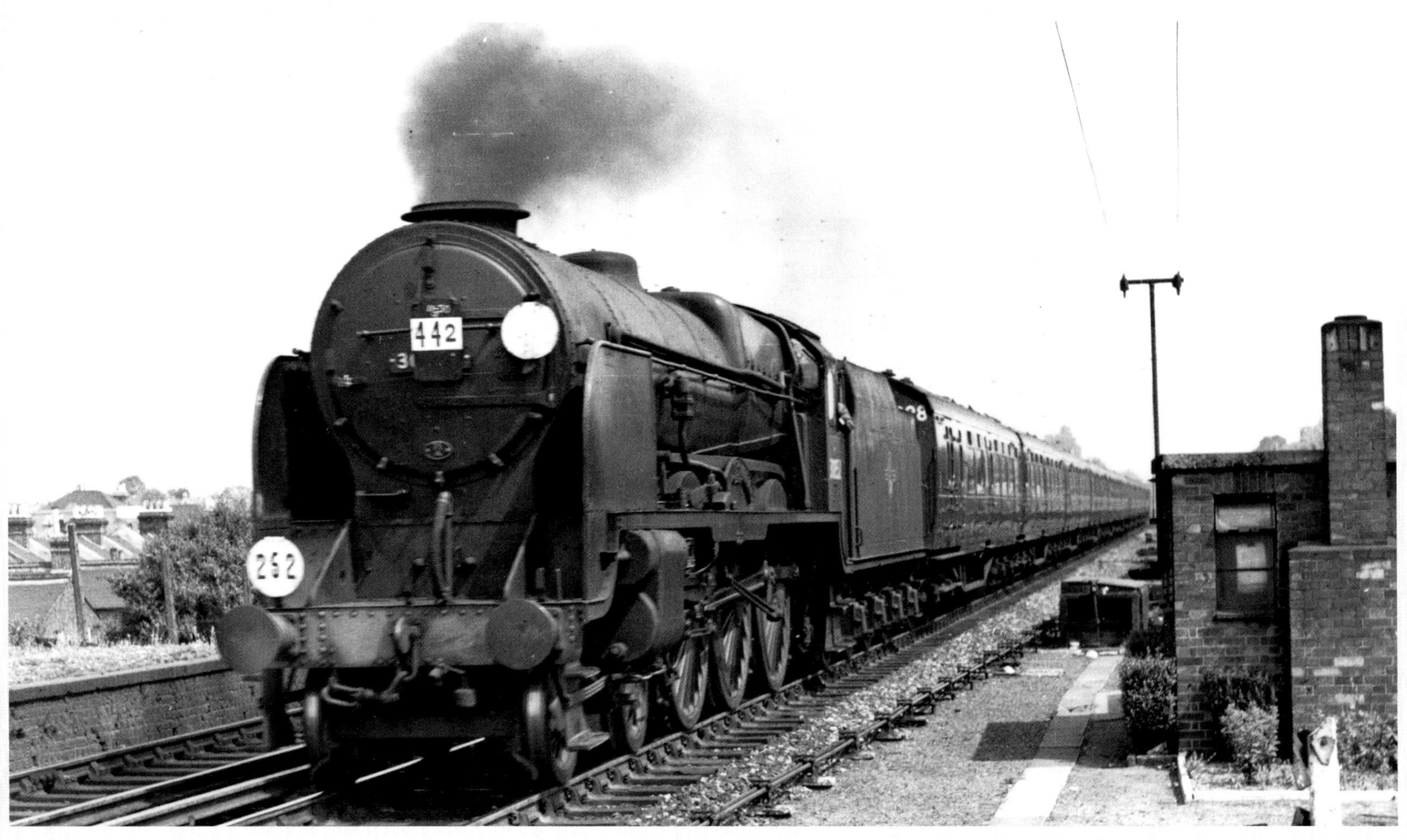

EARLSFIELD 'Lord Nelson' 4-6-0 No 30852 *Sir Walter Raleigh* is seen from a slightly different angle on the approach to Earlsfield. The train is the 11.30am Waterloo-Bournemouth on 25 July 1959.

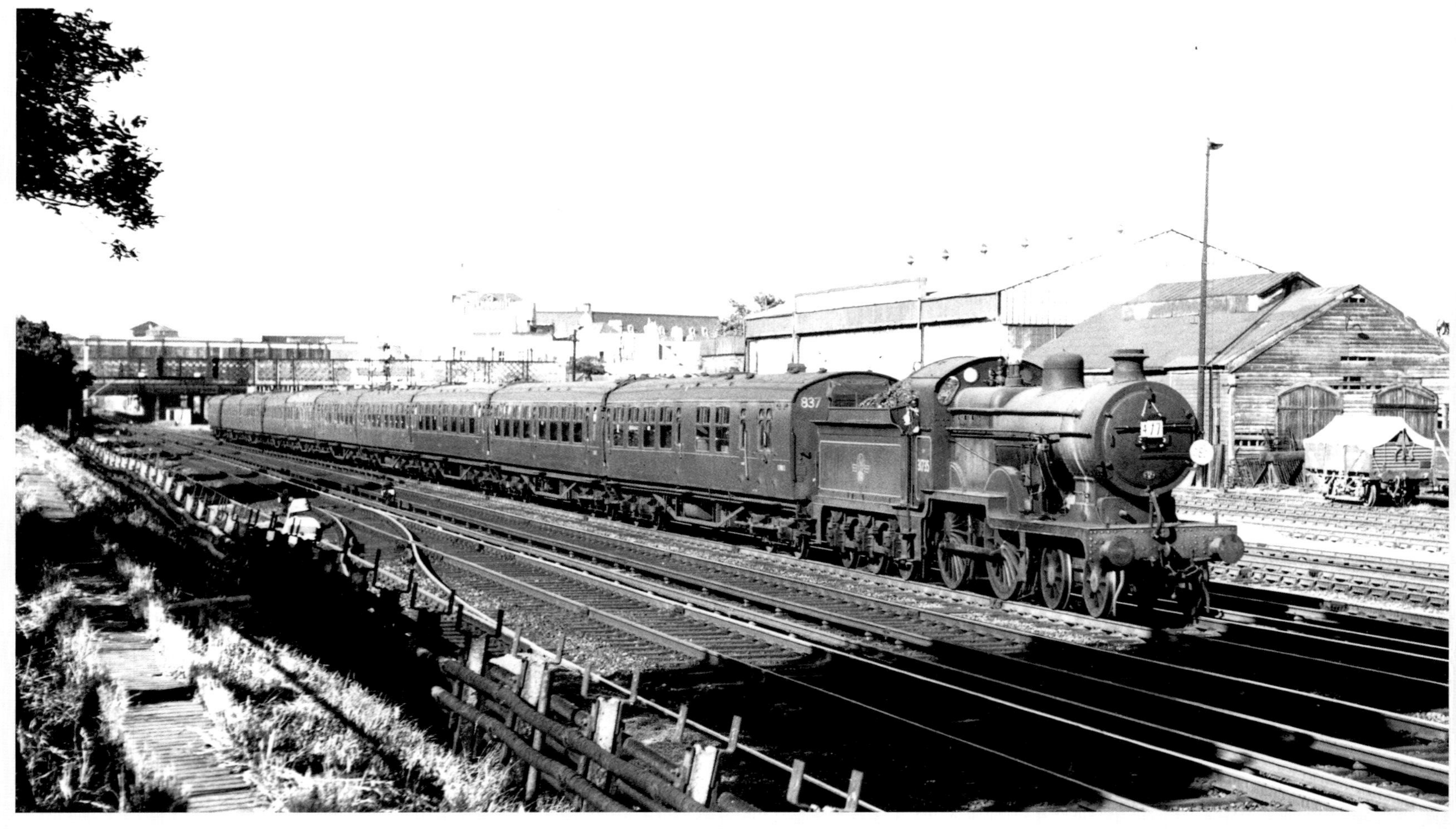

WIMBLEDON 'D1' 4-4-0 No 31735 passes the signal works at Wimbledon at the head of a own train of empty stock on 20 June 1959. The locomotive had been transferred to Eastleigh from the Eastern Section following the launch of Phase 1 of the Kent Coast electrification on 15 June 1959, and was being worked to its new home.

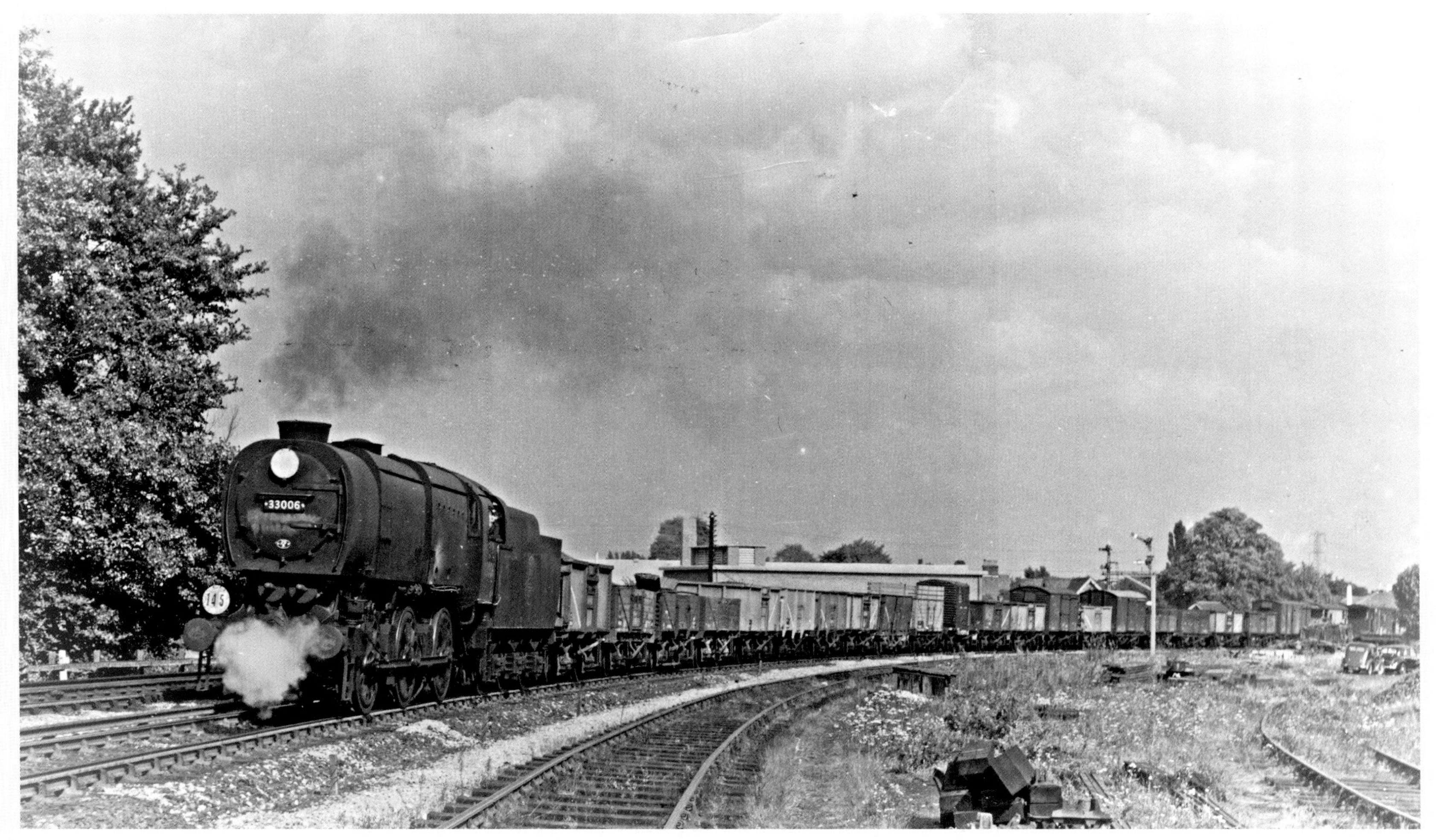

STAINES 'Q1' 0-6-0 No 33006 turns left out of Staines for Weybridge with the 2.10pm Feltham-Surbiton goods train on 15 September 1959. This working was usually taken by an 'H16' 4-6-2T.

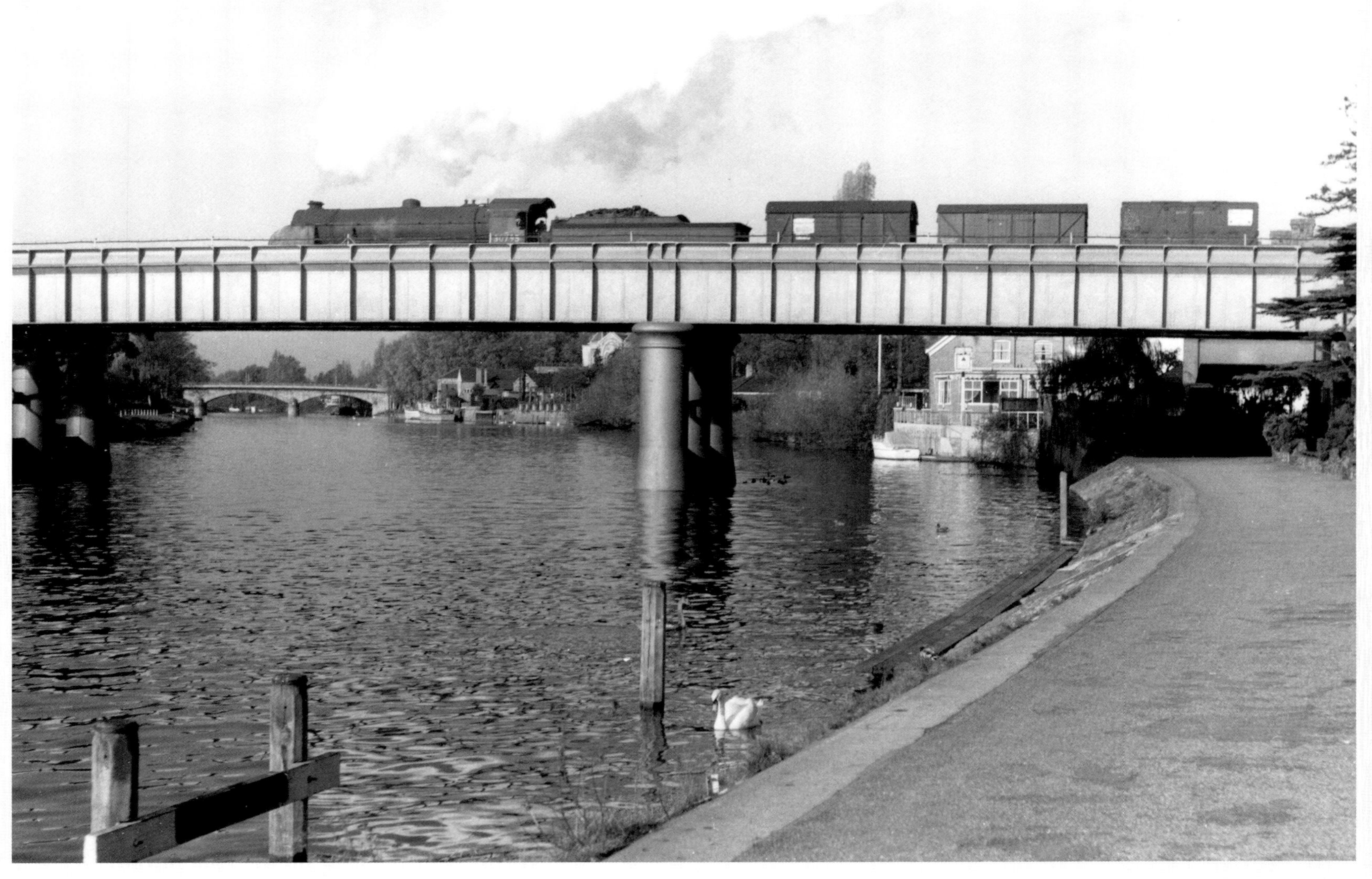

STAINES 'N15' 4-6-0 No 30795 *Sir Dinadan* crosses the Thames at Staines with a down goods train from Feltham on 4 November 1959. The arched bridge in the distance carried the A30 road until the Staines bypass was opened.

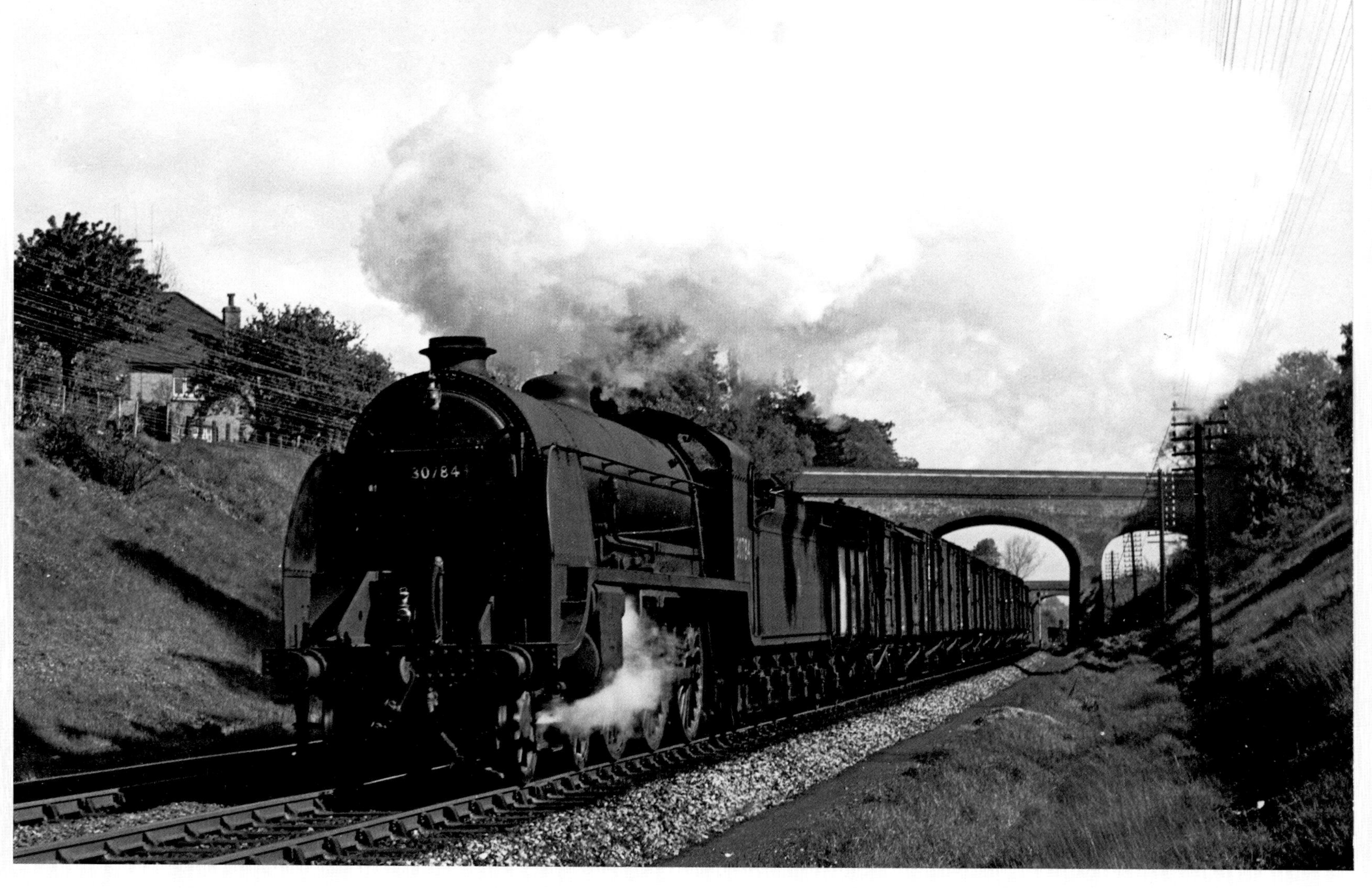

READING 'N15' 4-6-0 No 30784 *Sir Nerovens* brings a goods train for the Southern Region at Basingstoke from Reading West towards Southcote Junction on 2 May 1959. The nearer bridge carries the A4 Bath Road.

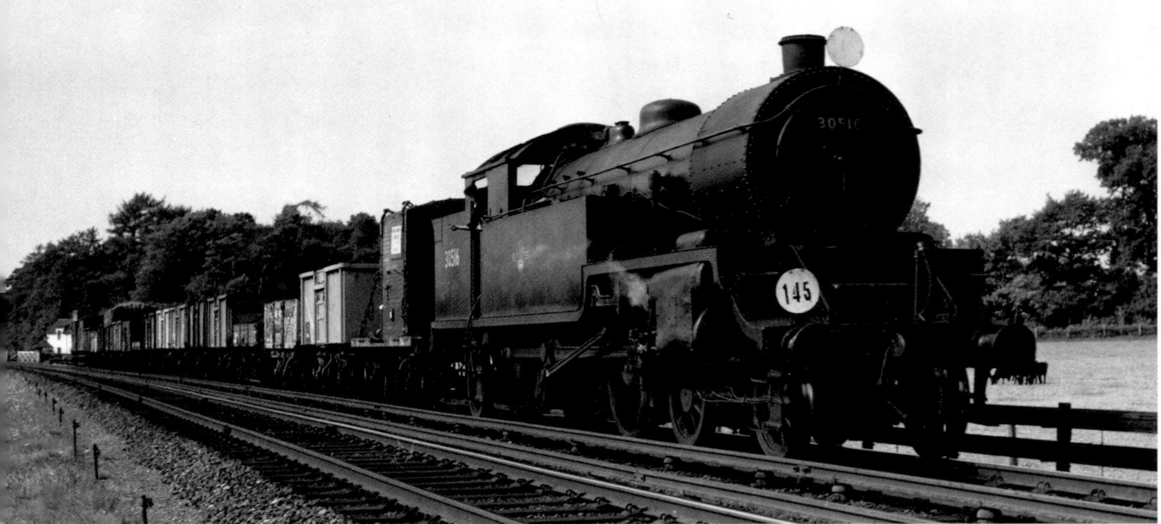

CHERTSEY The 2.10pm Feltham-Surbiton goods train is seen again, this time (on 17 September 1959) near Chertsey and headed by 'H16' 4-6-2T No 30516.

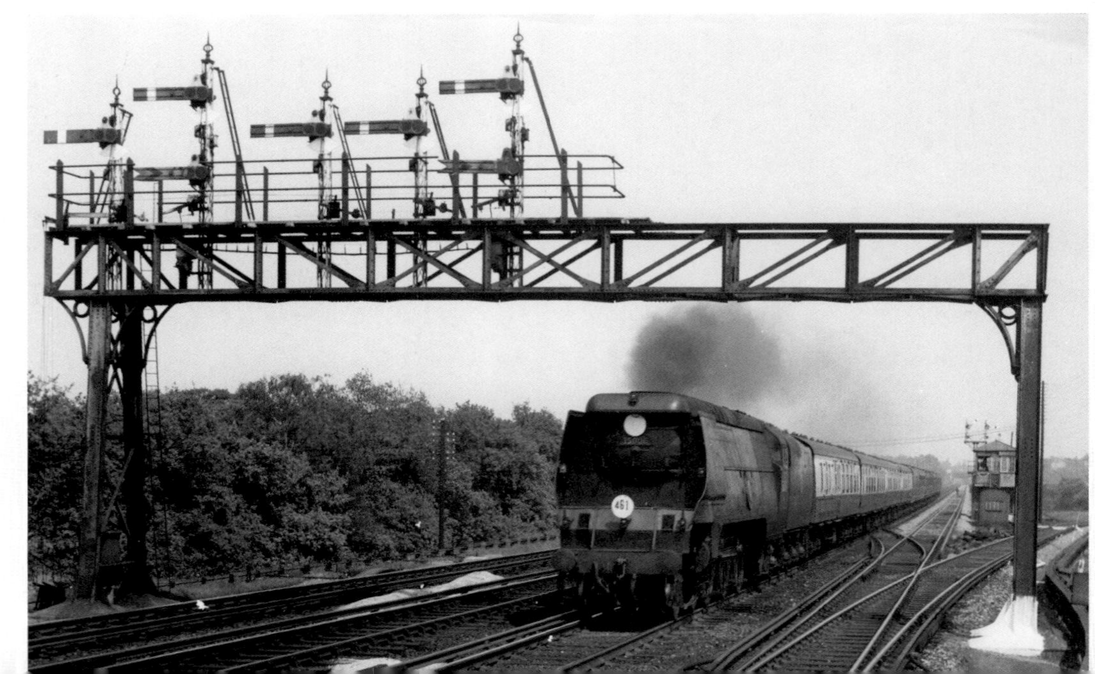

WEST WEYBRIDGE 'MN' 4-6-2 No 35006 *Peninsular & Oriental S.N. Co,* one of the last two of the class to be rebuilt in October 1959, approaches West Weybridge station at the head of the 1.00pm Waterloo-West of England on 12 May 1959. The line emerging from behind the signal box on the right is the western spur from the Virginia Water-Weybridge route.

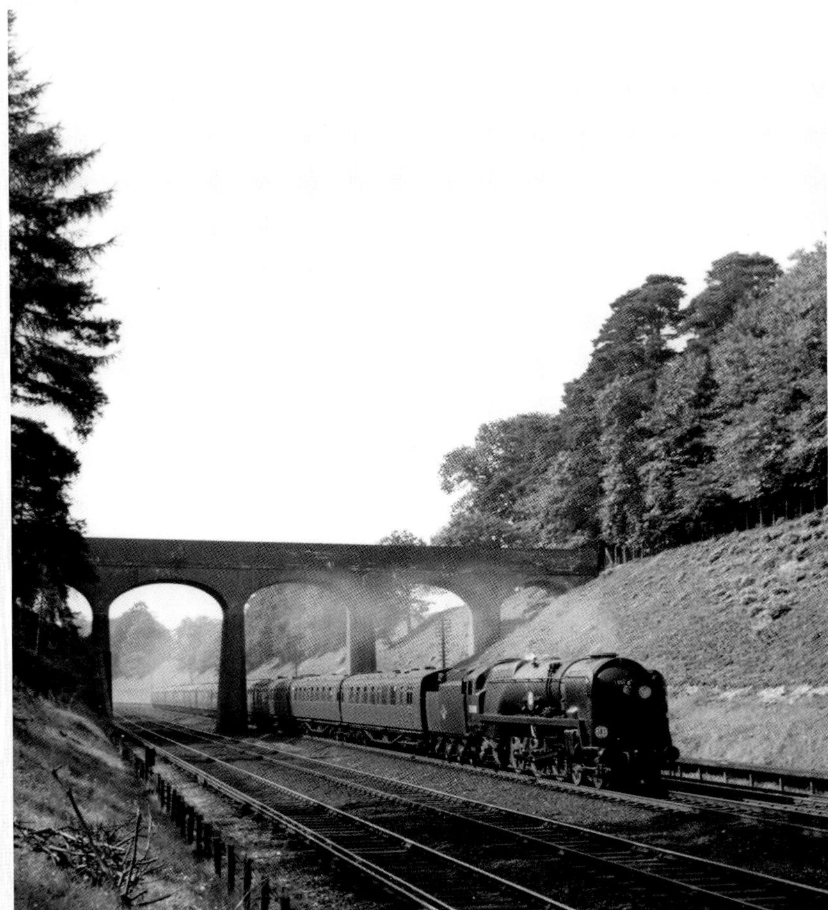

FARNBOROUGH 'MN' 4-6-2 No 35008 *Orient Line* heads the 12.10pm Bournemouth West-Waterloo train through Deepcut Cutting, east of Farnborough, on 10 September 1960.

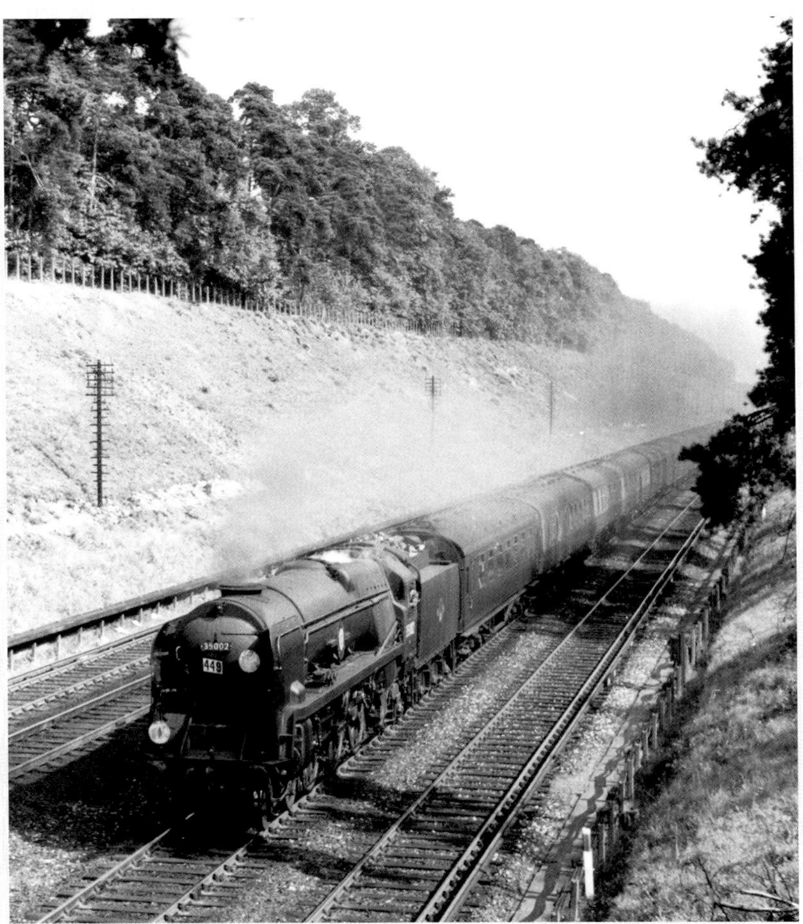

FARNBOROUGH Also in Deepcut Cutting on the same day, 'MN' 4-6-2 No 35002 *Union Castle* was captured at the head of the 1.30pm Waterloo-Bournemouth train.

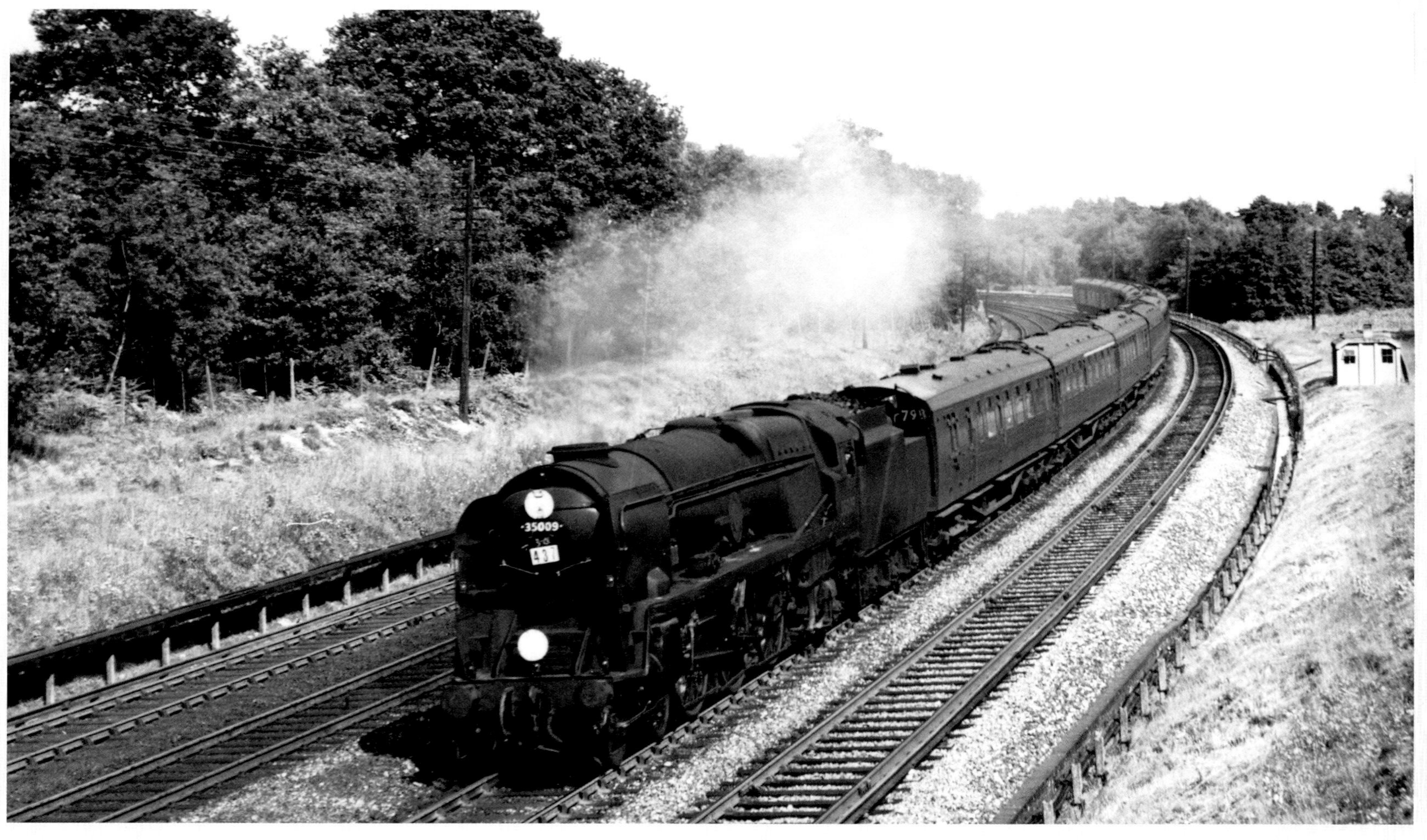

PIRBRIGHT Just west of Pirbright Junction, which is itself west of Brookwood, where the line to Aldershot, Farnham and, nowadays, the 'Watercress Line' leaves the main line to Basingstoke, 'MN' 4-6-2 No 35009 *Shaw Savill* heads the 3.00pm Waterloo-West of England on 7 August 1963.

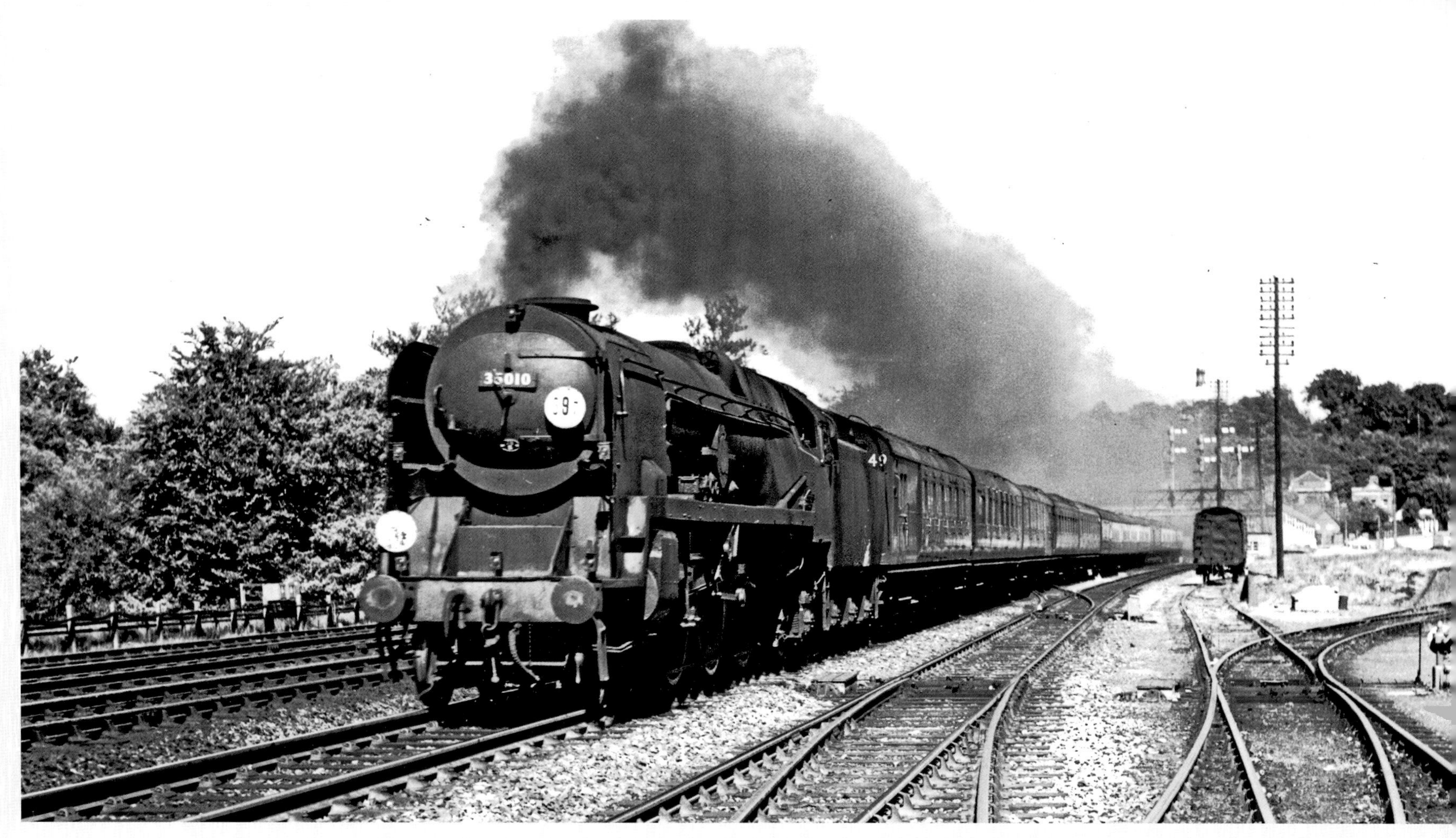

FARNBOROUGH With firing in progress, 'MN' 4-6-2 No 35010 *Blue Star* heads a Waterloo-Bournemouth train just west of Farnborough station on 20 June 1959. The down starting signals can be seen to the right of the train.

WINCHFIELD
A typical summer's Saturday morning at Winchfield, a deeply countrified station west of Farnborough: both down lines are signalled 'off', and 'N15' 4-6-0 No 30451 *Sir Lamorak,* the last Eastleigh 'Arthur' in service, runs into the almost deserted station with an up stopping train on 24 August 1961.

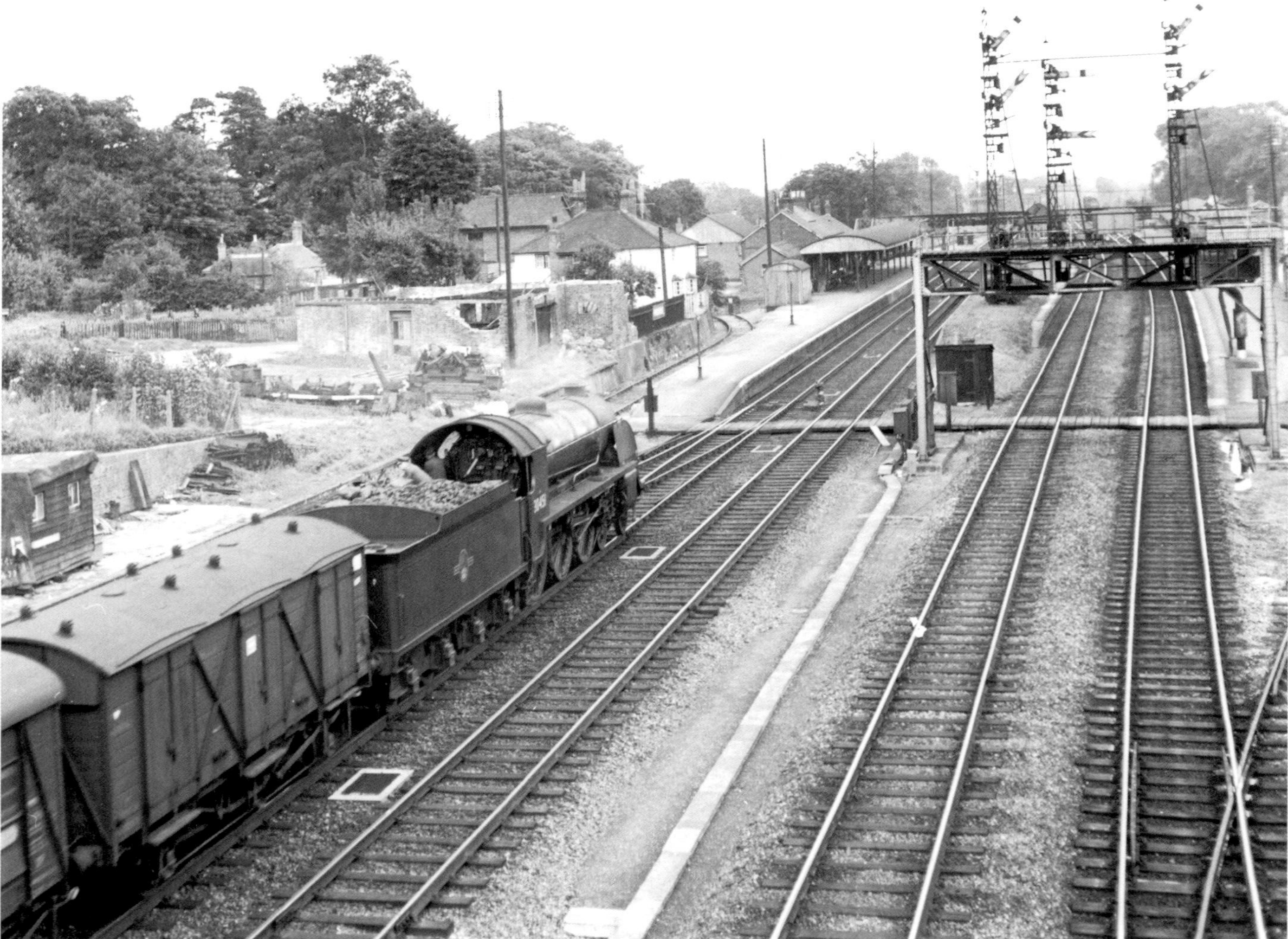

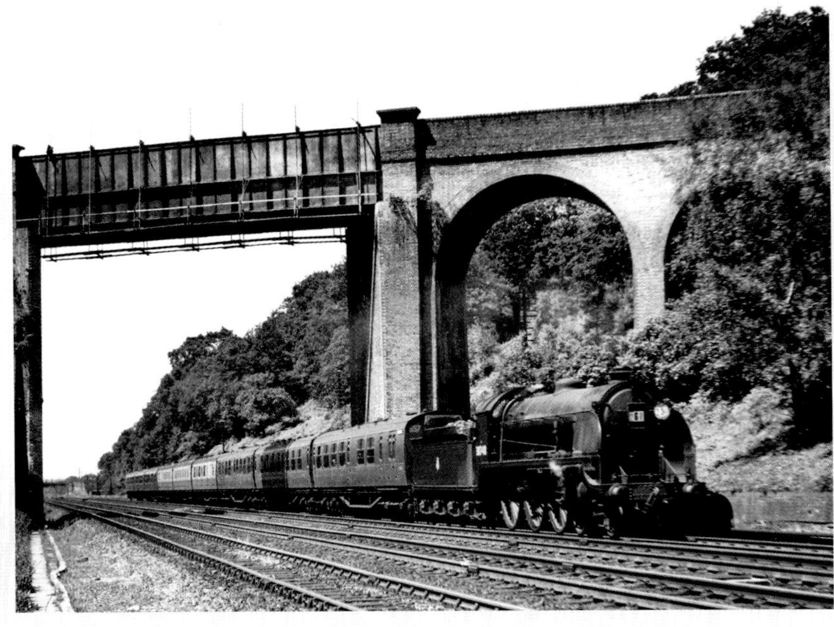

Above: **WINCHFIELD** Almost immediately west of Winchfield station the SR main line dives into a deep cutting. Here 'N15' 4-6-0 No 30748 *Vivien,* last survivor but one of the original LSWR 'N15s', passes with a Southampton Terminus-Waterloo stopping train on 27 July 1957. The imposing bridge carries a country lane, and is now masked by the M3 motorway.

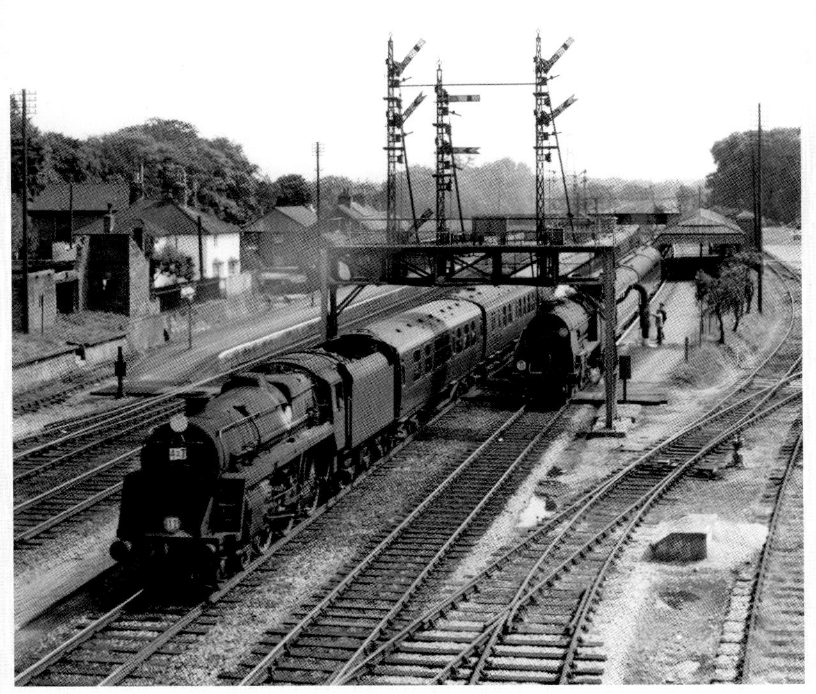

Left: **WINCHFIELD** 5MT 4-6-0 No 73089, not yet named *Maid of Astolat,* races through with a train for the West of England, while 'S15' 4-6-0 No 30512 with a train of empty LMR stock takes water at the Down Local platform on 13 August 1960.

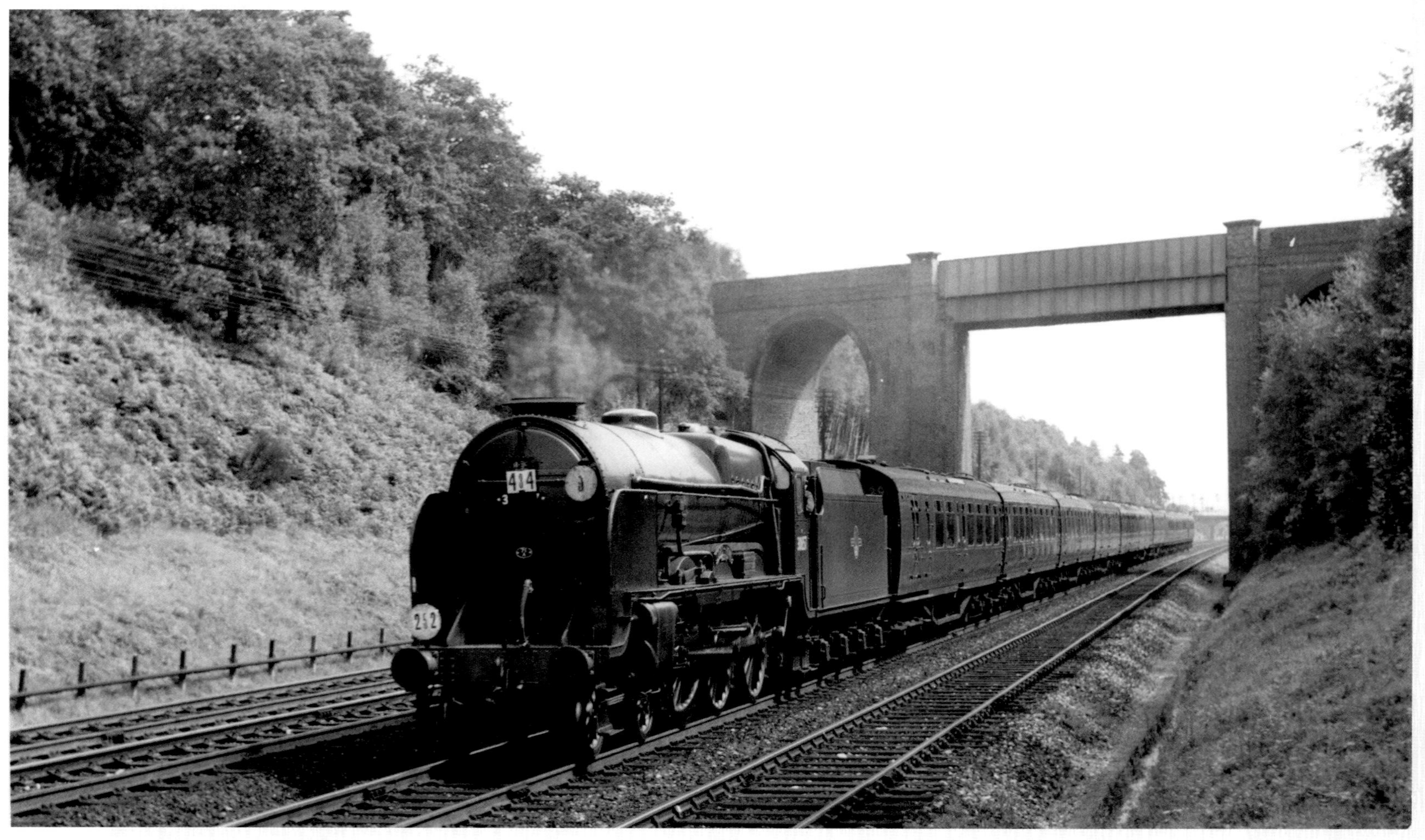

WINCHFIELD On the other side of the bridge, and on 13 August 1960, 'LN' 4-6-0 No 30857 *Lord Howe* heads the 11.30am Waterloo-Bournemouth West.

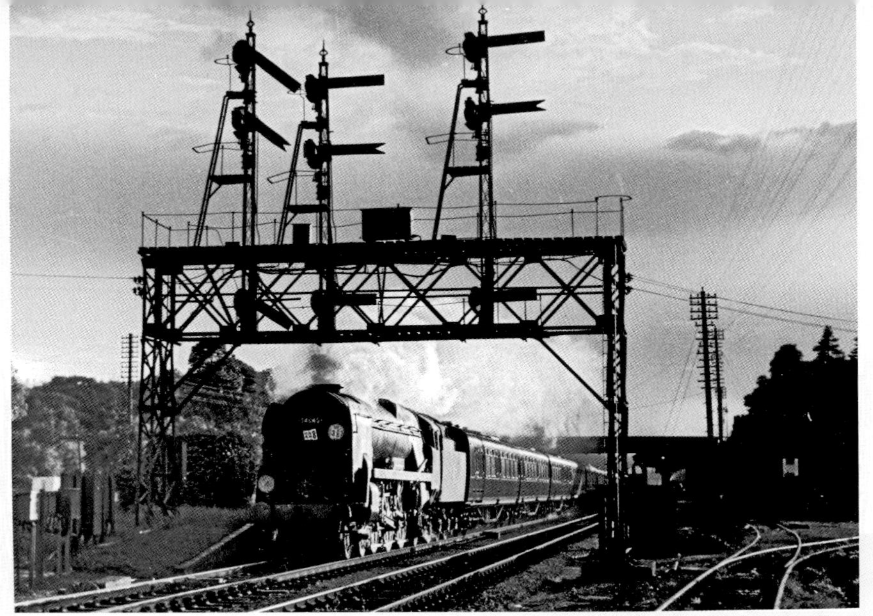

Left: **FLEET** 'WC' 4-6-2 No 34045 *Ottery St Mary* brings an up Bournemouth line train through Fleet station on the evening of 1 August 1960.

Below: **BASINGSTOKE** On 1 September 1962 'N15' 4-6-0 No 30782 *Sir Brian* hauls a Wadebridge and Bude to Waterloo train east of Basingstoke; it is believed to have been the last occasion that a 'King Arthur' worked a main-line express.

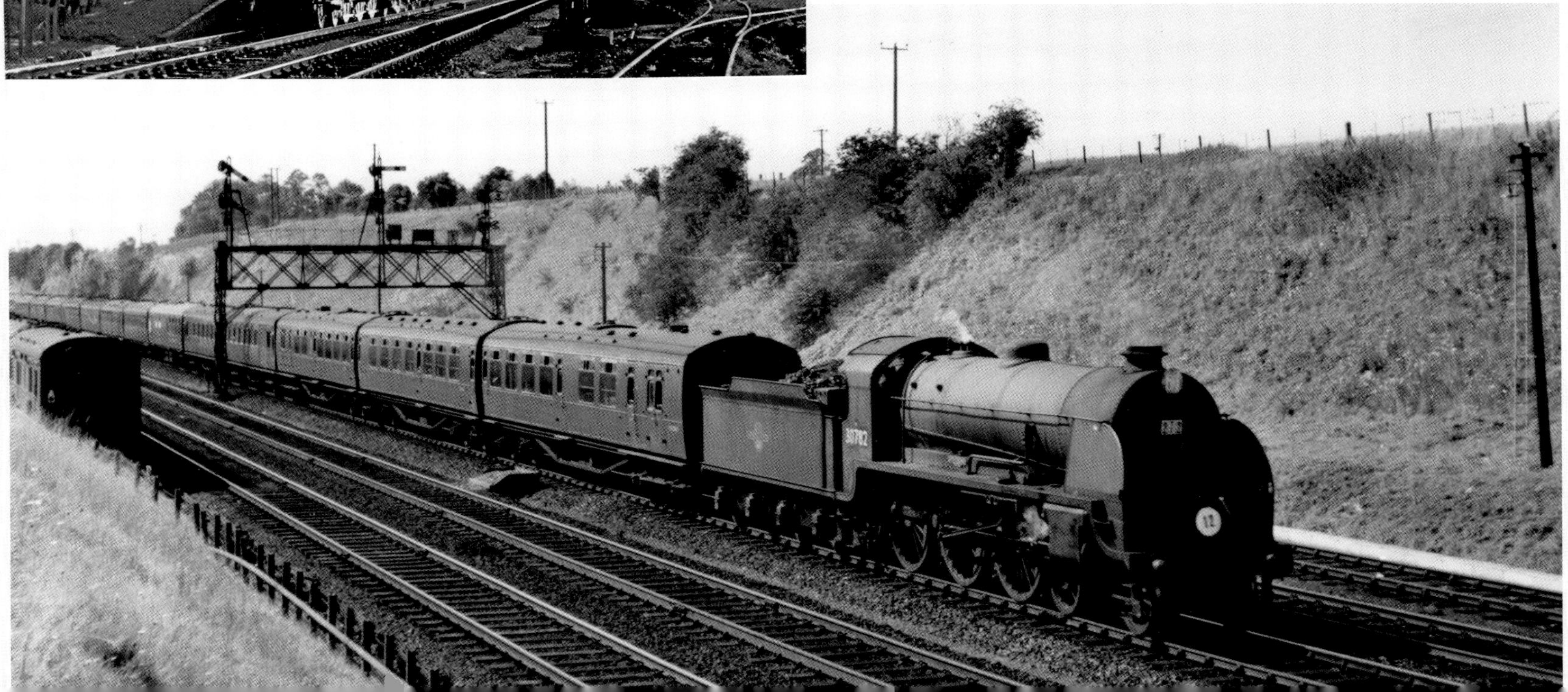

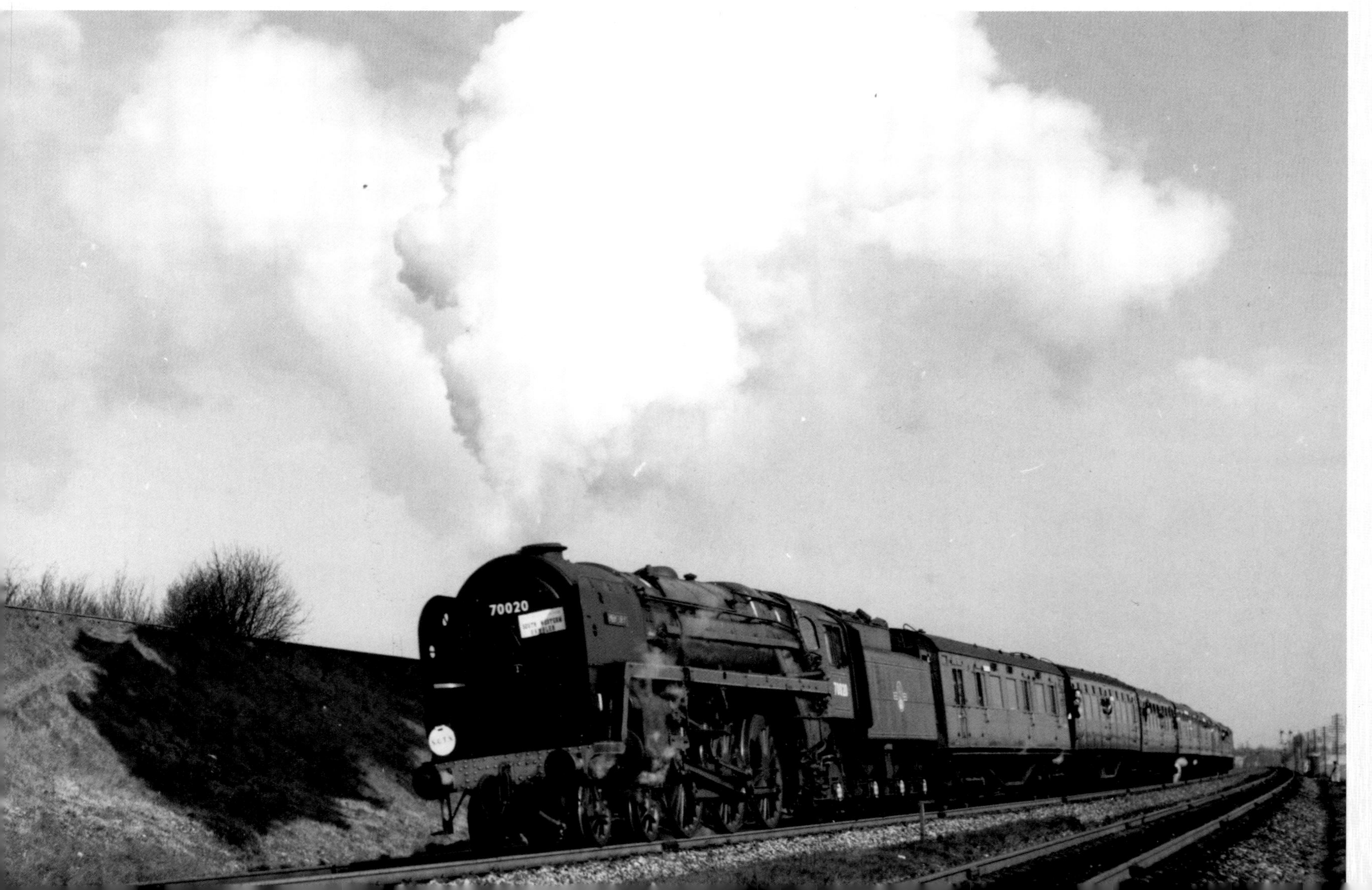

70020
SOUTH WESTERN
CLIPPER

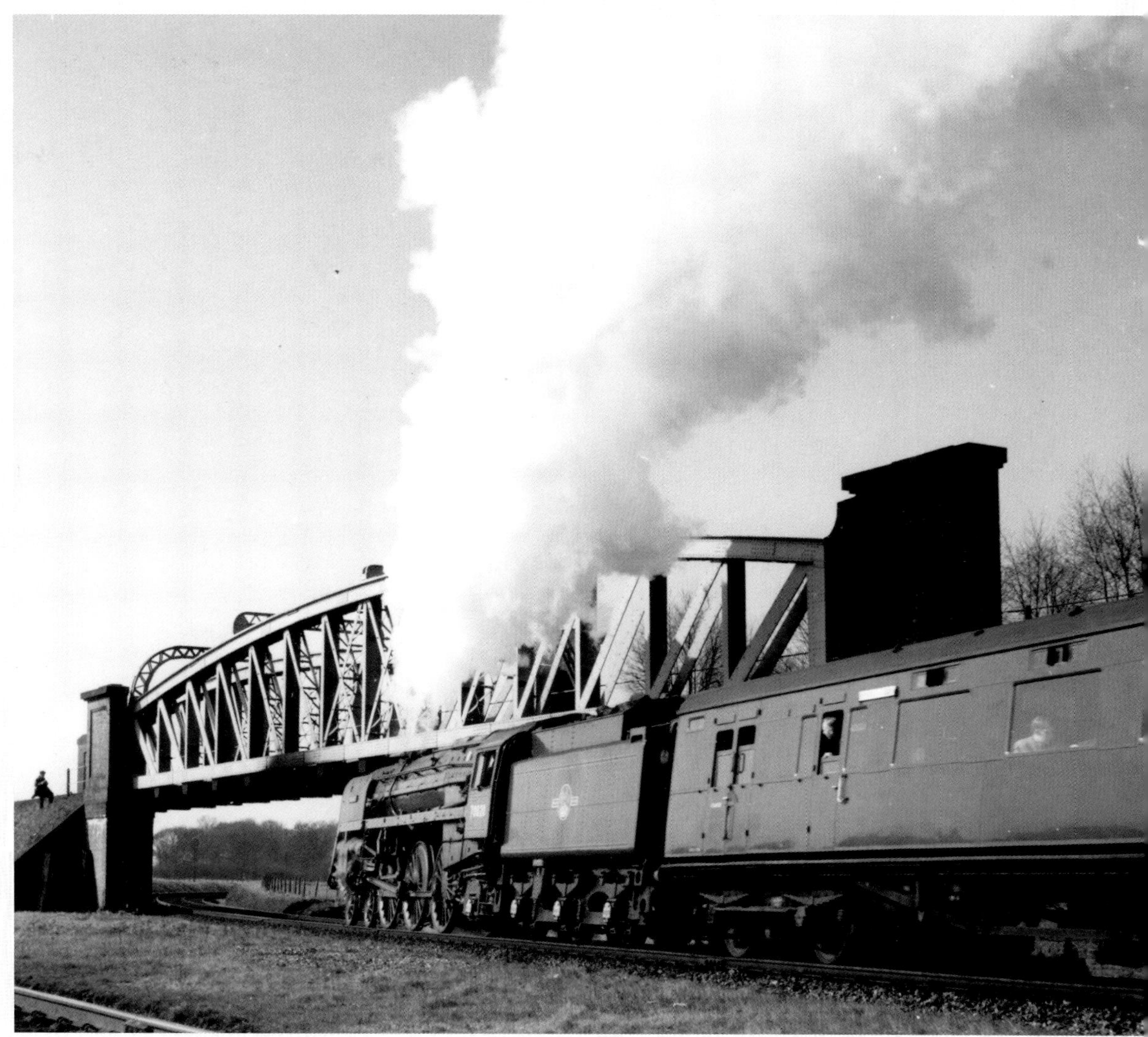

Leftt and right: **BATTLEDOWN** The Southern Counties Touring Society organised the 'South Western Rambler' excursion, which ran on 8 March 1964 from Waterloo to Waterloo via Reading, Basingstoke, Templecombe and Bournemouth. It was worked from Waterloo to Salisbury by 7P 'Britannia' 4-6-2 No 70020 *Mercury,* here seen approaching and diving under the Battledown Flyover.

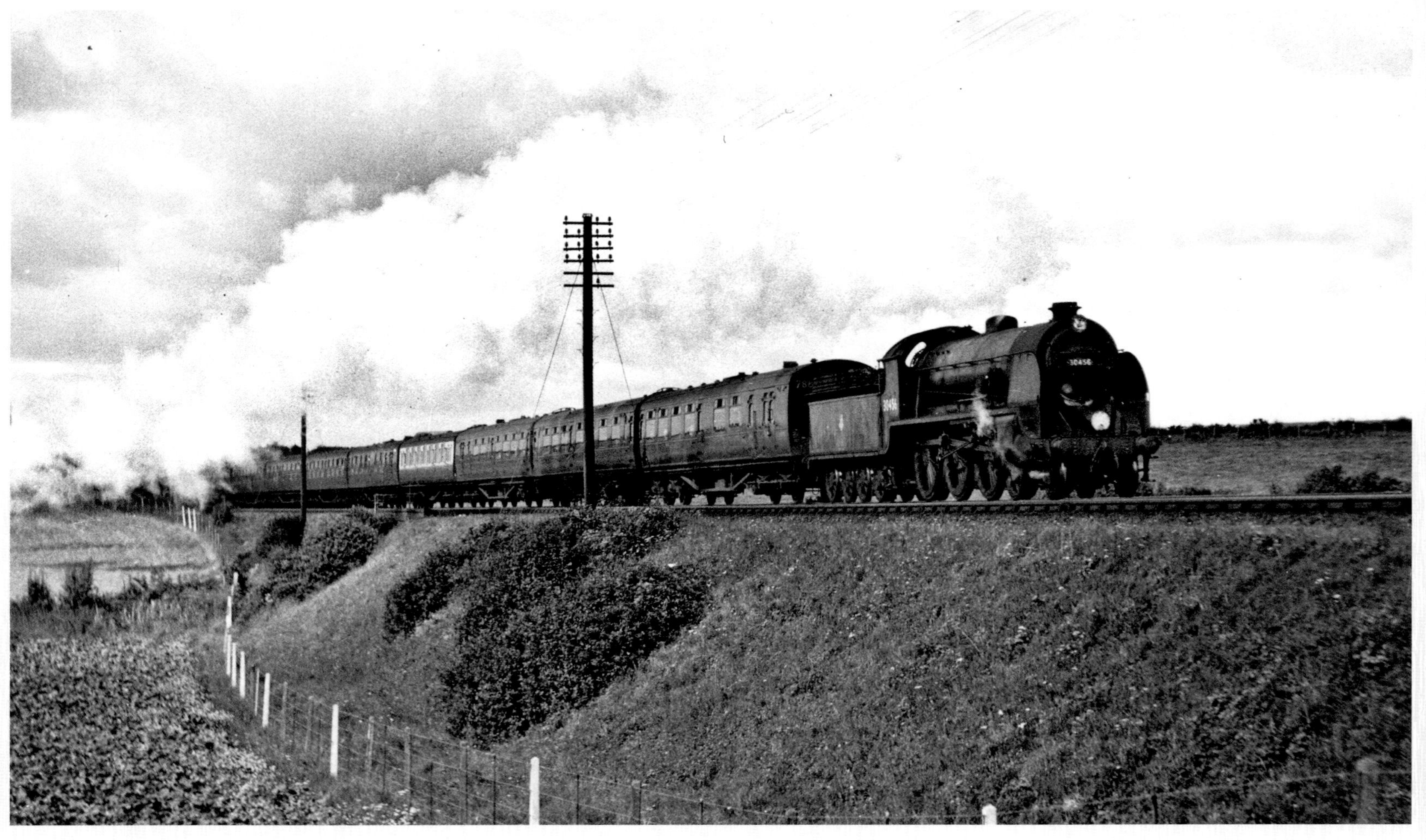

OVERTON 'N15' 4-6-0 No 30456 *Sir Galahad* heads the Sunday morning up semi-fast from Salisbury on 15 September 1957.
A year earlier this train had been a regular working for a Urie 'Arthur'.

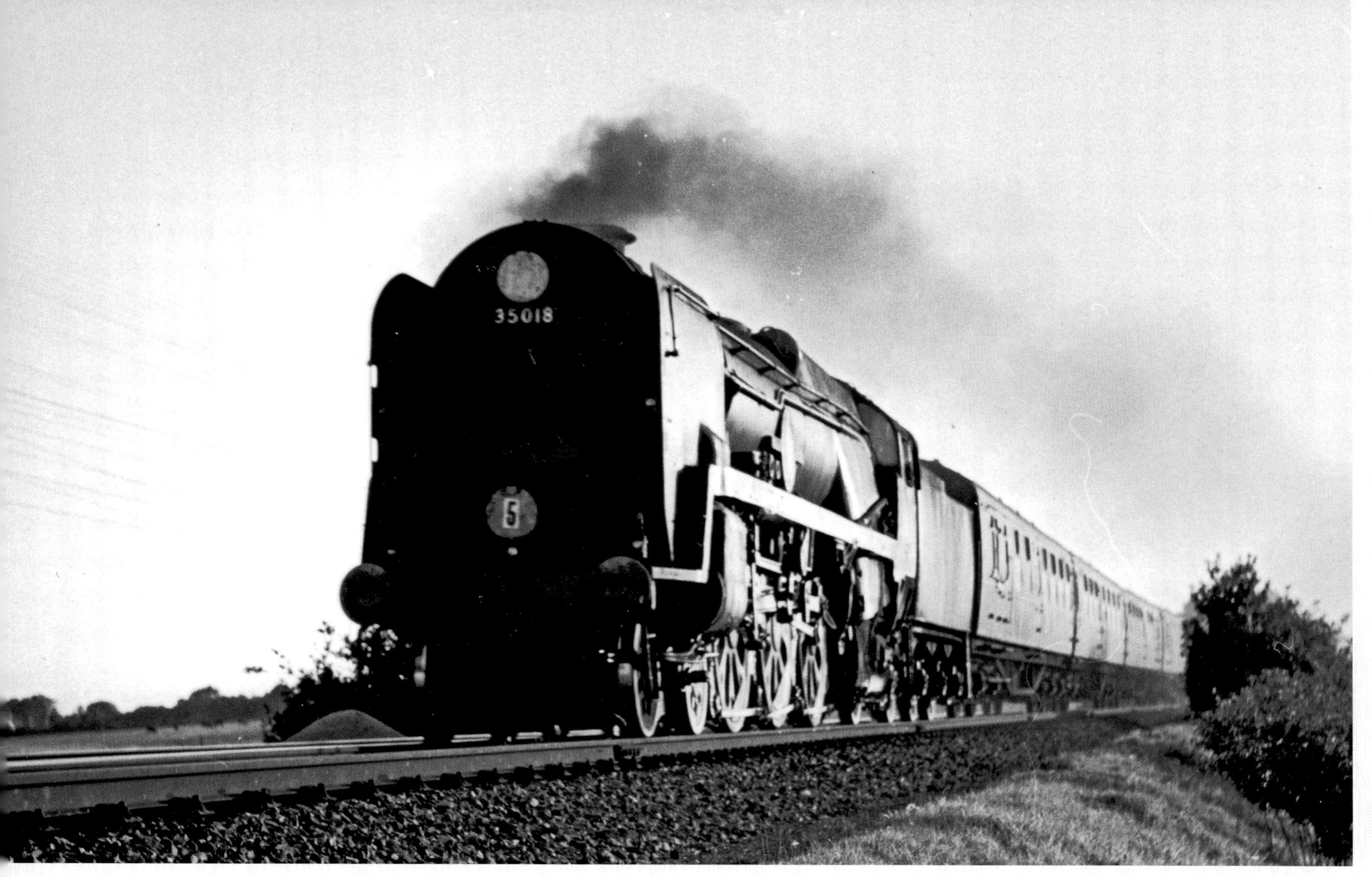

ANDOVER And from the other side of the line, 'MN' 4-6-2 No 35018 *British India Line* nears Andover with the 4.30pm Exeter Central-Waterloo on 9 September 1961.

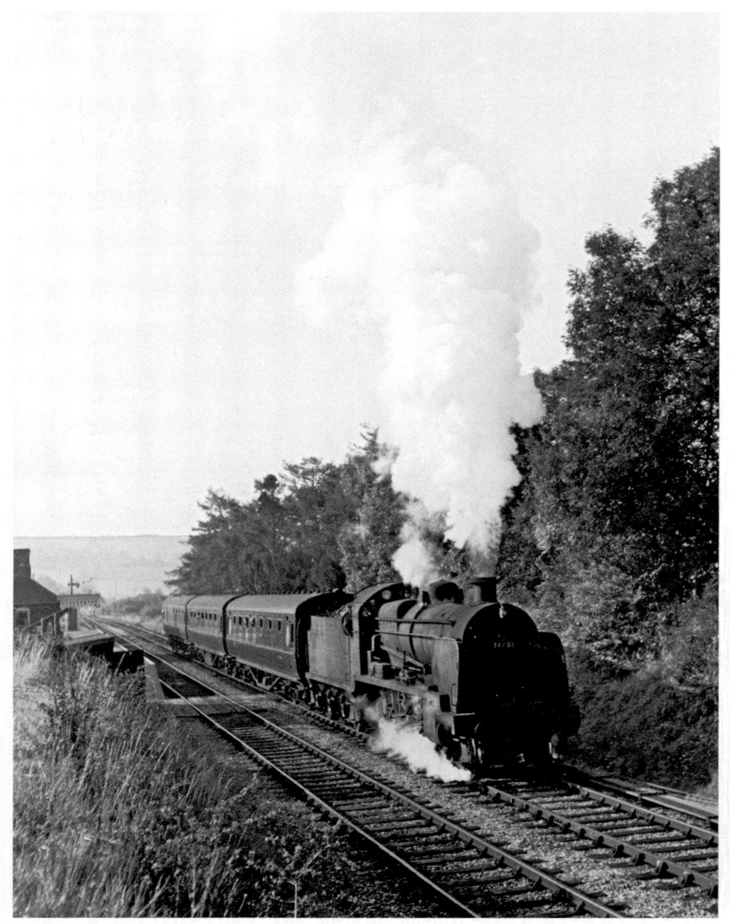

OGBOURNE On 9 September 1961, the last day of the service over the former Midland & South Western Junction (M&SWJ) route, 'U' 2-6-0 No 31791 pulls away from Ogbourne, south of Swindon, with the daily train from Southampton-Cheltenham.

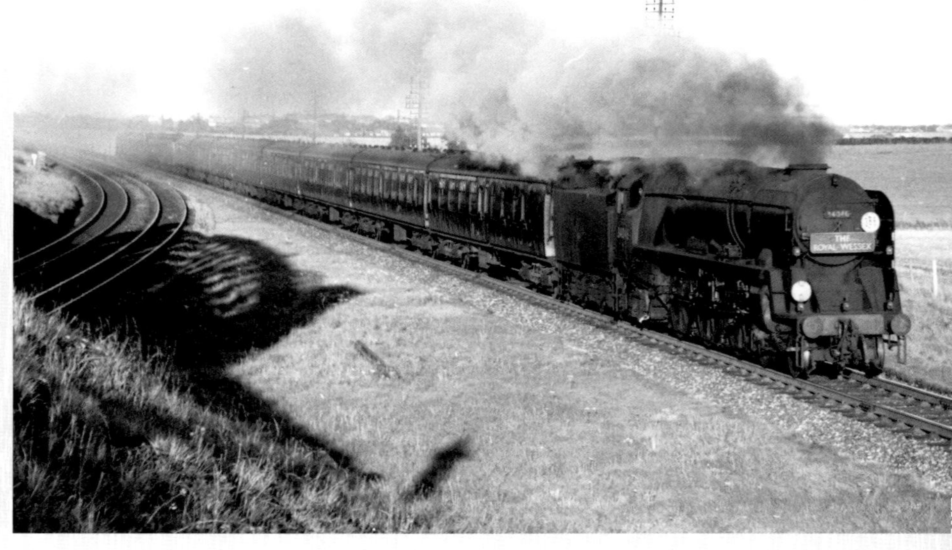

BATTLEDOWN Back to Battledown, this time for the Bournemouth line – the route to Salisbury curves left – as 'WC' 4-6-2 No 34046 *Braunton* passes at the head of the down 'Royal Wessex' on 30 September 1961. The photographer apologises for the intrusion of his shadow.

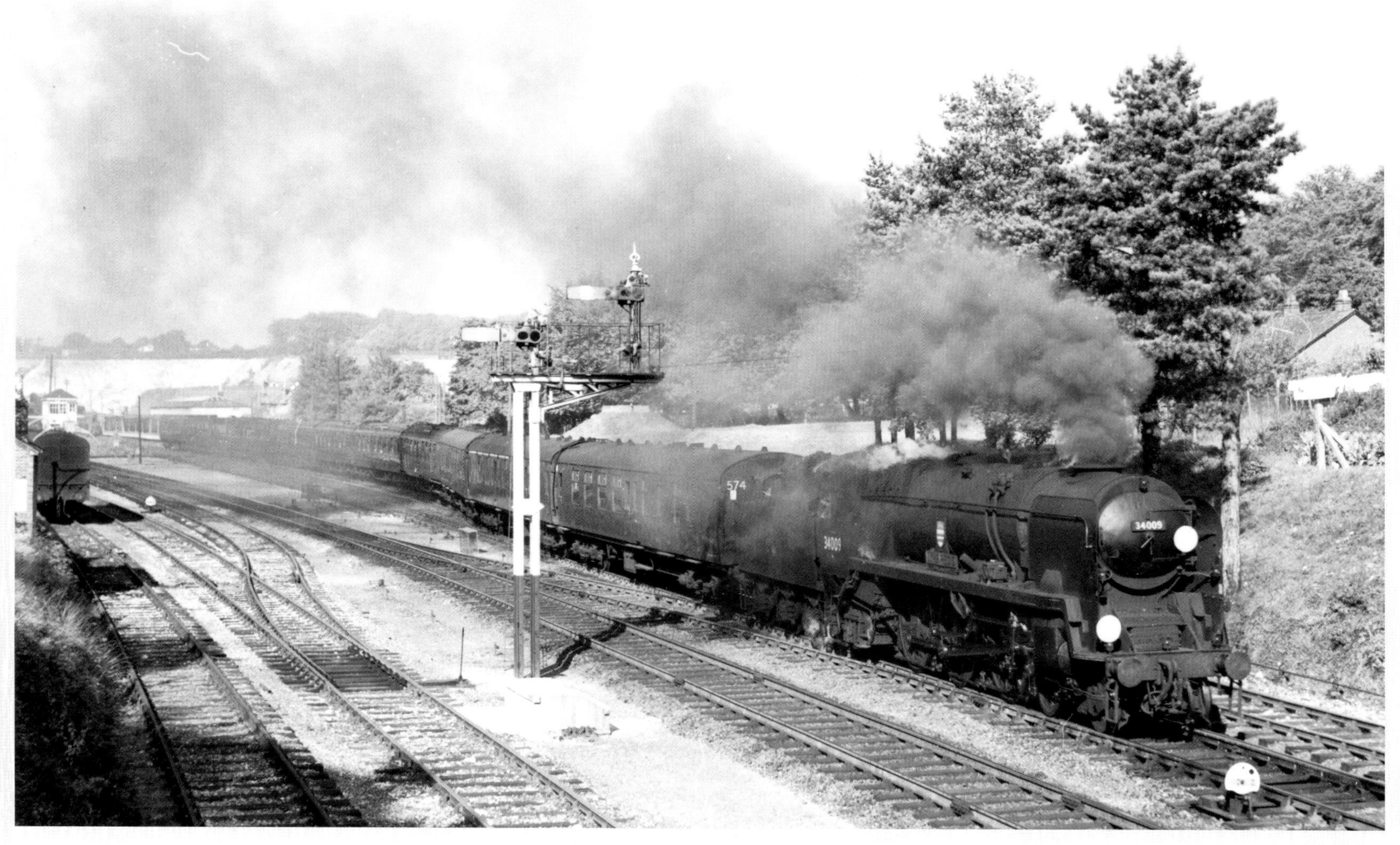

MICHELDEVER 'WC' 4-6-2 No 34009 *Lyme Regis* pulls away from Micheldever with a down train to Bournemouth on 20 July 1966. The wind is clearly favouring the washing on the right!

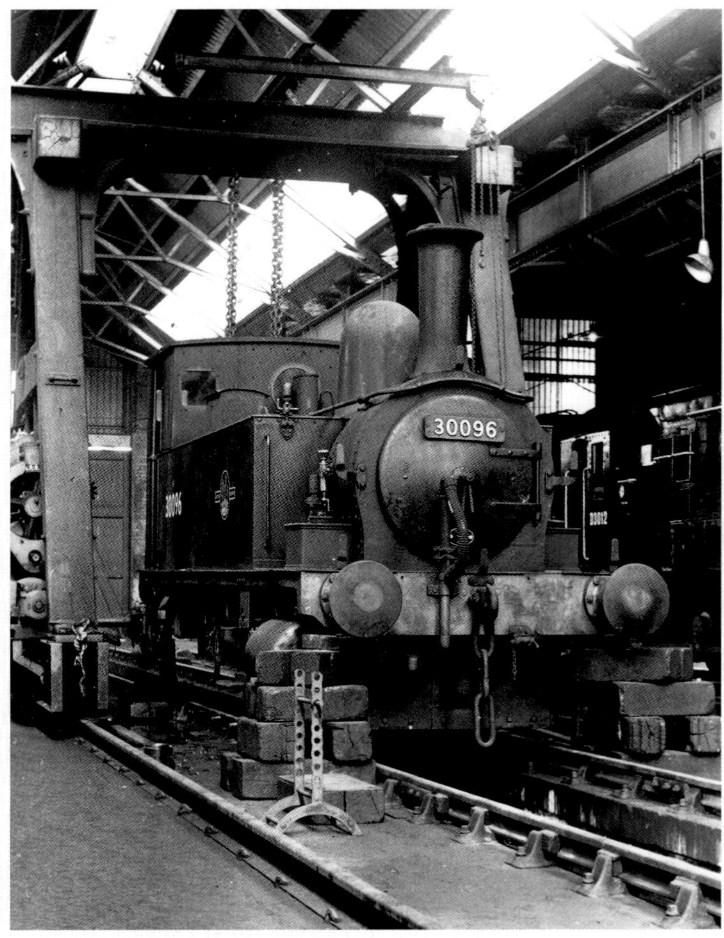

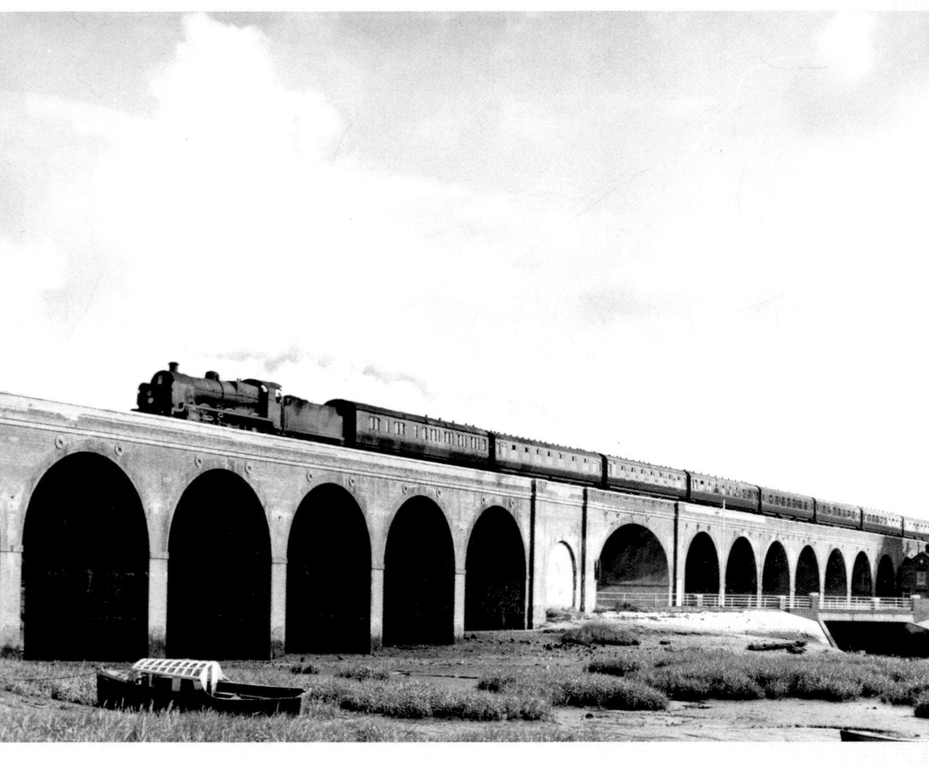

Above: **FAREHAM** A 'U' 2-6-0, unidentifiable even at the time but one of the batch converted from the 2-6-4T 'River' Class, crosses Fareham Viaduct at the head of the 9.31am Portsmouth-Cardiff train on 19 August 1961.

EASTLEIGH In the depths of Eastleigh depot, 'B4' 0-4-0T No 30096, formerly *Normandy* (and now preserved on the Bluebell Railway), receives attention on 30 April 1961.

Right: **WICKHAM** 'E1' 0-6-0T No 32694 and 'O2' 0-4-4T No 30200 head the LCGB 'Solent Limited' rail tour up to Droxford on the freight-only stub at the south end of the former Meon Valley line, near Wickham, on 30 April 1961.

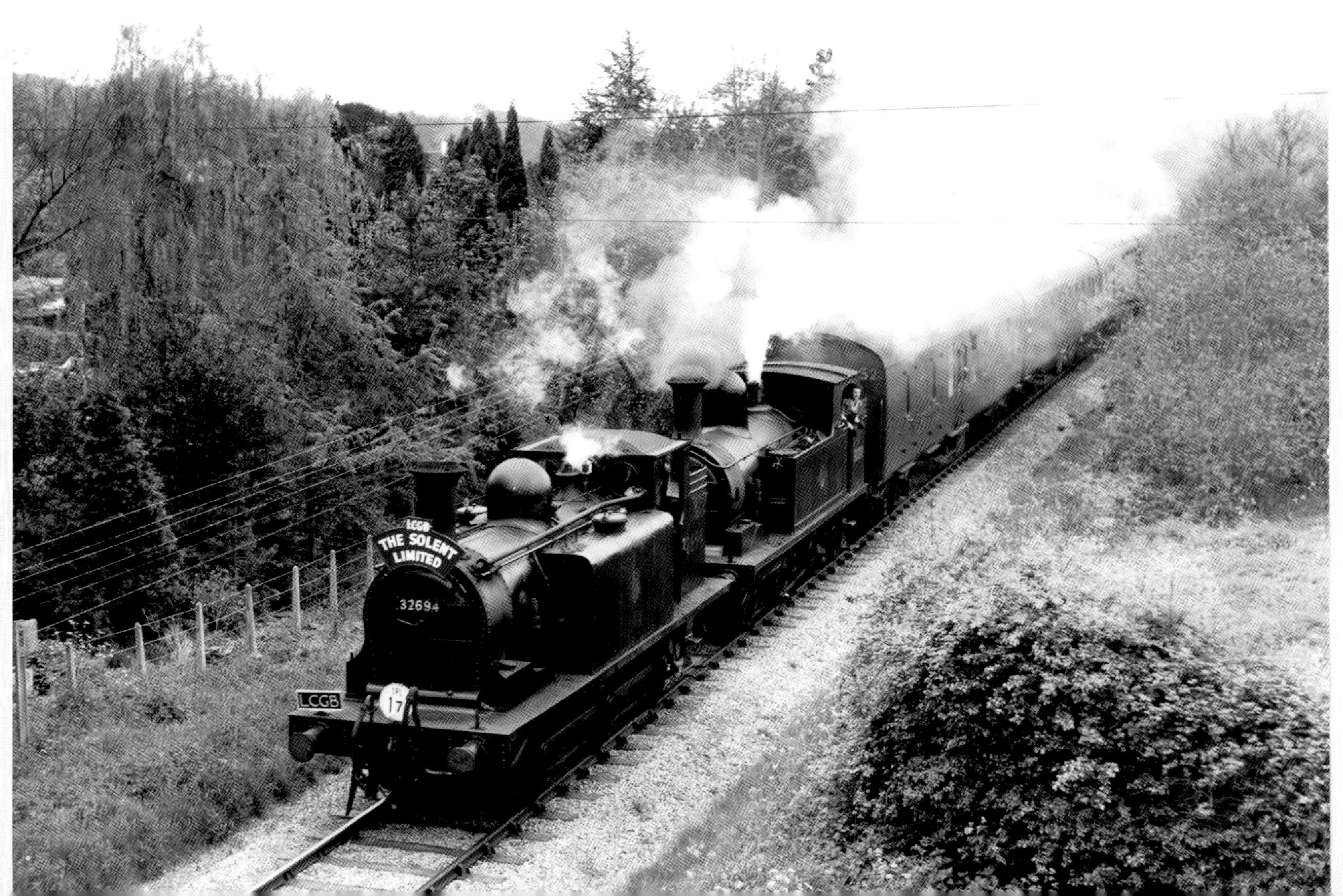
LCGB
THE SOLENT
LIMITED
32694
LCGB
17

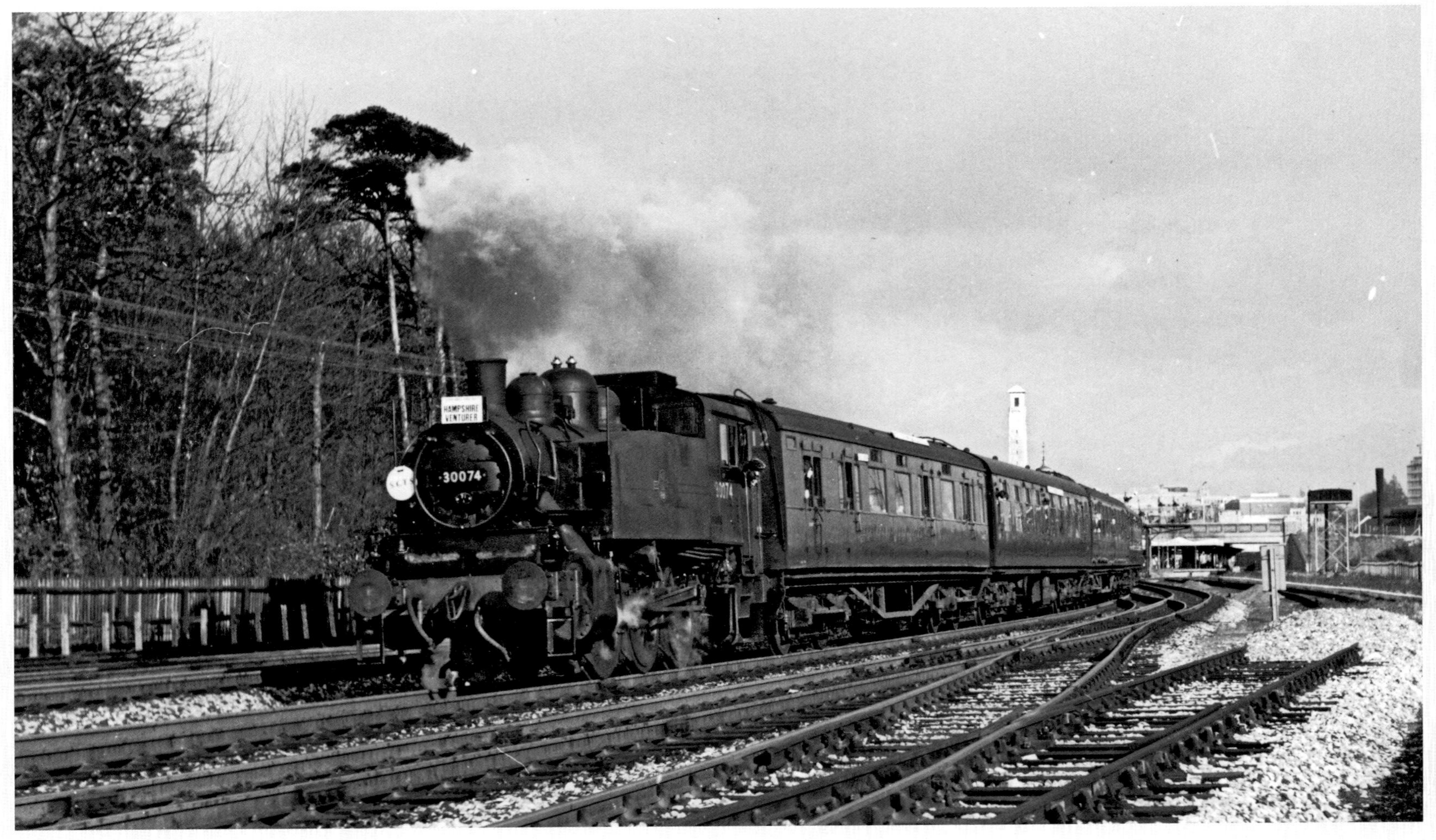

SOUTHAMPTON With the station clock tower and some of the platforms clearly visible, 'USA' 0-6-0T No 30074 pulls out of Southampton Central when heading the SCTS 'Hampshire Venturer' rail tour to Fawley on 10 March 1963.

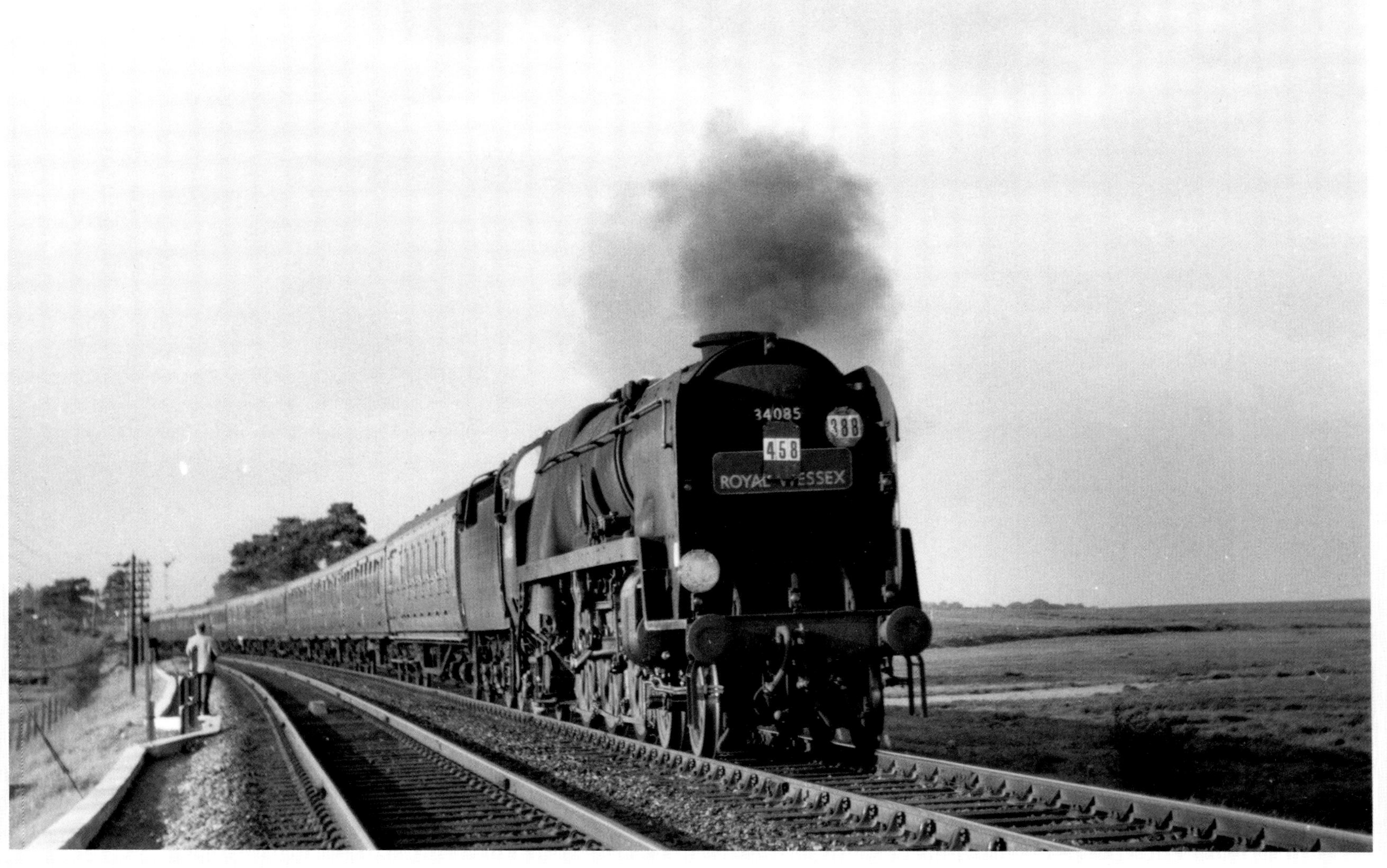

BEAULIEU ROAD The down 'Royal Wessex' is seen north of Beaulieu Road against a background of heath typical of large areas of the New Forest. 'BB' 4-6-2 No 34085 *501 Squadron*, however, appears very work-worn to be hauling an important express train in 1961 – on 19 August.

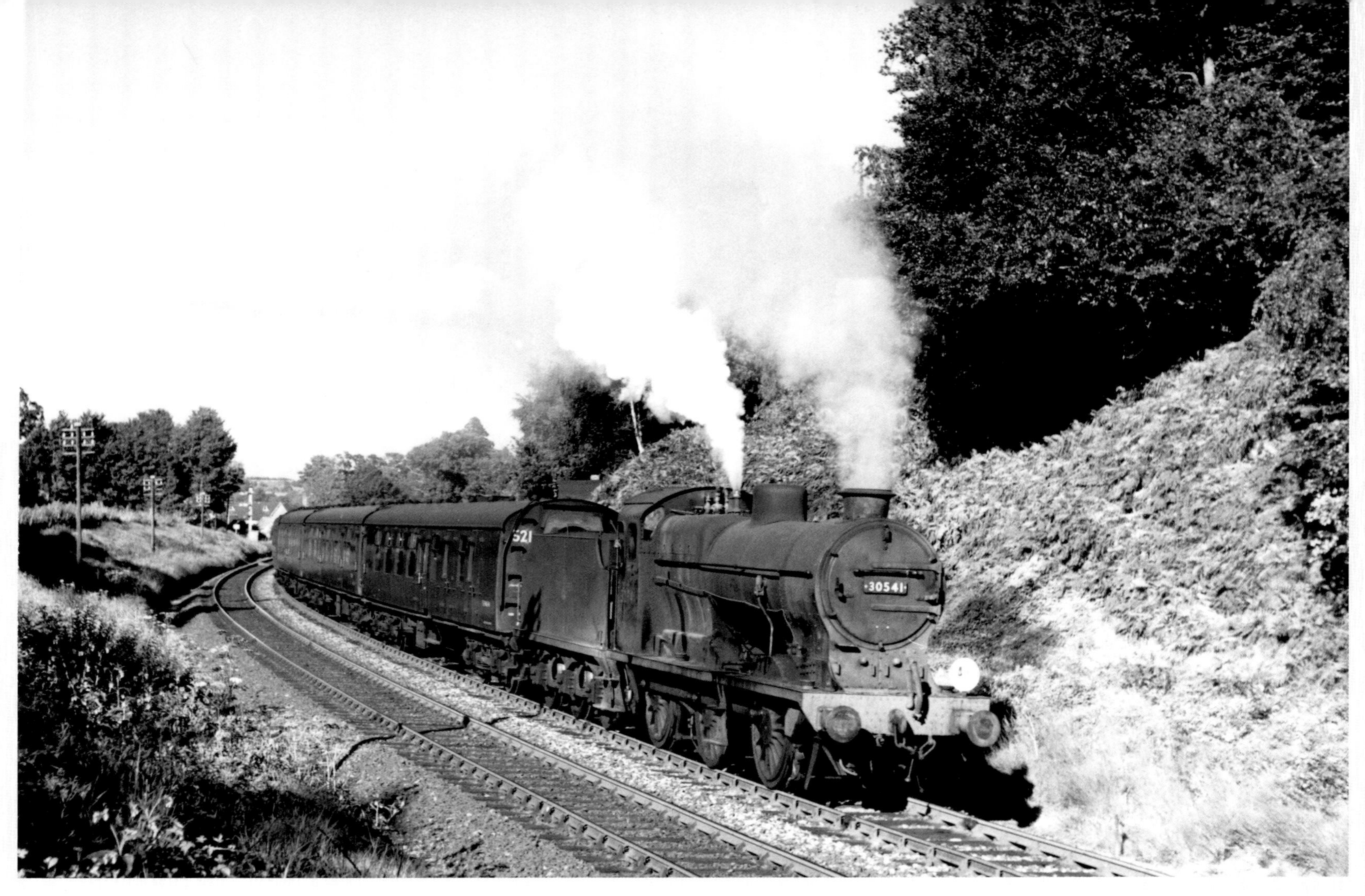

WIMBORNE On 7 September 1962 'Q' 0-6-0 No 30541 climbs out of Wimborne with the 4.07pm Brockenhurst-Bournemouth stopping train over the 'old' main line, which formed part of the LSWR route to Dorchester from 1847 until 1888. In the latter year the direct line through Sway was opened.

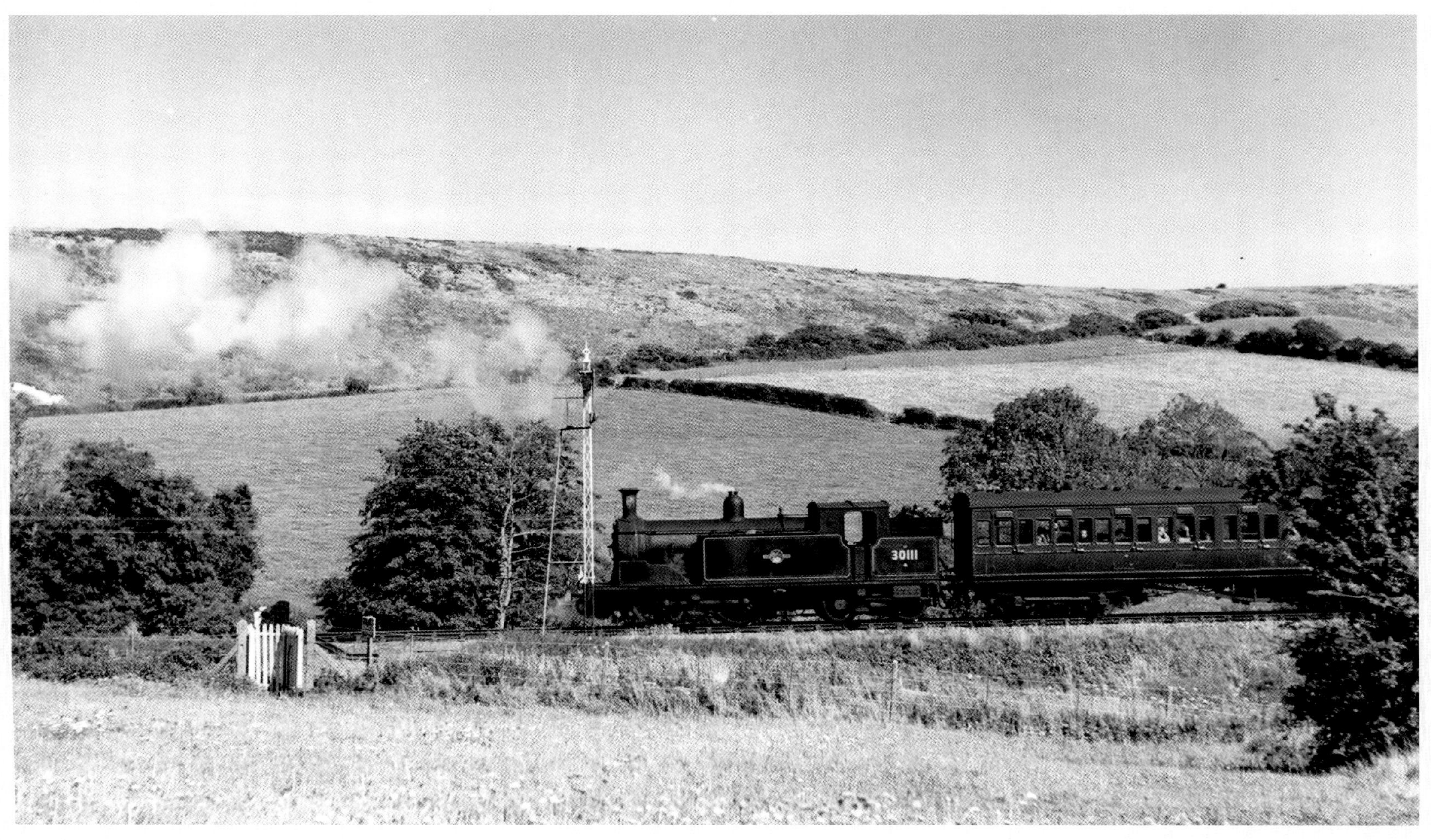

CORFE CASTLE 'M7' 0-4-4T No 30111 propels the 1.35pm from Wareham to Swanage past the up home signal towards Swanage on 9 September 1962. The coach, an ex-SECR ten-compartment 100-seater, was being used to strengthen the branch's normal two-coach set.

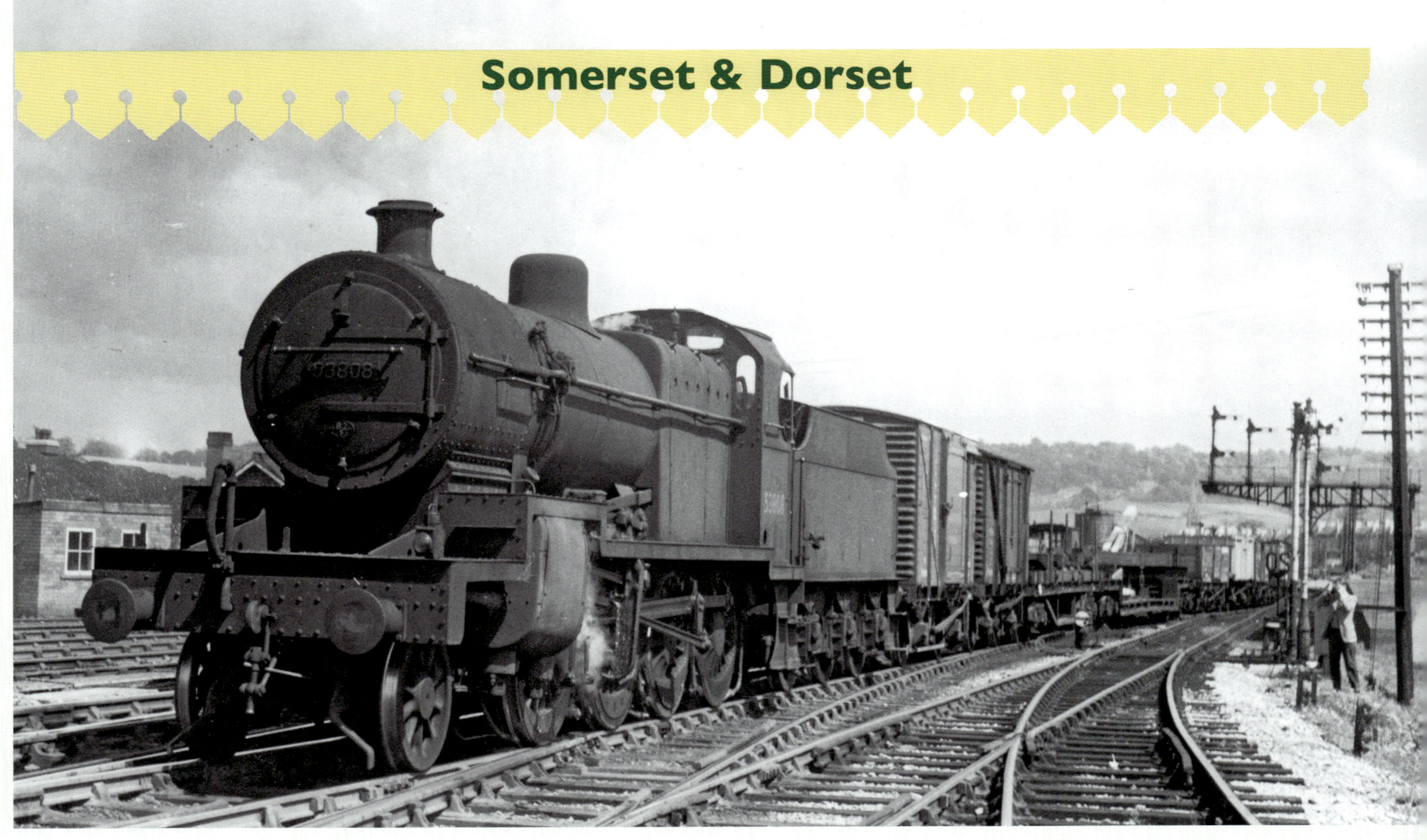

BATH JUNCTION 7F 2-8-0 No 53808 crosses the junction on 23 April 1960 at the head of the 2.00pm goods train to Mangotsfield. The Somerset & Dorset line swings right in the foreground.

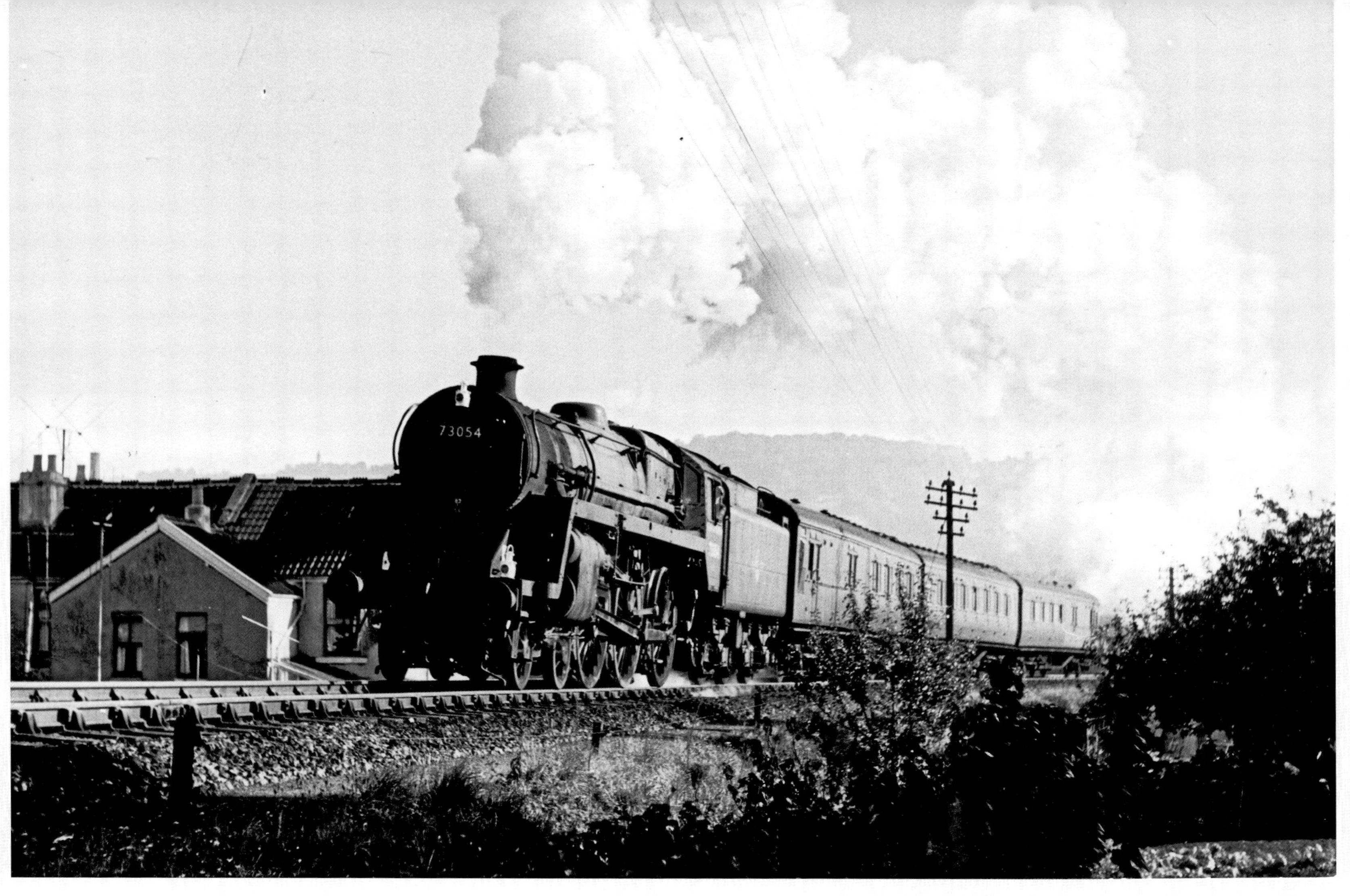

BATH JUNCTION 5MT 4-6-0 No 73054 is rounding the curve immediately above Bath Junction on 7 August 1961 with the 8.15am stopping train to Templecombe. The train is obviously climbing the 1 in 50 gradient to Combe Down Tunnel.

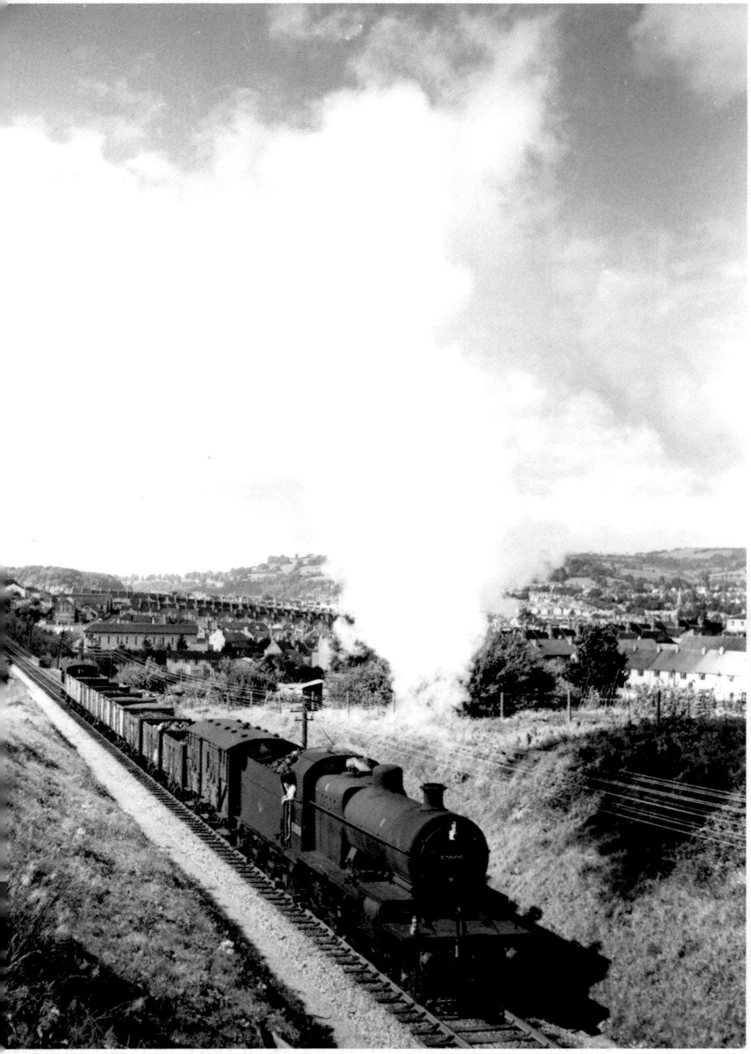

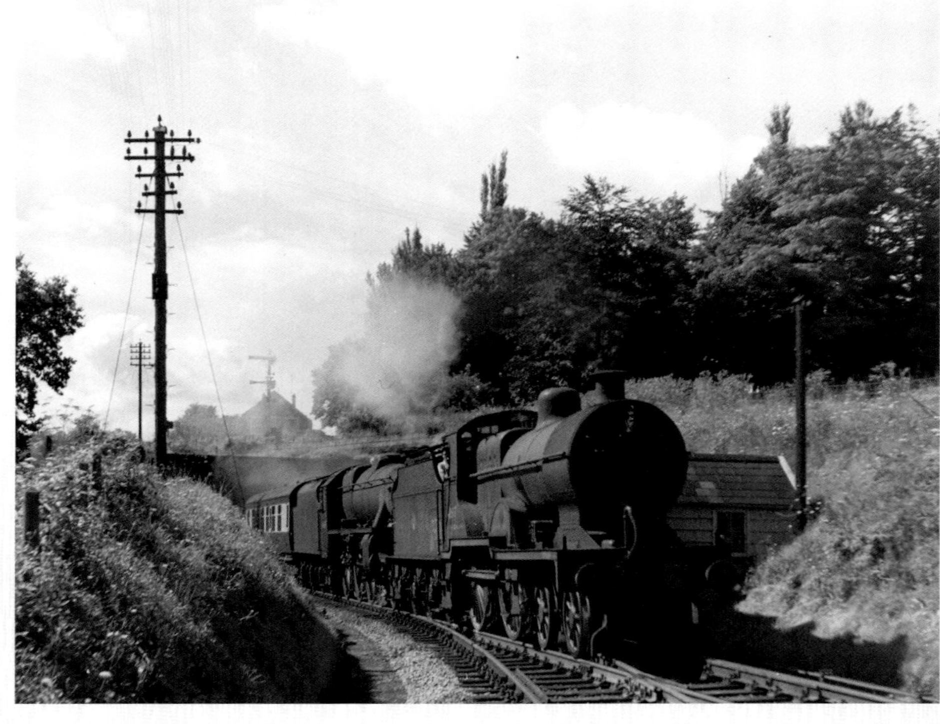

Left: **DEVONSHIRE BANK** 7F 2-8-0 No 53808 is seen again, heading the 2.00pm goods train from Bath Green Park, but this time for Evercreech Junction. The train is nearing Devonshire Tunnel on 12 September 1962.

Above: **MIDFORD** 2P 4-4-0 No 40697 pilots an unidentified 'Black 5' 4-6-0 out of Midford 'tunnel' on 23 August 1958 at the head of the 8.40am Bournemouth-Bradford train. Behind the 2P can be seen the ground frame - Midford 'A' - which controlled the entrance — right foreground — to Midford goods yard. The station stood at the other end of the 'tunnel'. This was the only time I photographed a 'Black 5' on the Somerset & Dorset.

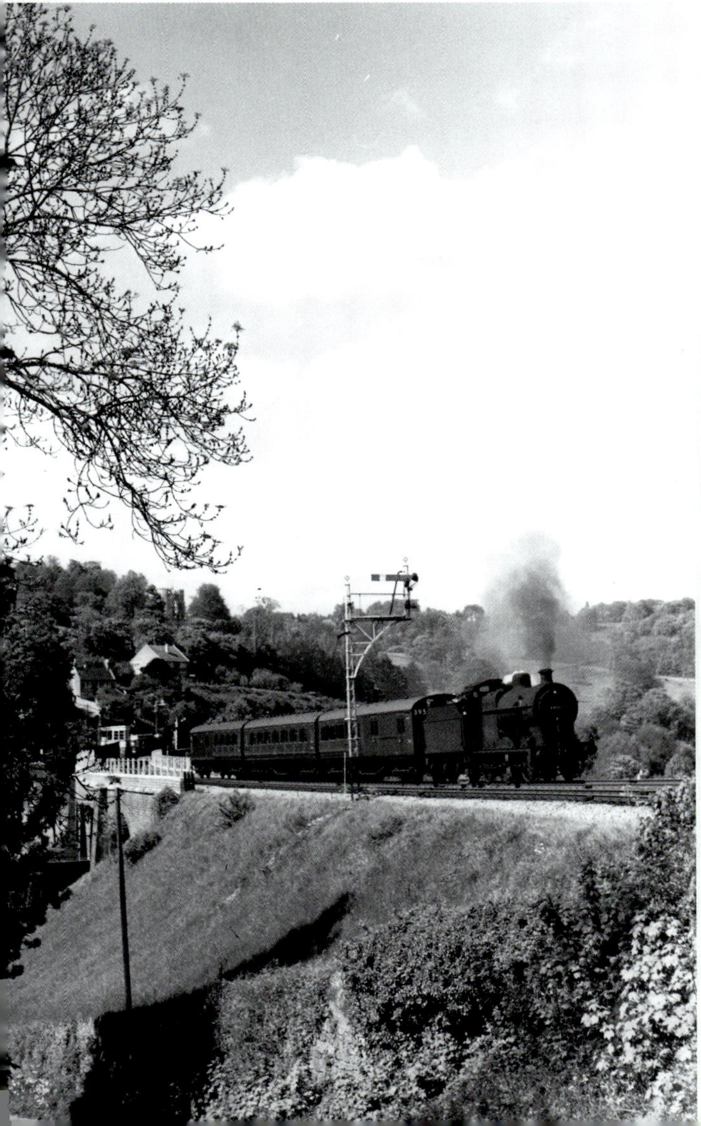

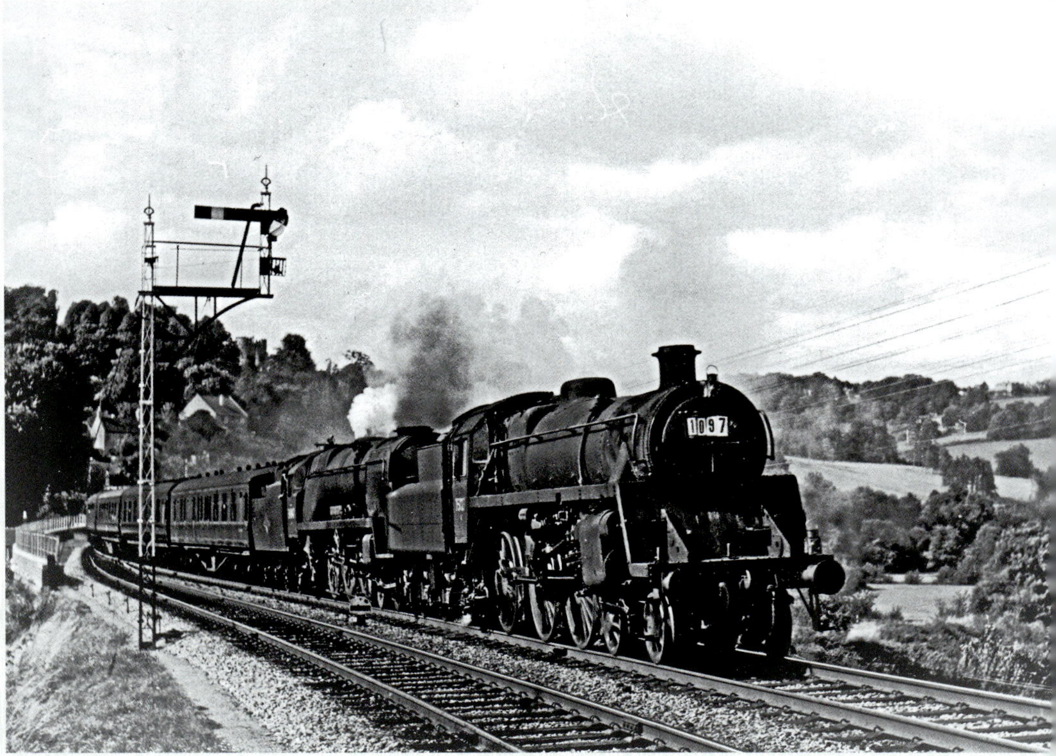

Above: **MIDFORD** 4MT 4-6-0 No 75027 pilots 'WC' 4-6-2 No 34047 *Callington* off Midford Viaduct, which started at the south end of the station's platform, with the 3.30pm Bristol-Bournemouth on 5 August 1961.

Left: **MIDFORD** 4F 0-6-0 No 44557 leaves Midford Viaduct with a late-afternoon stopping train from Bath to Templecombe on 23 April 1960. This was one of my favourite shots at Midford.

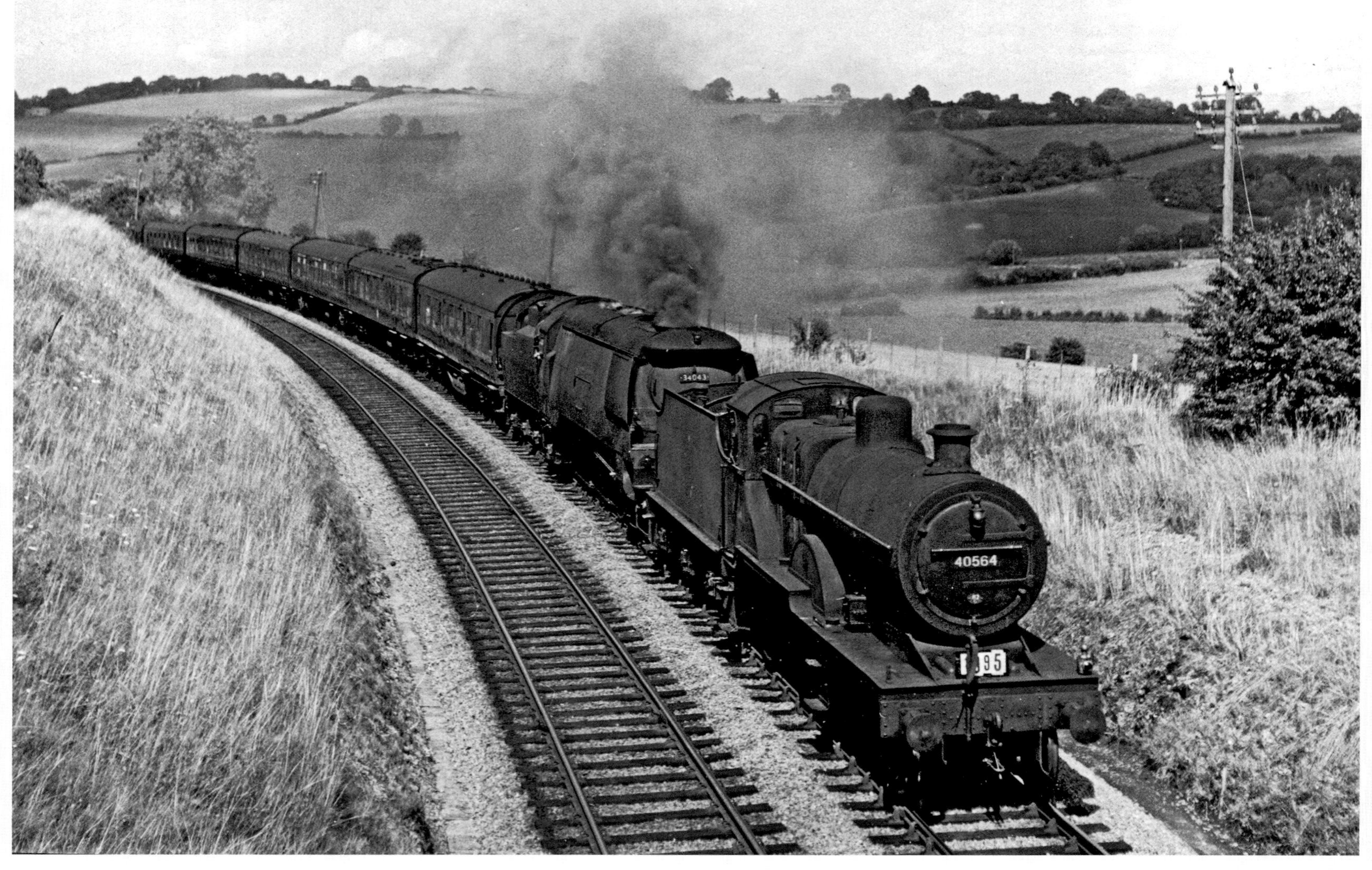

MIDFORD 2P 4-4-0 No 40564 leads 'WC' 4-6-2 No 34043 *Combe Martin* as they recover from the slack through Midford with the southbound 'Pines Express' on 5 August 1961.

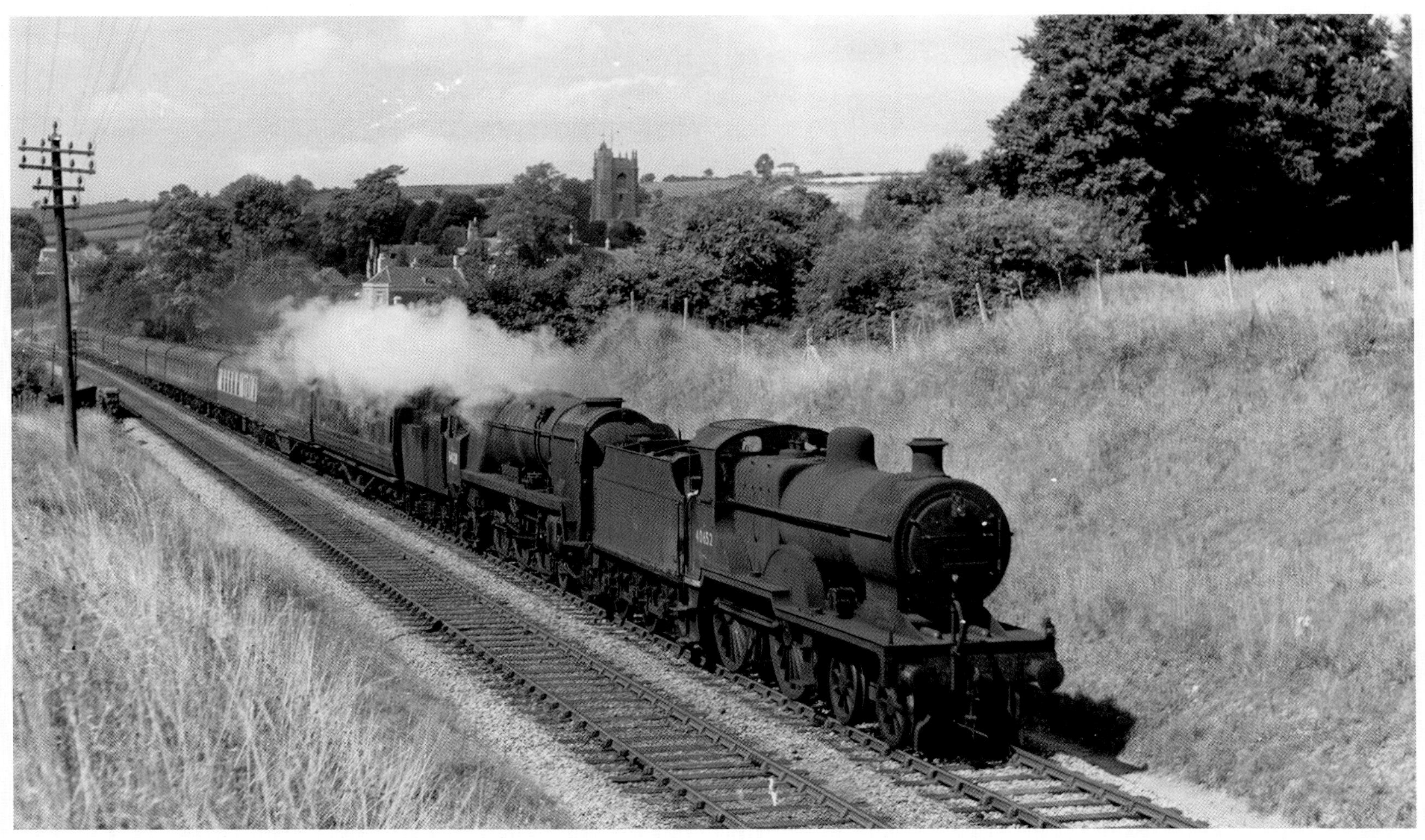

WELLOW The church of St Julian overlooks village and scene as 2P 4-4-0 No 40652 pilots 'WC' 4-6-2 No 34028 *Eddystone* past Wellow with a train for the London Midland Region on 29 August 1959.

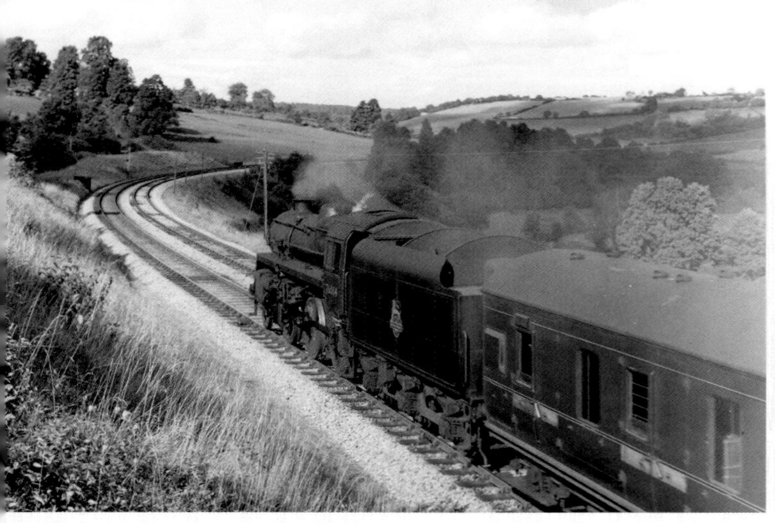

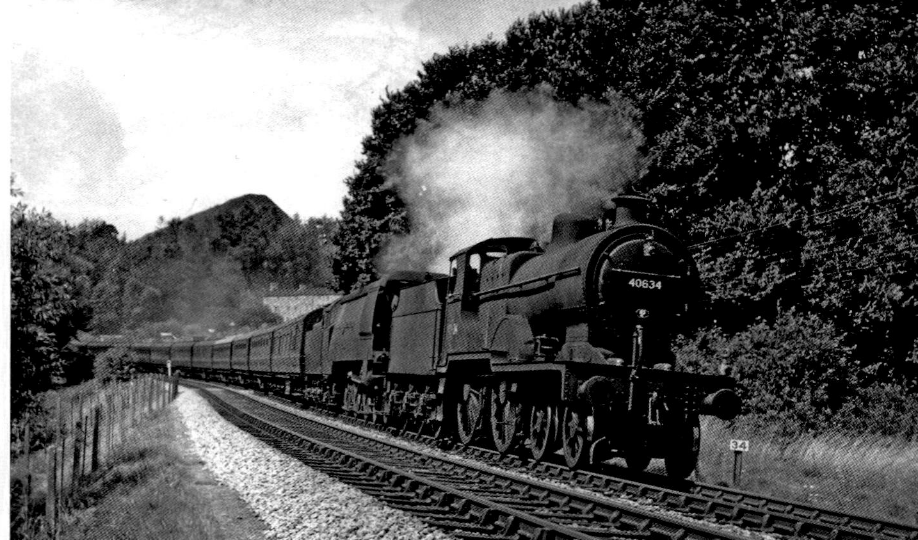

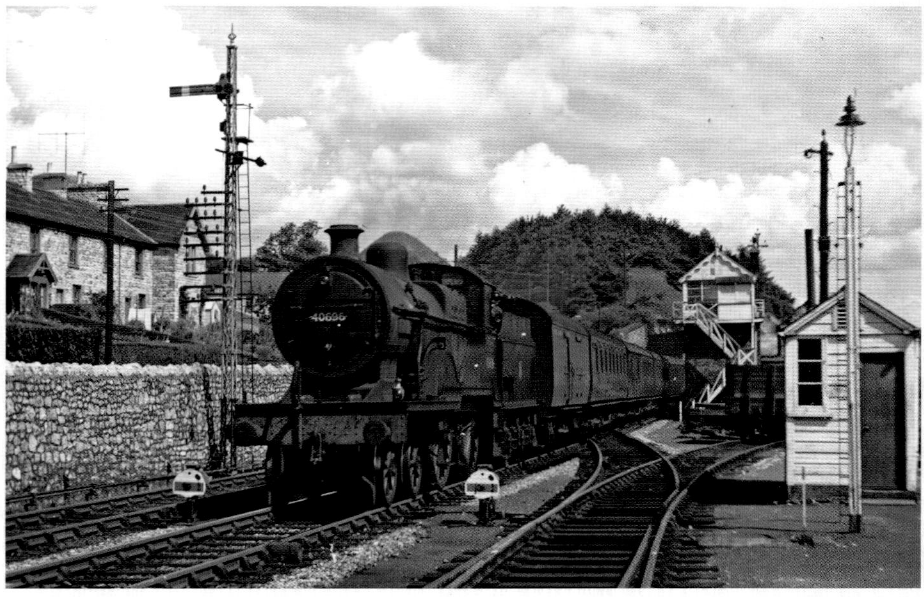

Above: **MIDFORD** 4MT 2-6-0 No 76064 sweeps down the valley towards Midford with a Bournemouth-Bath stopping train on 3 September 1960.

Above right: **WRITHLINGTON** 2P 4-4-0 No 40634 pilots 'WC' 4-6-2 No 34043 *Combe Martin* through the curves near Writhlington, 1 mile east of Radstock, with what is believed to have been the 8.40am Bournemouth-Bradford train on 5 August 1961. The slagheap in the background was a memento of the North Somerset coalfield, which had provided much traffic for the railway.

Right: **RADSTOCK** 2P 4-4-0 No 40696 drifts into Radstock at the head of the 1.10pm Bath-Templecombe stopping train on 23 August 1958. The same slagheap can be seen above the locomotive's dome.

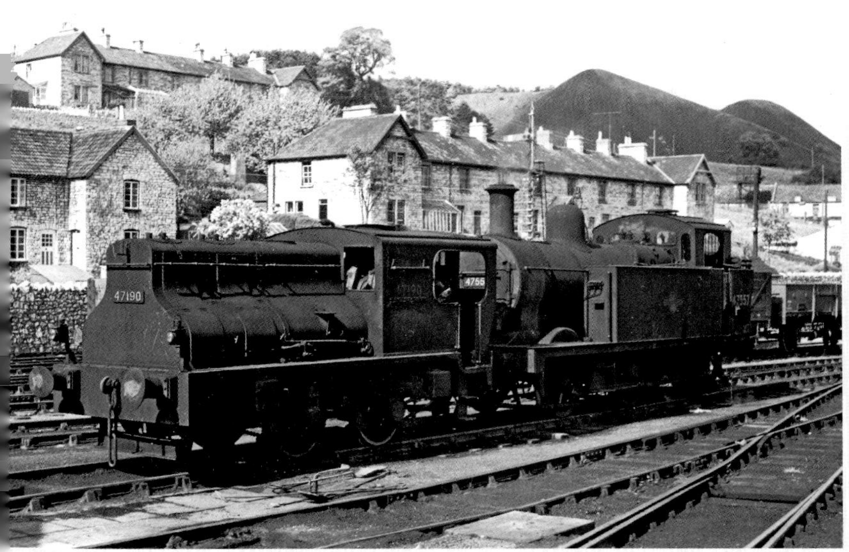

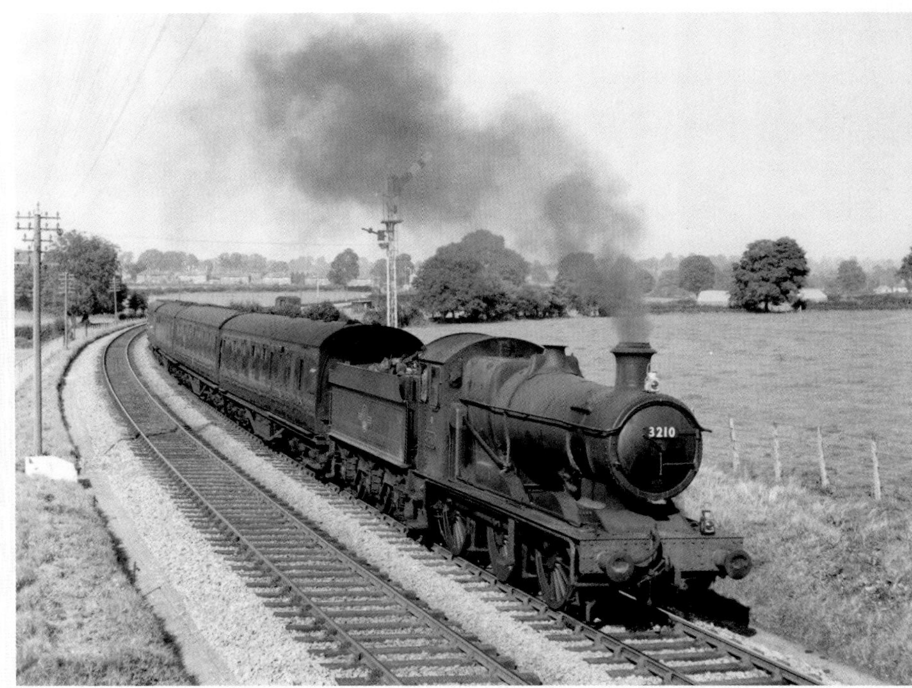

Above: **RADSTOCK** Yet more slagheaps dominate the background of this shot. In Radstock locomotive depot yard on 23 April 1960 are two contrasting shunting engines, Sentinel 0-4-0T No 47190 and 3F 0-6-0T No 47557. The latter was for general shunting and banking trains on the main line, while the former had been bought to service some sidings in Radstock yard with very limited headroom.

Above right: **BINEGAR** '2251' 0-6-0 No 3210 brings a down stopping train away from Binegar on its way from Bath to Templecombe on 31 August 1961.

Right: **BINEGAR** 4MT 4-6-0 No 75009 and 7F 2-8-0 No 53808 head the Cleethorpes-Exmouth through train near Binegar on 25 August 1962.

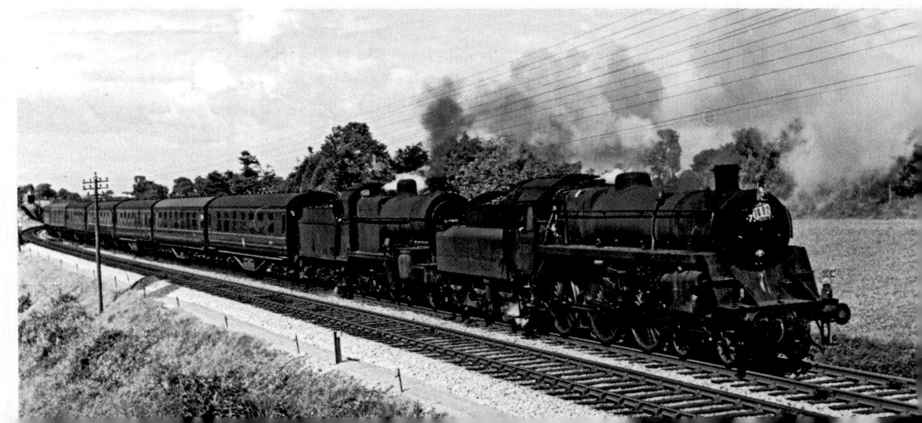

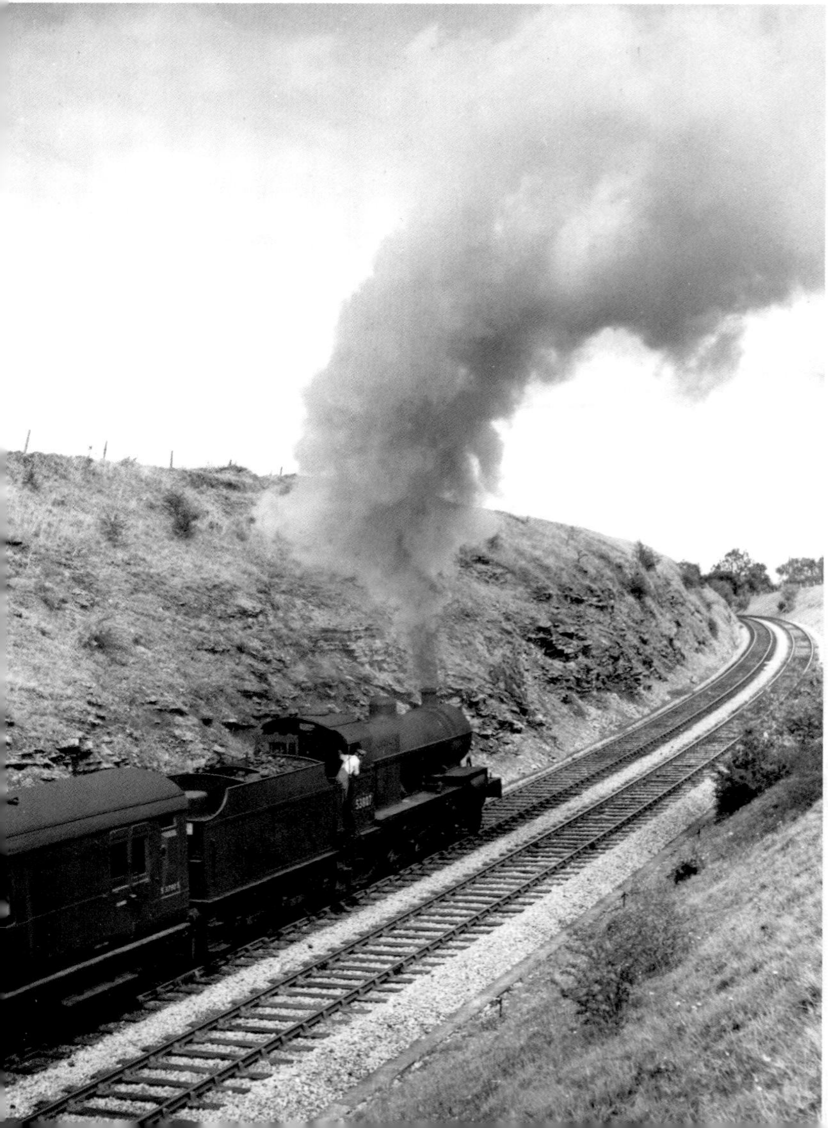

Left: **MASBURY** Also on 25 August 1962 7F 2-8-0 No 53807 clambers up the last stretch to the summit cutting at Masbury – the grade can be seen to be changing in the distance – with the Exmouth-Cleethorpes through train. The smoke was keeping ahead of the engine, and had blown down in front of it as the train approached.

Below: **MASBURY** 7F 2-8-0 No 53807 is on the last mile of the climb to Masbury from the south with what is thought to be the 3.40pm Bournemouth-Bath on 29 August 1959.

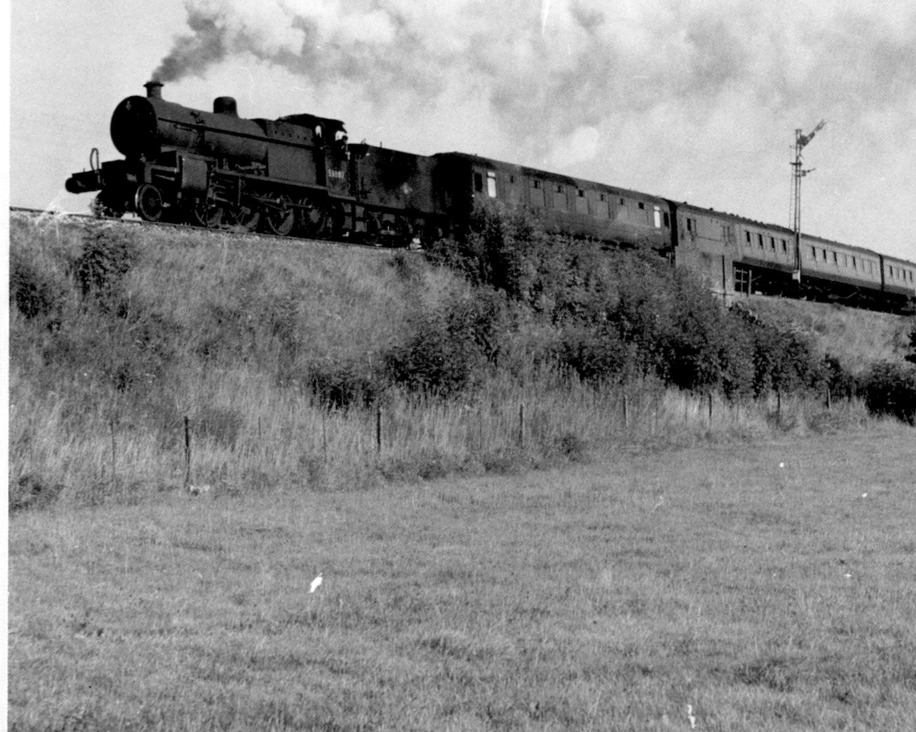

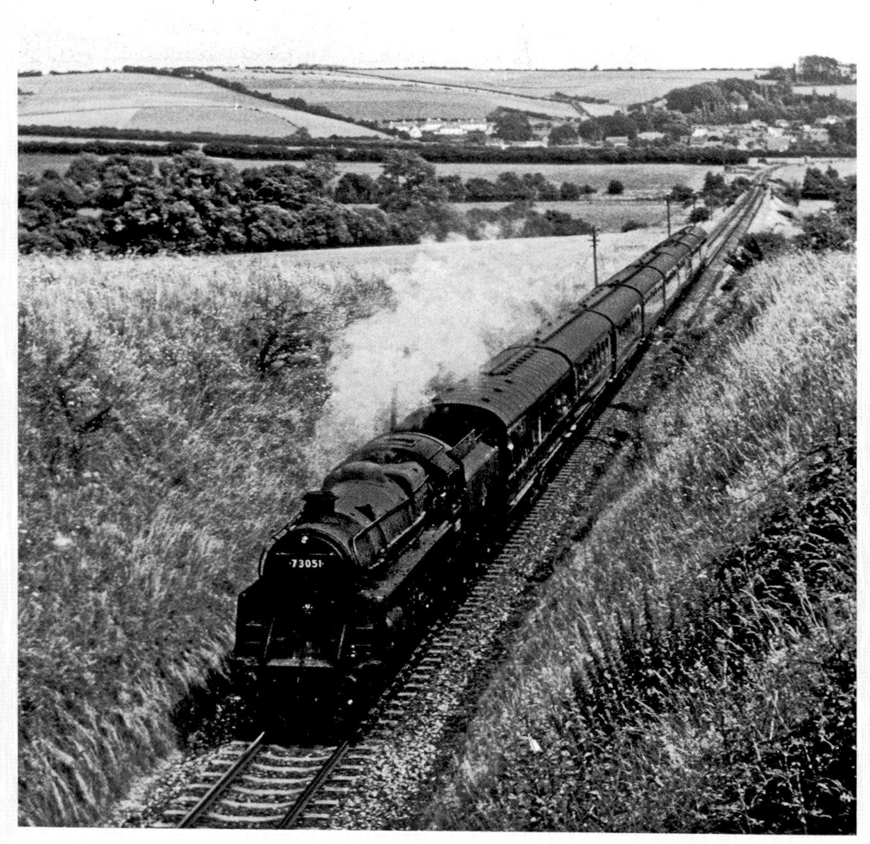

SHILLINGSTONE 5MT 4-6-0 No 73051 nears Shillingstone with the 2.45pm Bournemouth-Bristol train on 9 July 1960. The village of Stourpaine can be seen in the background across the valley.

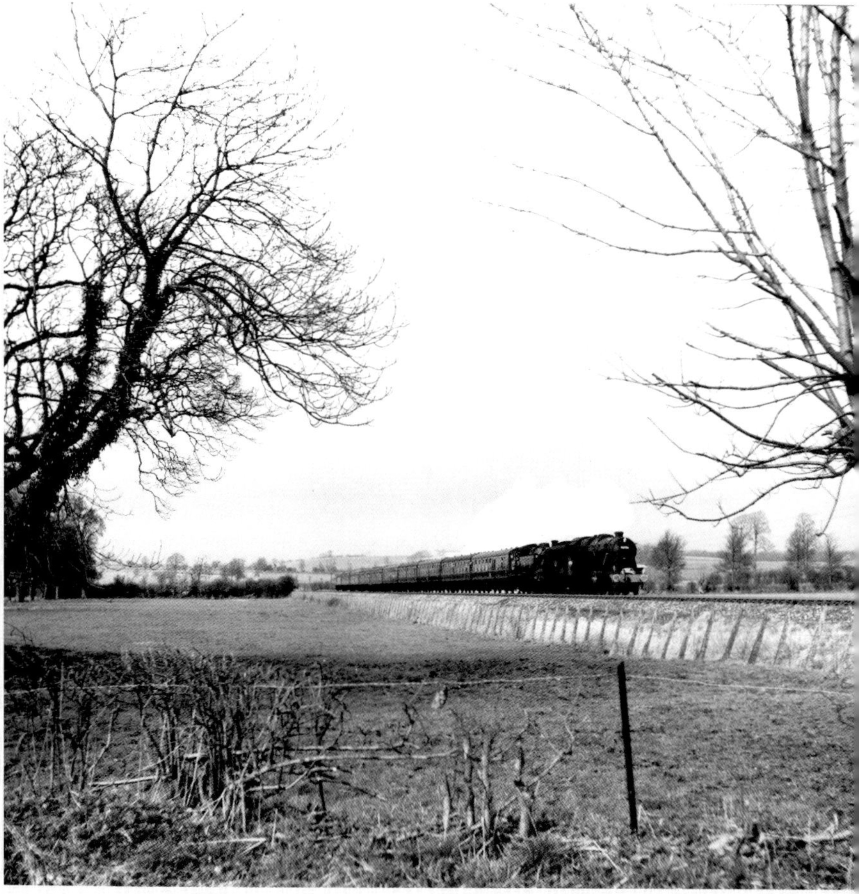

WINCANTON 8F 2-8-0 No 48706 pilots 4MT 2-6-4T No 80043 towards Wincanton with the SLS special train run to commemorate the closure of the Somerset & Dorset line on 6 March 1966. Normal services had ceased the day before.

London & South Western lines west of Salisbury

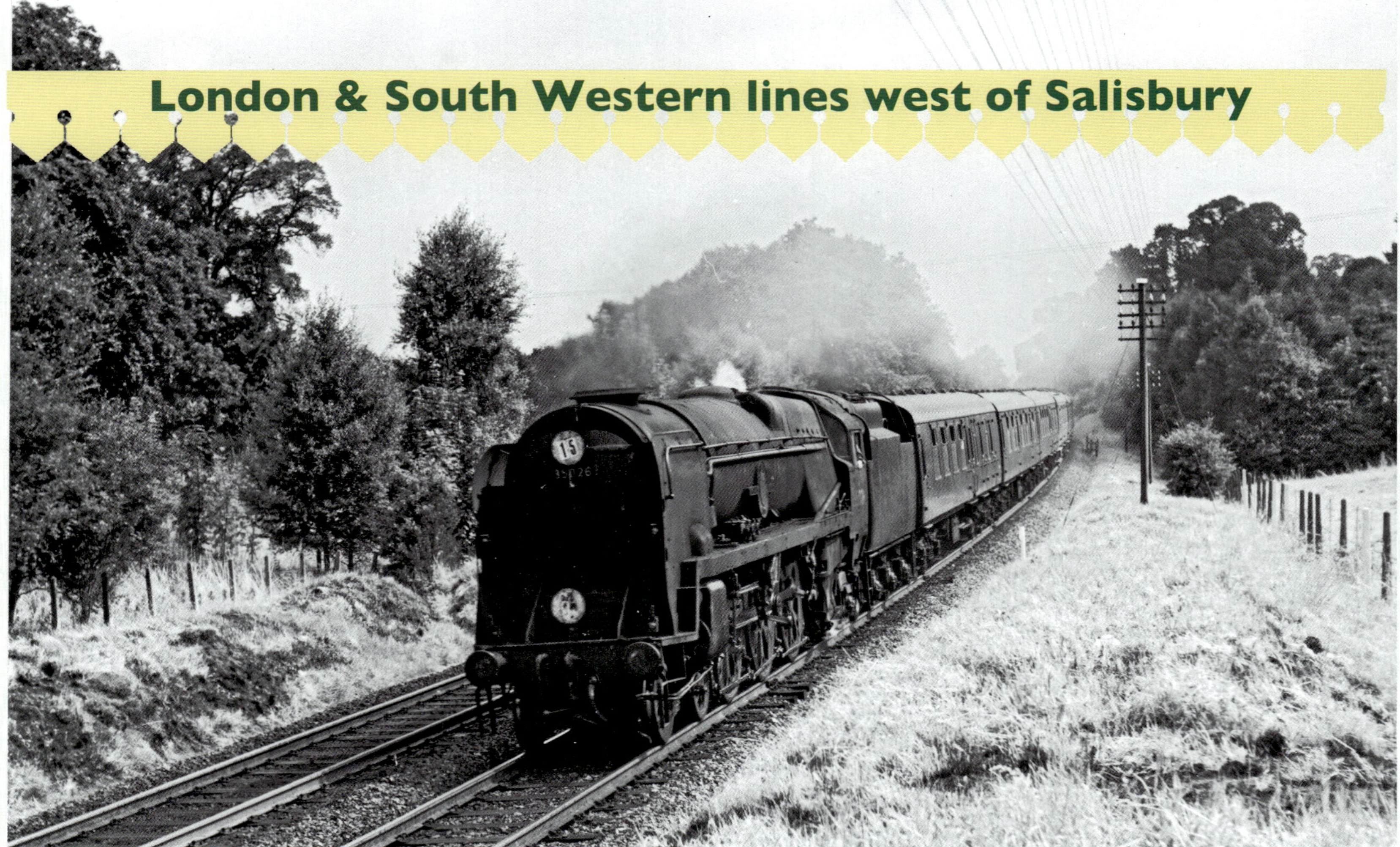

BUCKHORN WESTON TUNNEL Just east of the tunnel 'MN' 4-6-2 No 35026 *Lamport & Holt Line* brings the 9.00am Waterloo-West of England train up the climb from Gillingham on 3 August 1964. In steam days this was one of the relatively few places between Salisbury and Exeter where the telegraph wires did not interfere with photography. Nowadays a communications tower has been placed, that now impairs the shot.

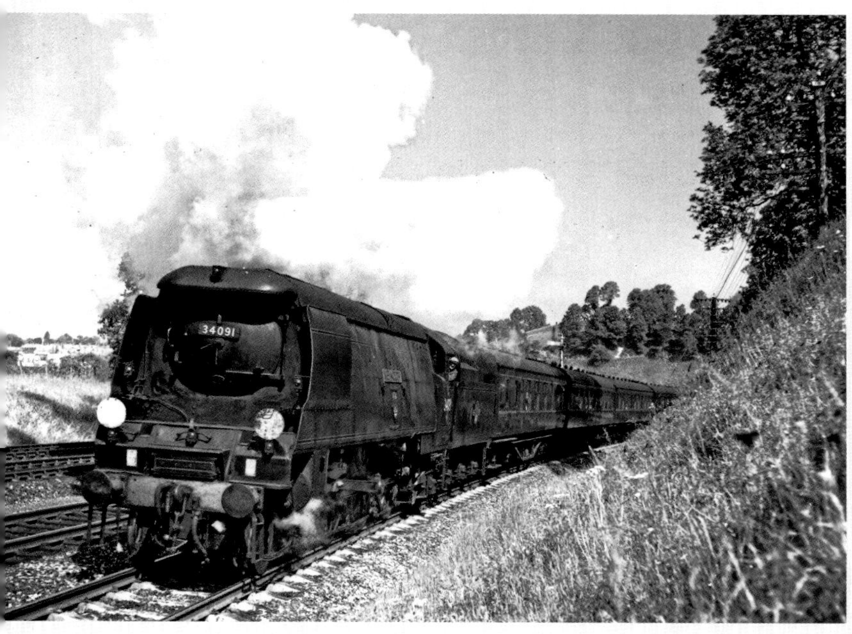

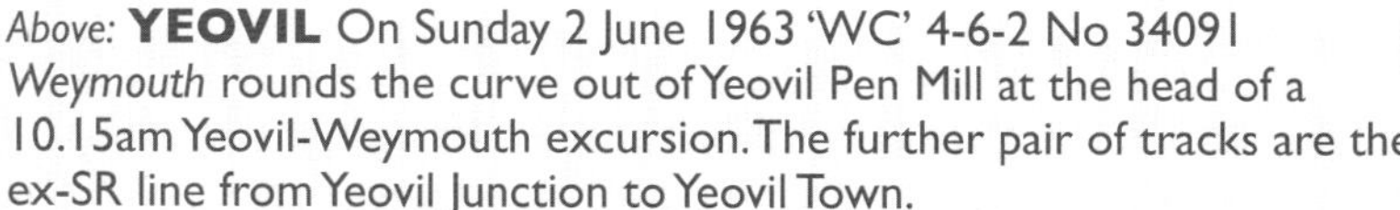

Above: **YEOVIL** On Sunday 2 June 1963 'WC' 4-6-2 No 34091 *Weymouth* rounds the curve out of Yeovil Pen Mill at the head of a 10.15am Yeovil-Weymouth excursion. The further pair of tracks are the ex-SR line from Yeovil Junction to Yeovil Town.

Above right: **YEOVIL** However, something seems to have gone wrong on the same day for the 10.30am excursion to Weymouth, which is plodding south behind 0-6-0PT No 8759, running bunker-first; a 3MT 2-6-2T is assisting in the rear. The line to Yeovil Junction cuts a diagonal across the front of the trees on the left.

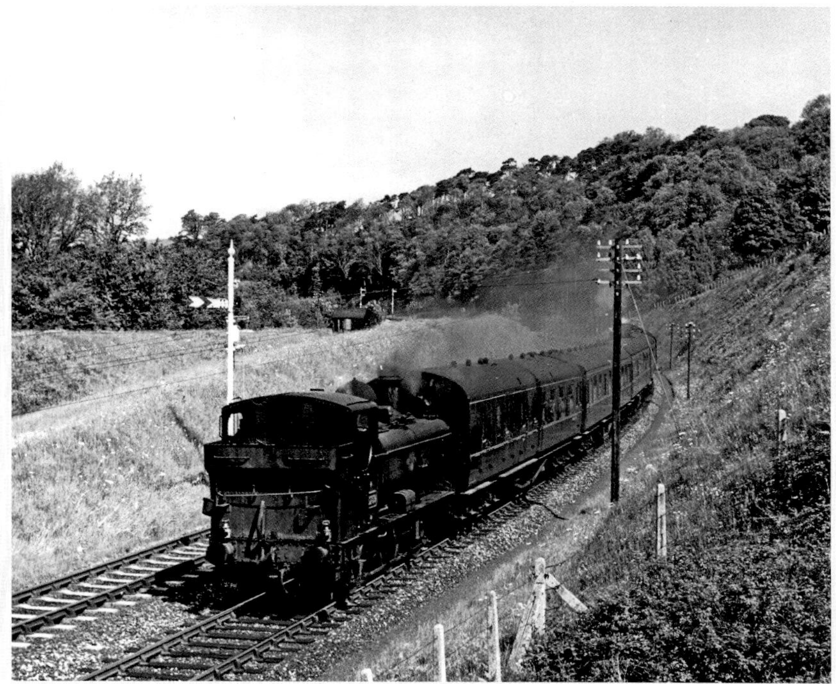

Right: **AXMINSTER** '0415' 4-4-2T No 30584 heads a train to Lyme Regis past the wood near Bulmoor Cross on 16 April 1960.

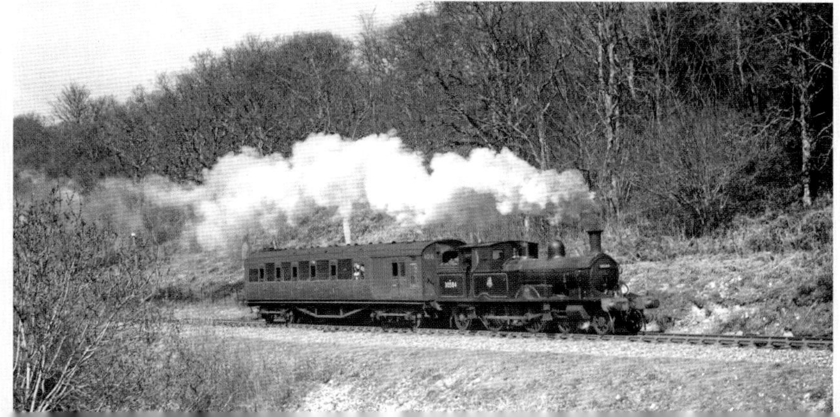

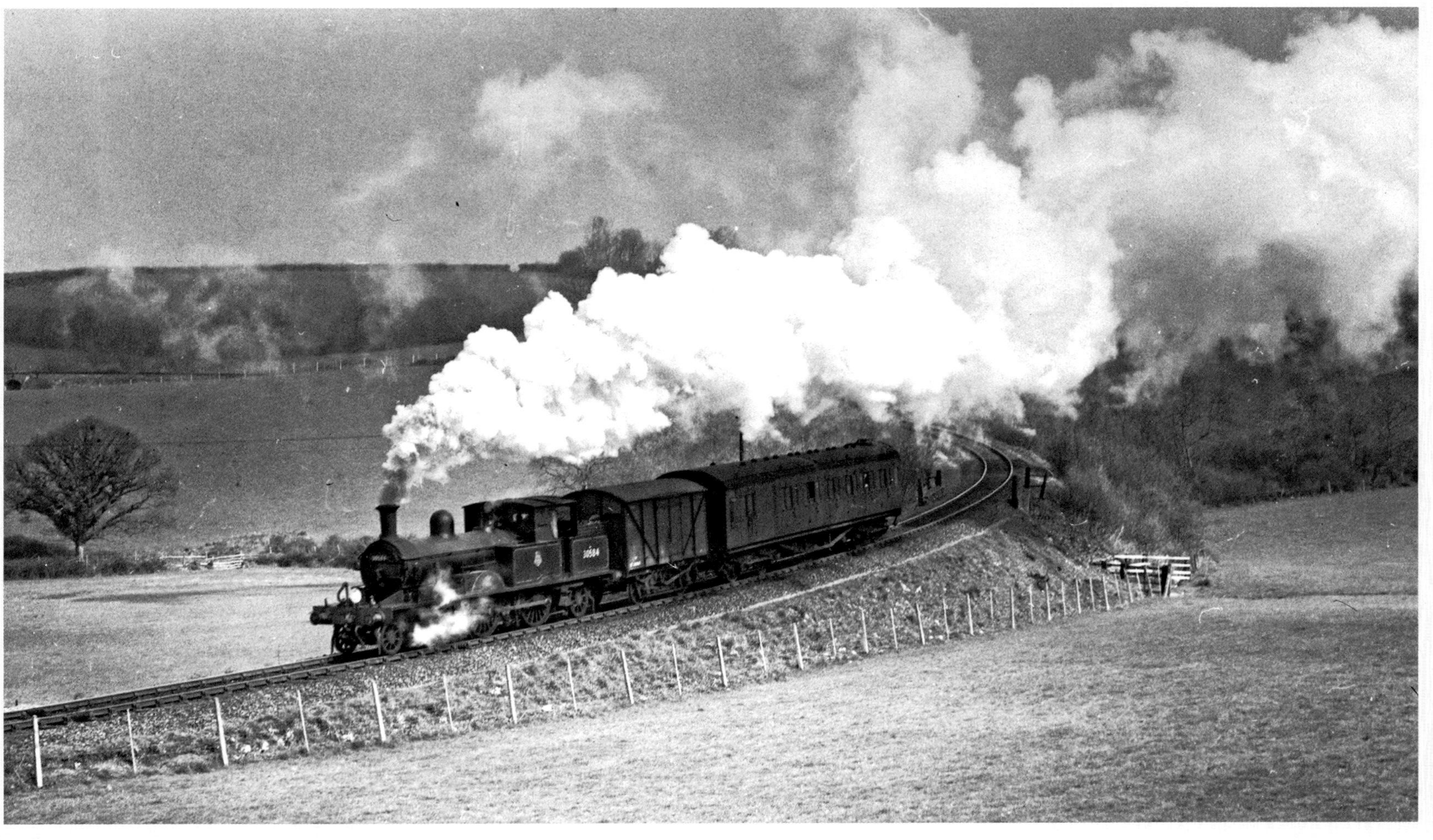

AXMINSTER Also on 16 April 1960 '0415' 4-4-2T No 30584 emerges from the shadow cast by her smoke as she leads a train for Lyme Regis round the curve above the farm of Trill; an earlier length of the curve can be seen in the left background. Trill is out of frame to the left.

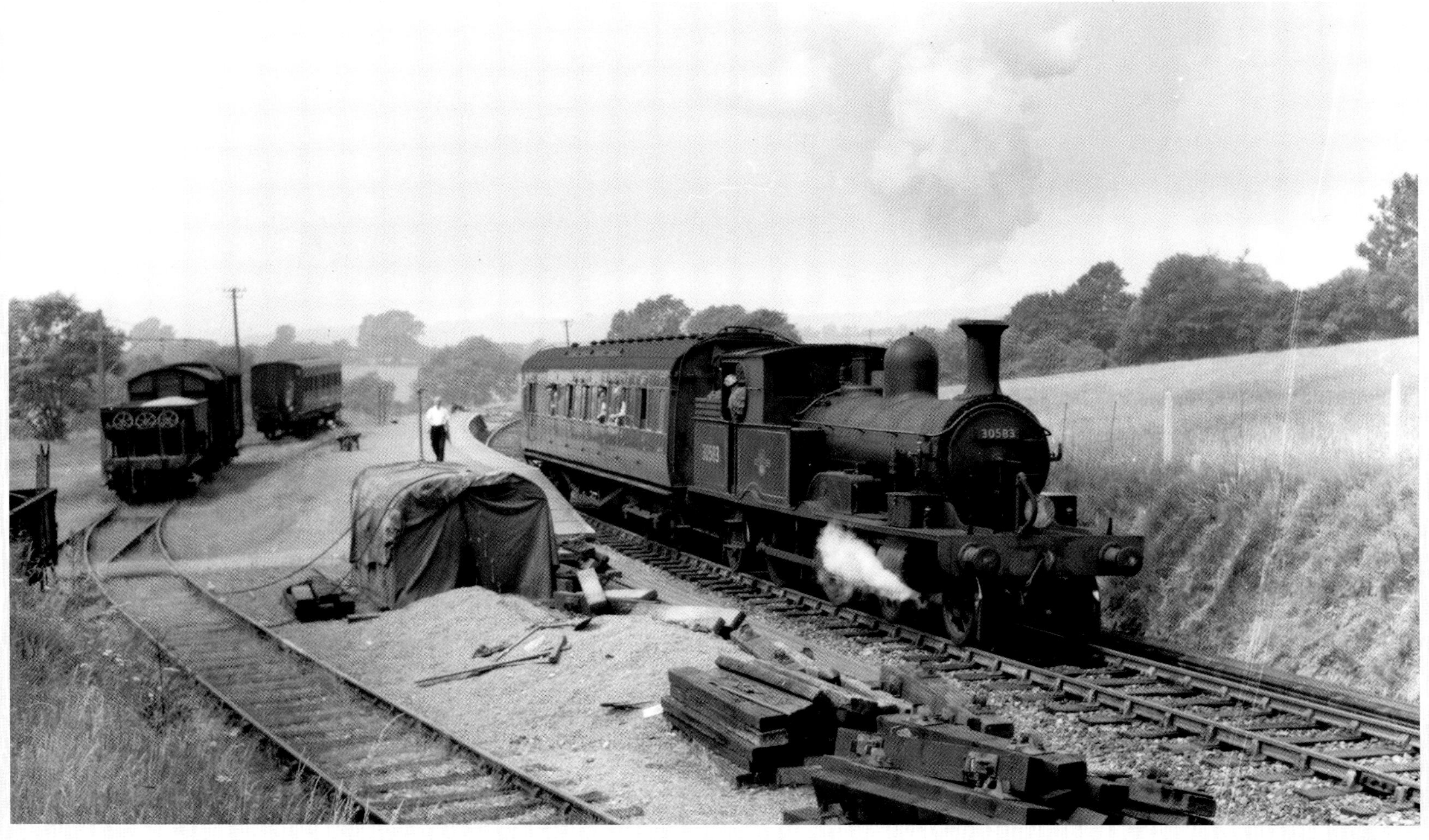

COMBPYNE '0415' 4-4-2T No 30583 restarts the 1.48pm train from Axminster for Lyme Regis on 27 June 1960. A camping coach is present in the siding, and the permanent way material lying in the foreground and the siding indicate that works are in progress to fit the line for 2MT 2-6-2Ts.

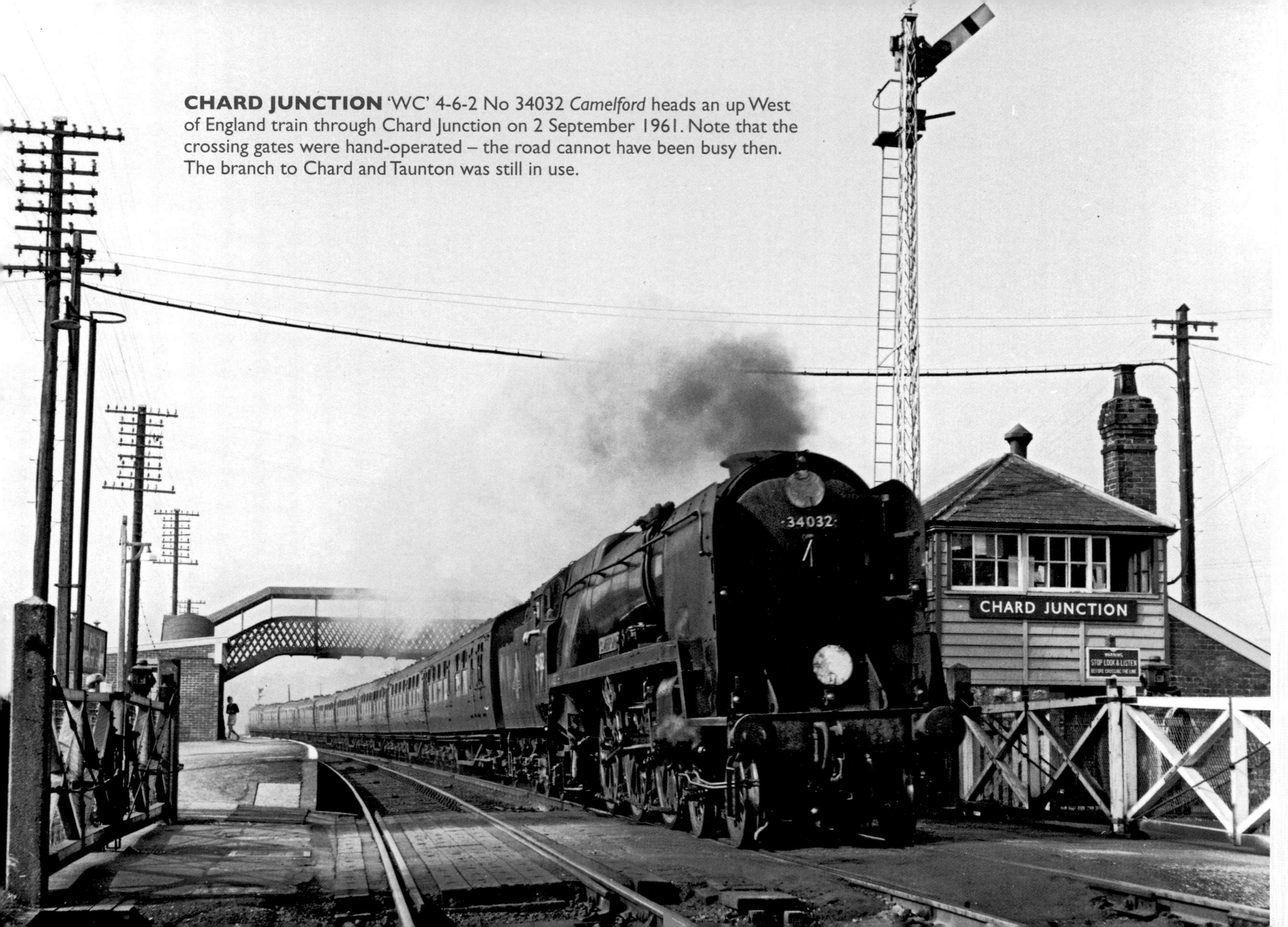

CHARD JUNCTION 'WC' 4-6-2 No 34032 *Camelford* heads an up West of England train through Chard Junction on 2 September 1961. Note that the crossing gates were hand-operated – the road cannot have been busy then. The branch to Chard and Taunton was still in use.

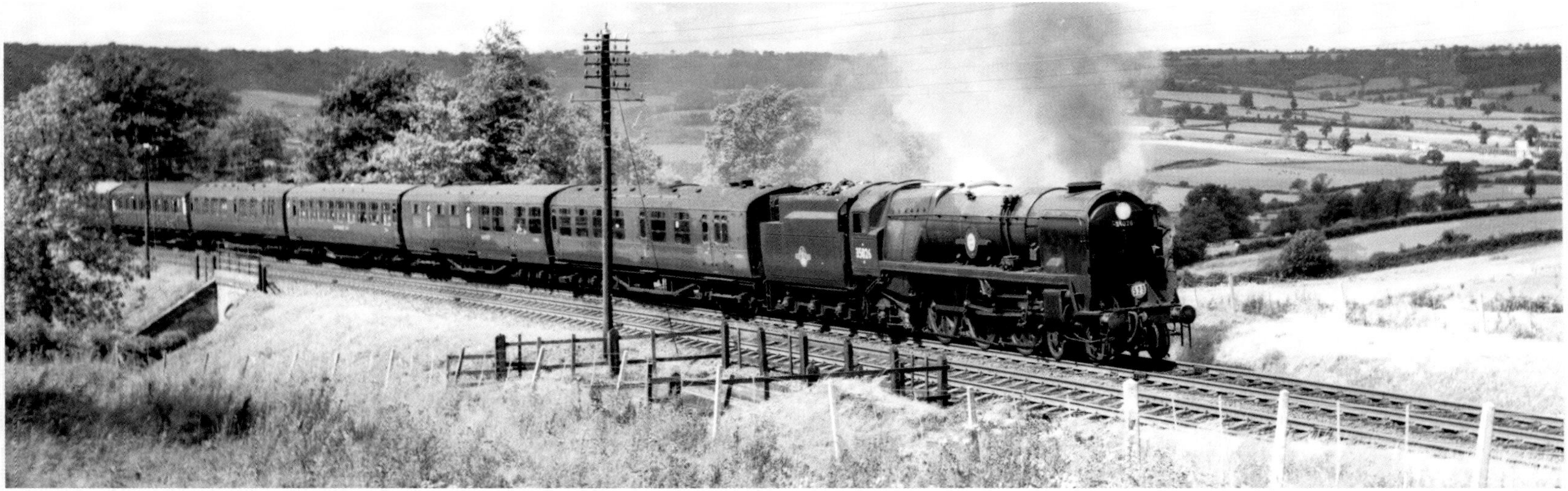

Above: **HONITON** The up 'Atlantic Coast Express', hauled by 'MN' 4-6-2 No 35026 *Lamport & Holt Line*, approaches Honiton Tunnel on 4 August 1962.

Right: **TIPTON ST JOHN'S** 3MT 2-6-2T No 82017 takes to the hills above Tipton St John's with the 10.55am Sidmouth Junction to Sidmouth train on 9 June 1961. The station is immediately beyond the junction (right background), while the branch to Budleigh Salterton and Exmouth stretches across the river flats in the background.

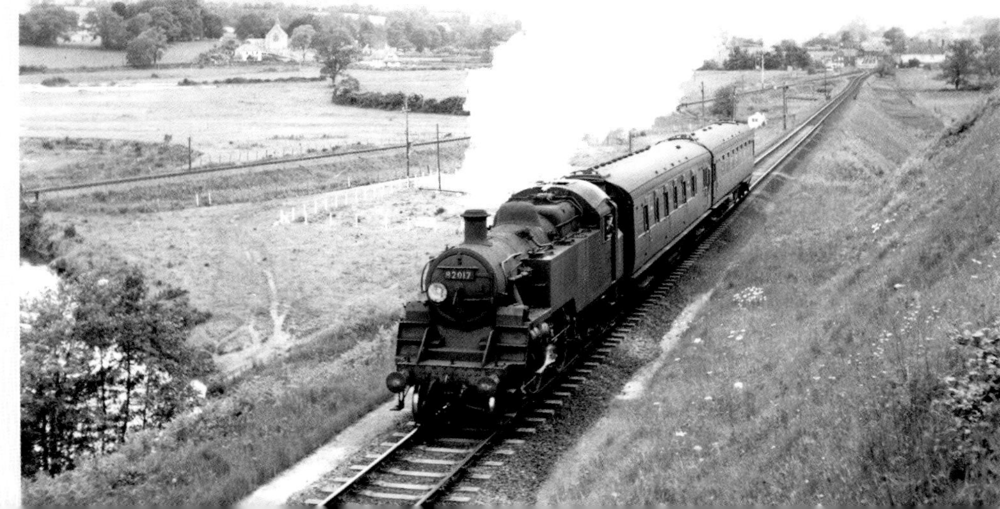

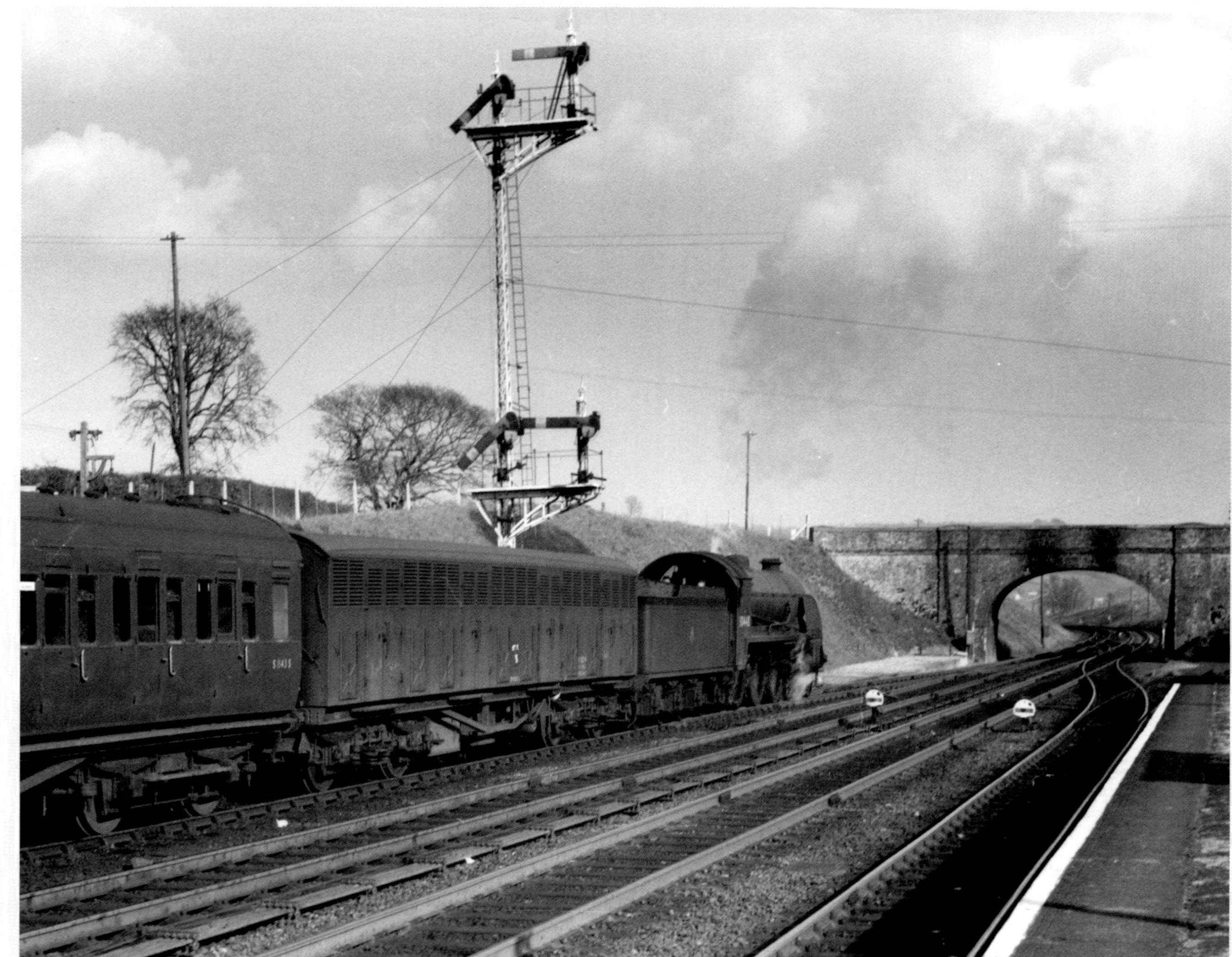

SEATON JUNCTION
'N15' 4-6-0 No 30448 *Sir Tristram* pulls out of the up platform loop with a main-line stopping train on 16 April 1960. The unusually tall signal post was intended to make the signals visible above the station buildings to the crews of locomotives on the up through line.

MORTEHOE & WOOLACOMBE 'BB' 4-6-2 No 34072
257 Squadron brings the 5.05pm Exeter Central-Ilfracombe train up
the last few yards of the 1 in 40 gradient to Mortehoe & Woolacombe
station, and the summit of the line from Barnstaple, on 18 June 1963.

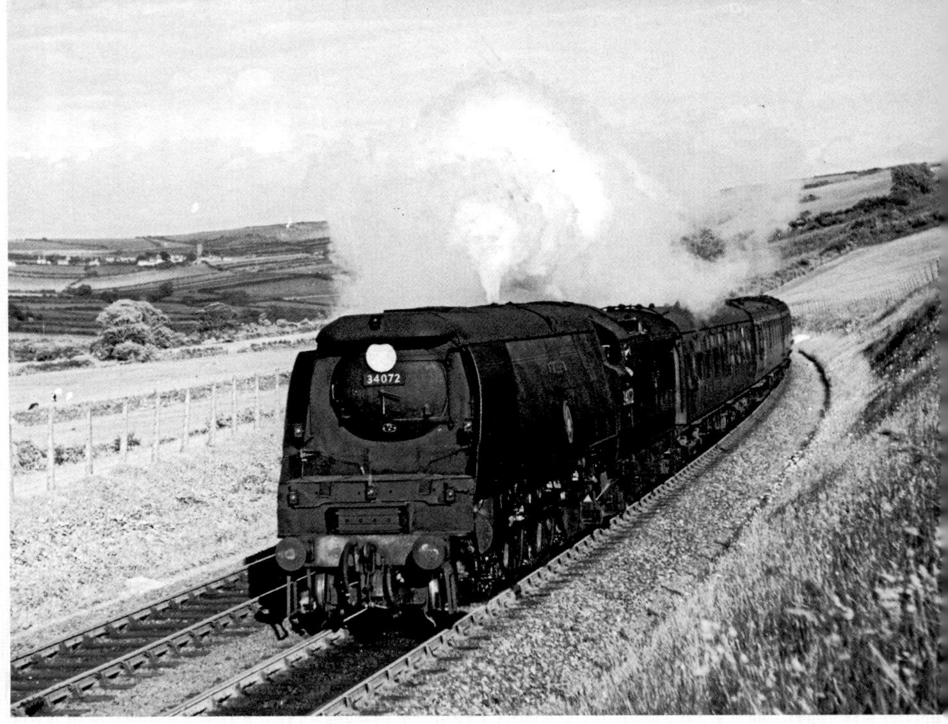

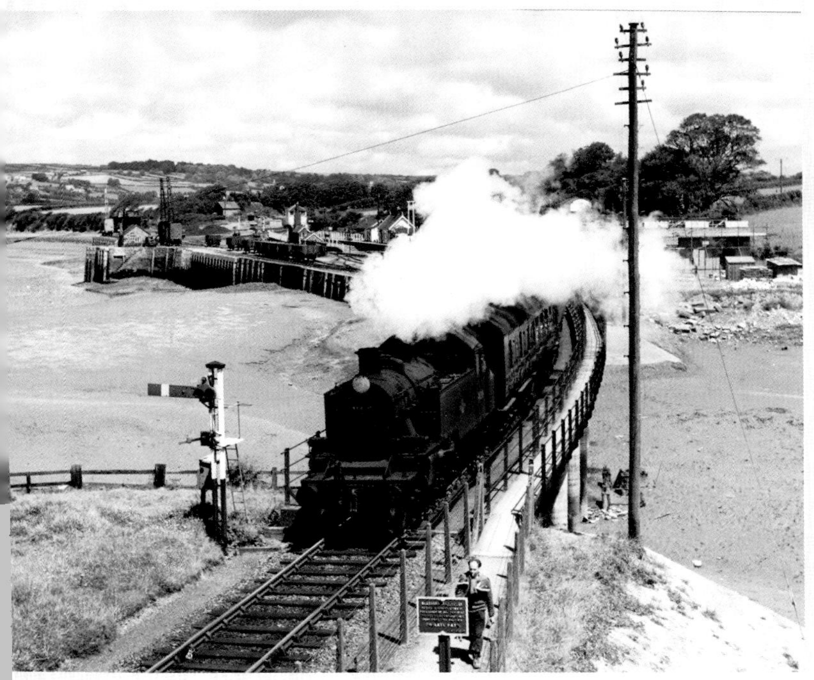

FREMINGTON On 22 June 1963 the 2.00pm Barnstaple Junction-Torrington
train is headed away from Fremington by 2MT 2-6-2T No 41216. The Southern
Region's coal supply for the South West was still brought to Fremington Quay,
alongside the station, by coasters. When the tide ebbed, the coaster dried out,
and sat on the mud until the next flood tide.

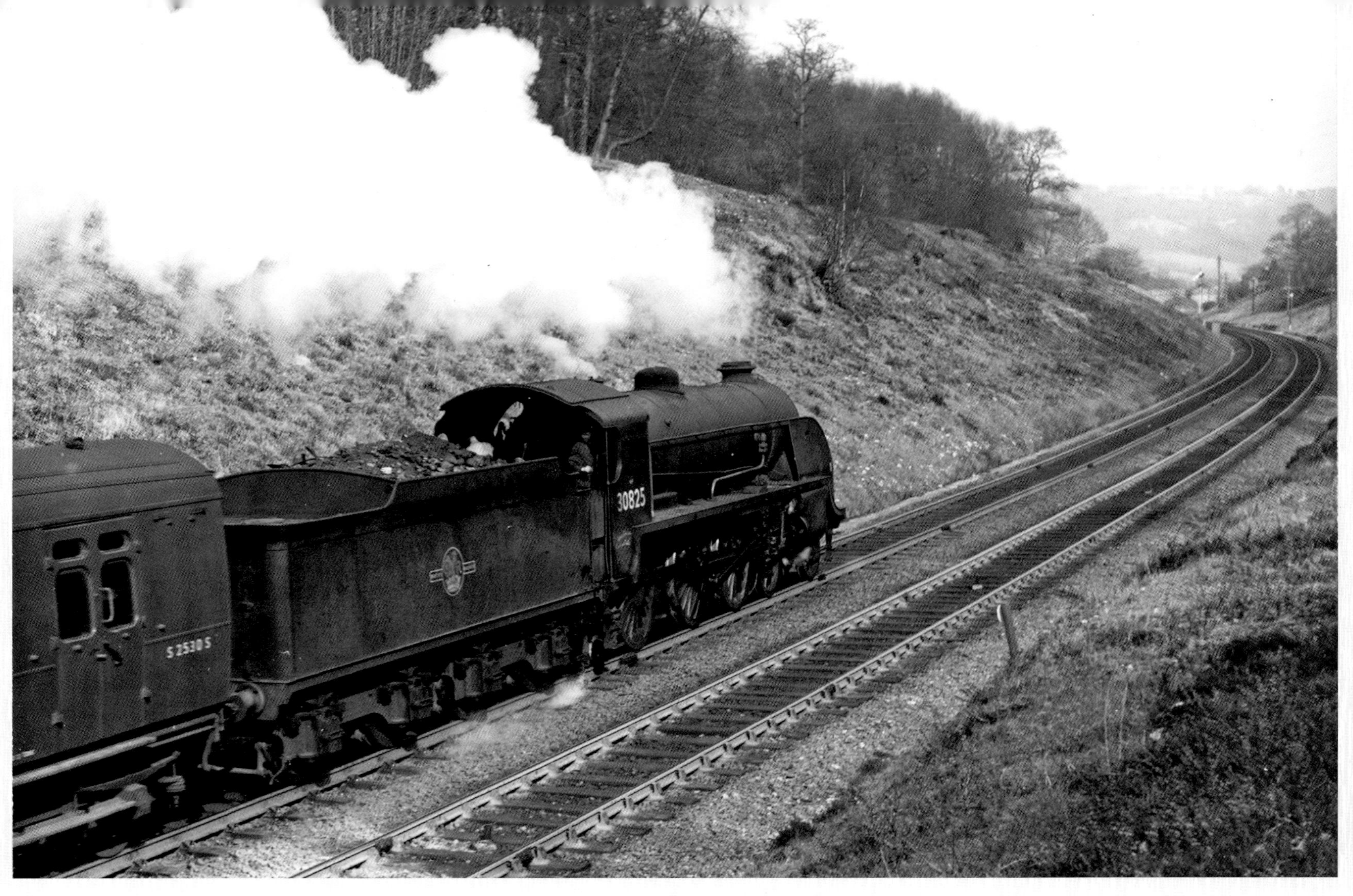

HONITON BANK The 3.20pm Exeter Central-Templecombe stopping train is led down the grade from Honiton Tunnel by 'S15' 4-6-0 No 30825 on 16 April 1960.

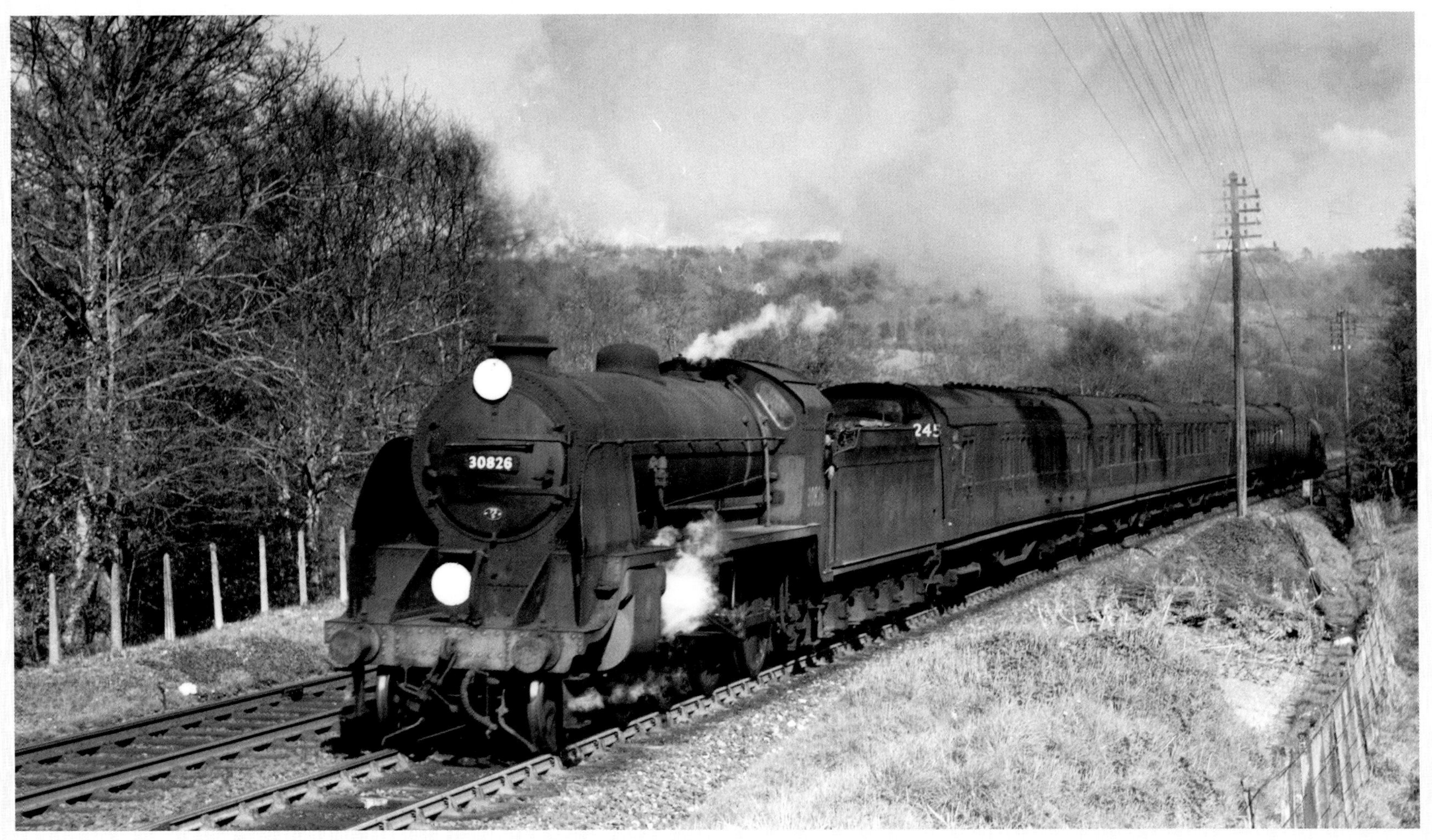

HONITON BANK Here we see 'S15' 4-6-0 No 30826 climbing the bank with a down stopping train on the same April day. Just visible at the back of the train is a milk tanker.

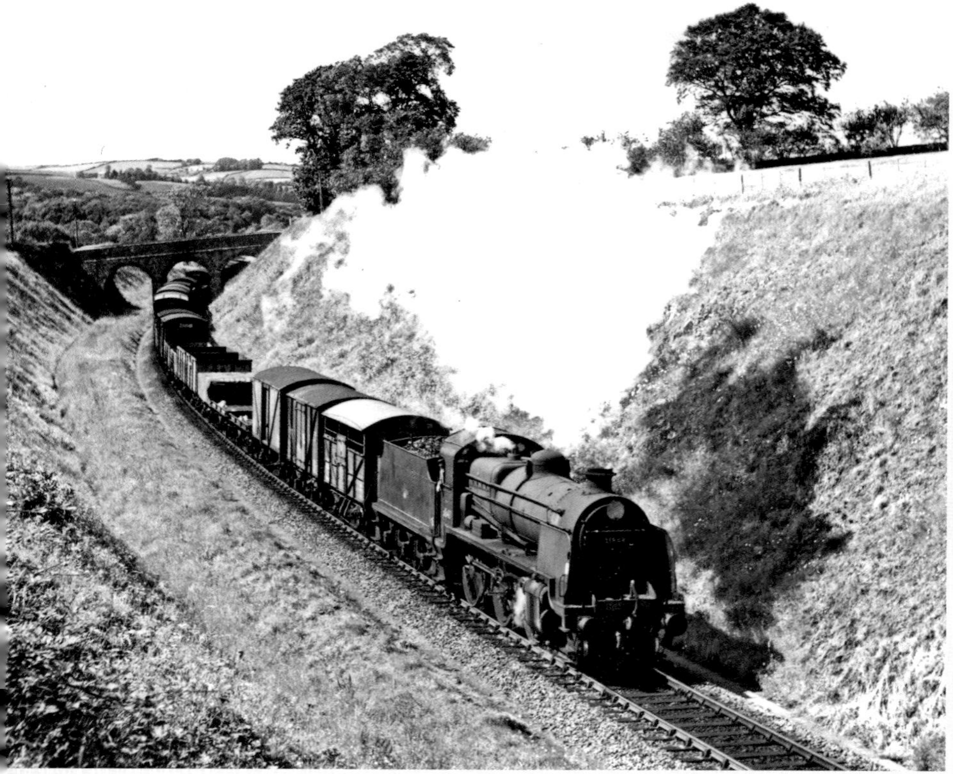

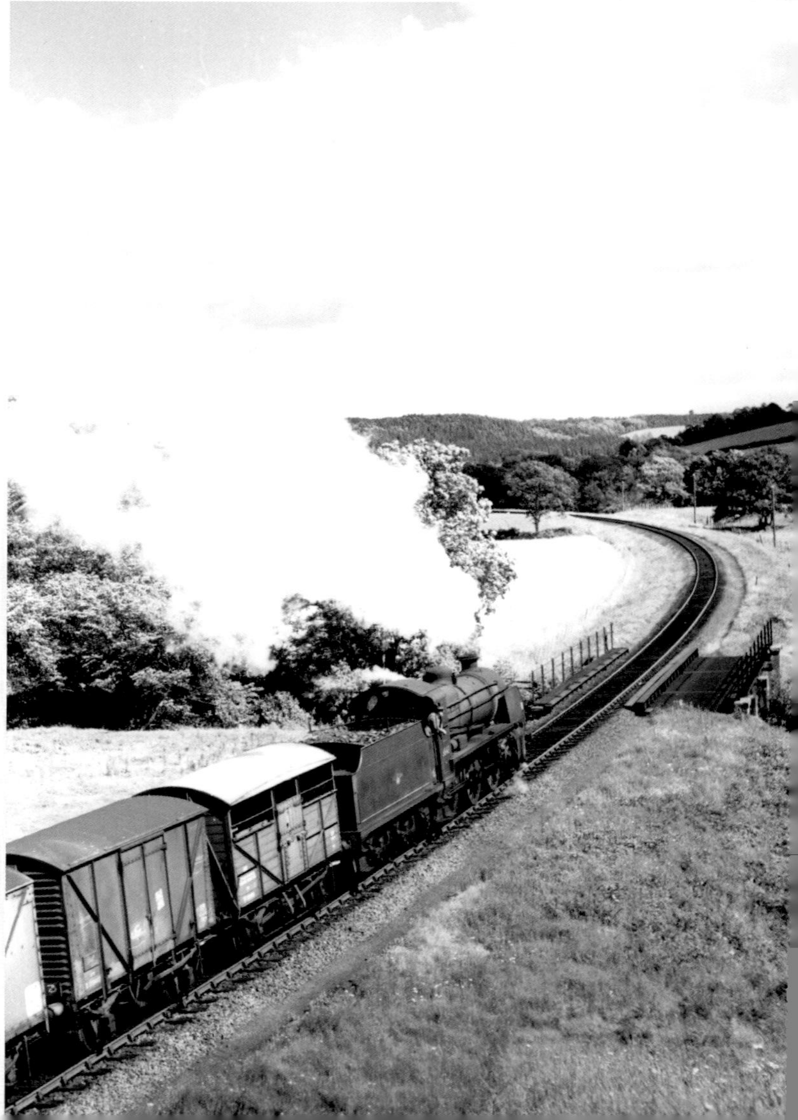

Above and right: **EGGESFORD** 'N' 2-6-0 No 31843 hauls the afternoon up goods train along the North Devon line near Eggesford on 26 June 1963.

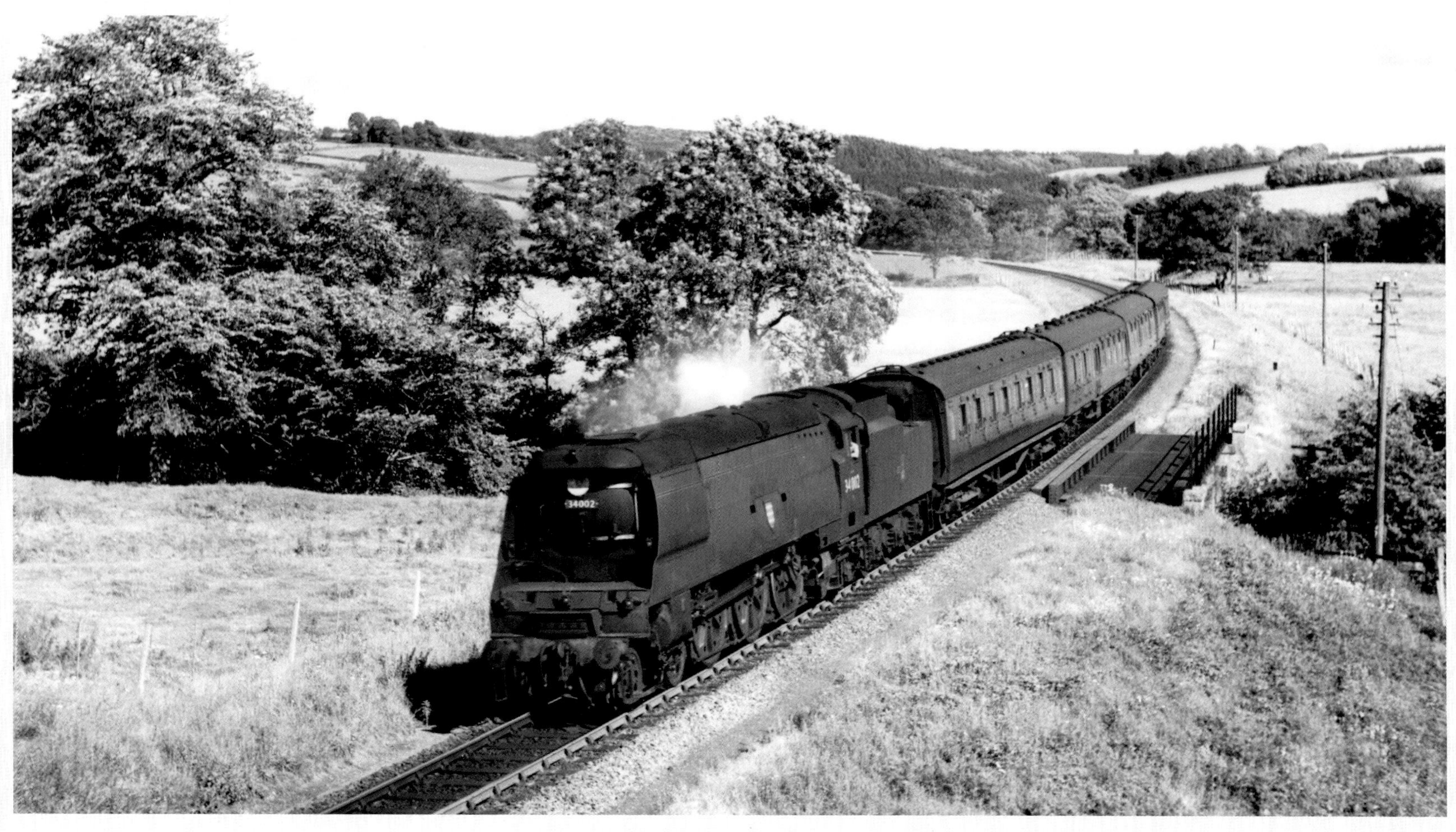

EGGESFORD Hauled by 'WC' 4-6-2 No 34002 *Salisbury*, the North Devon portion of the down 'Atlantic Coast Express' – three coaches for Ilfracombe and one for Torrington – heads down the Taw valley north of Eggesford on the same day. Bridges were built wide enough to permit doubling of the line, but this has never been done.

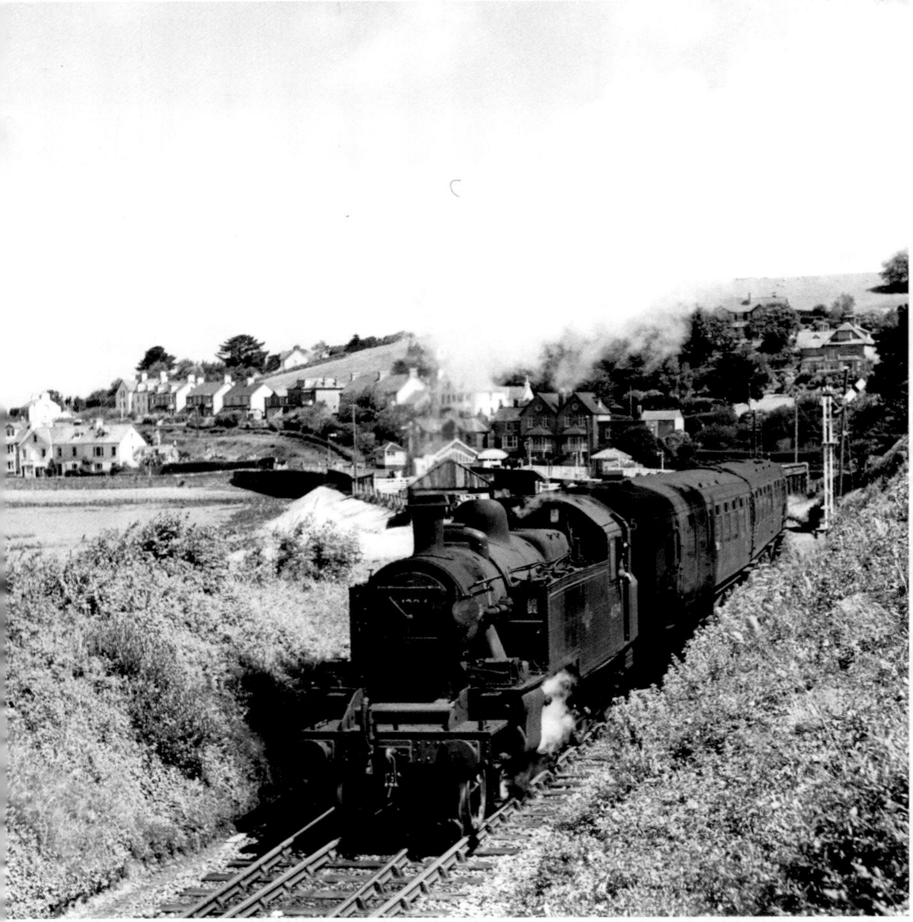

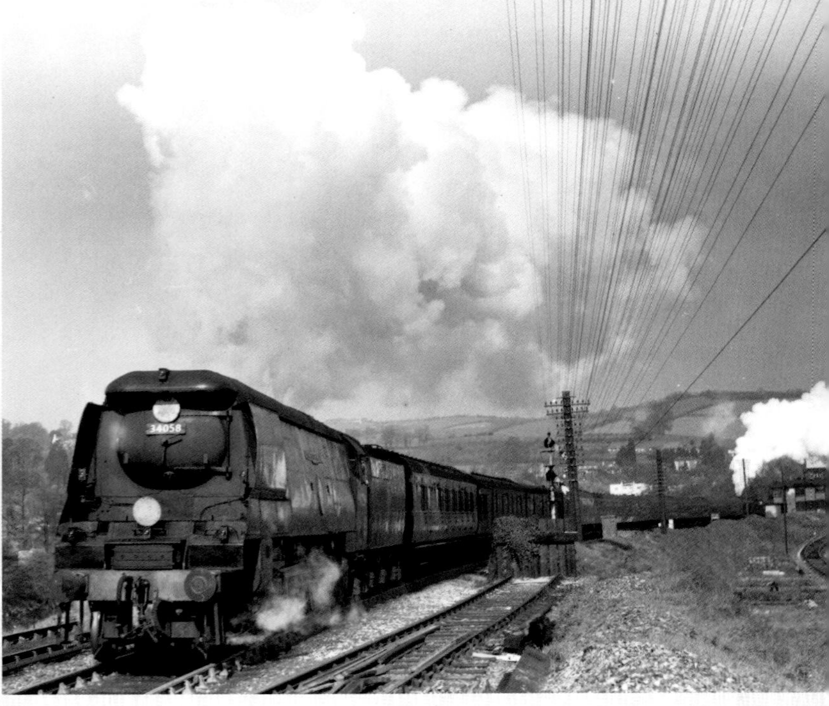

Above: **EXETER CENTRAL** The Plymouth portion of an express to Waterloo is brought up the 1 in 37 bank from Exeter St Davids on 18 April 1960 by 'BB' 4-6-2 No 34058 *Sir Frederick Pile*. An unidentified 'Z' 0-8-0T is helping at the rear.

Right: **COWLEY BRIDGE JUNCTION, EXETER** The Plymouth portion of the 3.00pm train from Waterloo passes the junction on 17 April 1963. The train is headed by diesel-hydraulic locomotive No D868 *Zephyr*. The Western Region had taken over Southern Region lines west of Salisbury at the end of 1962, and diesel locomotives were gradually taking over the workings.

Above: **INSTOW** 2MT 2-6-2T No 41294 leaves Instow at the head of the 11.35am train from Barnstaple Junction to Torrington on 22 June 1963. Instow station can be seen above the train.

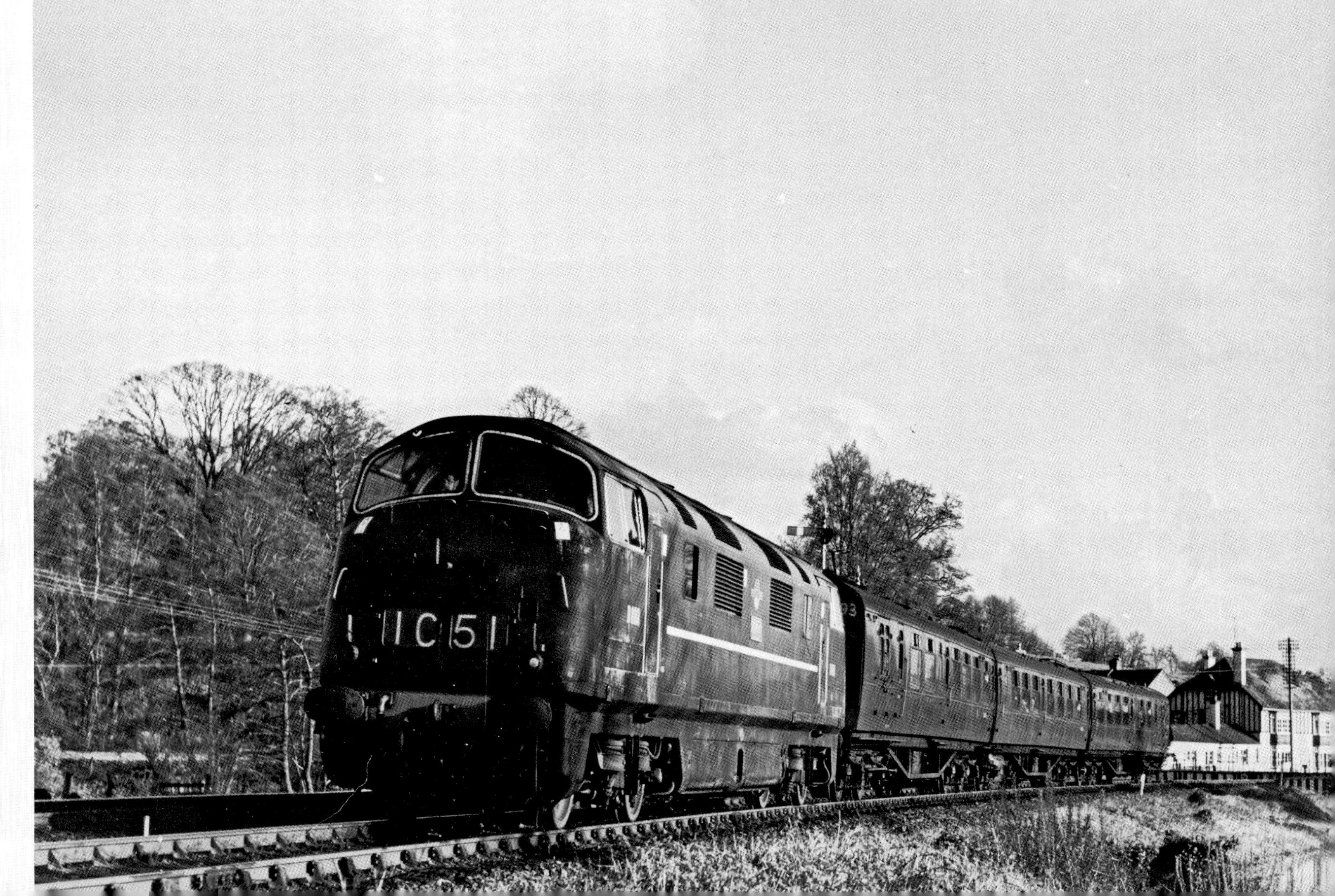

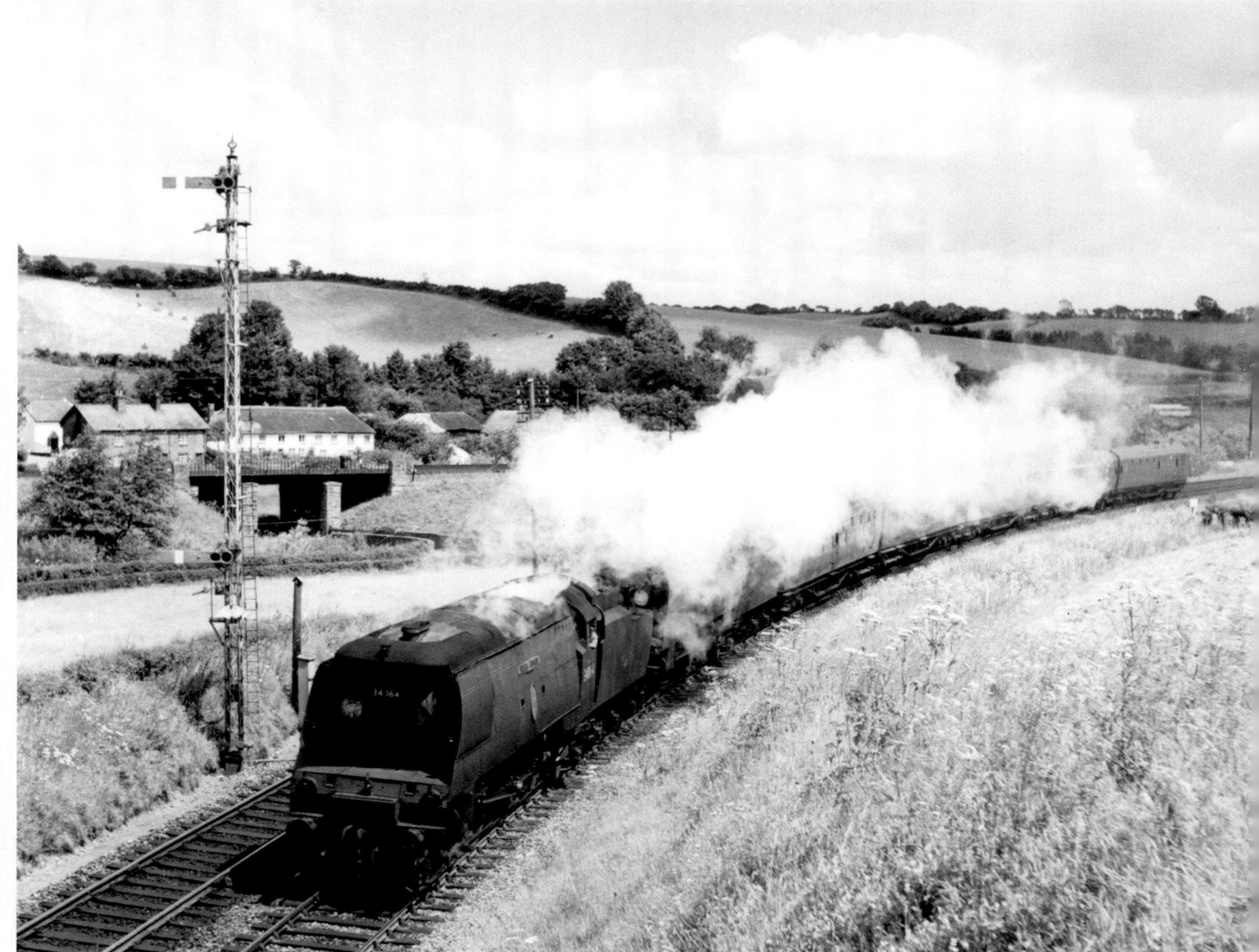

COLEFORD JUNCTION The combined Plymouth, Bude and Padstow portions of the down 'Atlantic Coast Express' of 27 June 1963 pass Coleford Junction, where the North Devon line (seen in the background) diverges. The train is hauled by 'BB' 4-6-2 No 34075 *264 Squadron*, piloted by No 34064 *Fighter Command*, fitted with a Giesl ejector.

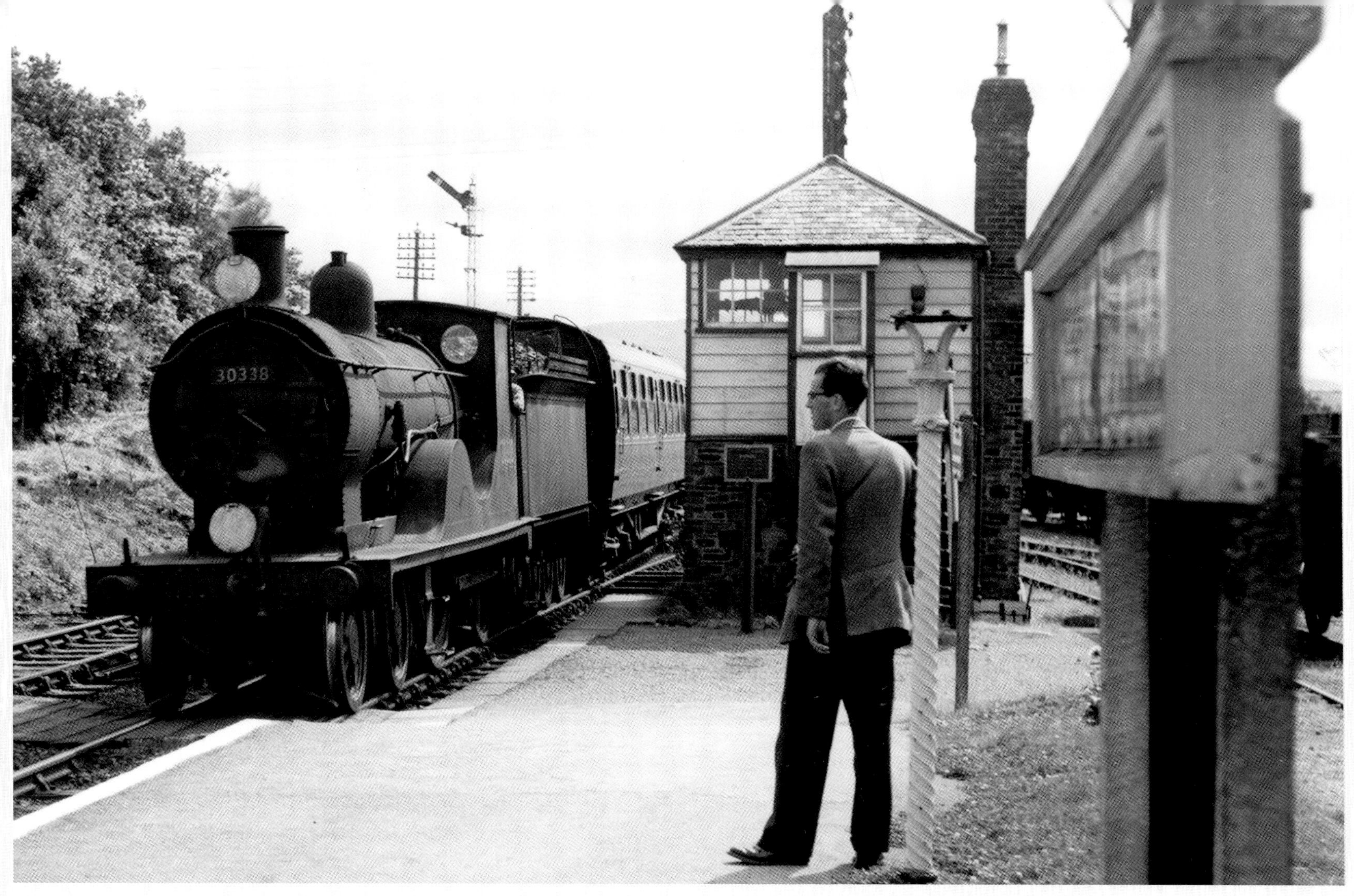

SAMPFORD COURTENAY Headed by 'T9' 4-4-0 No 30338, the 3.39pm from Okehampton to Exeter sweeps through Sampford Courtenay on 1 August 1959.

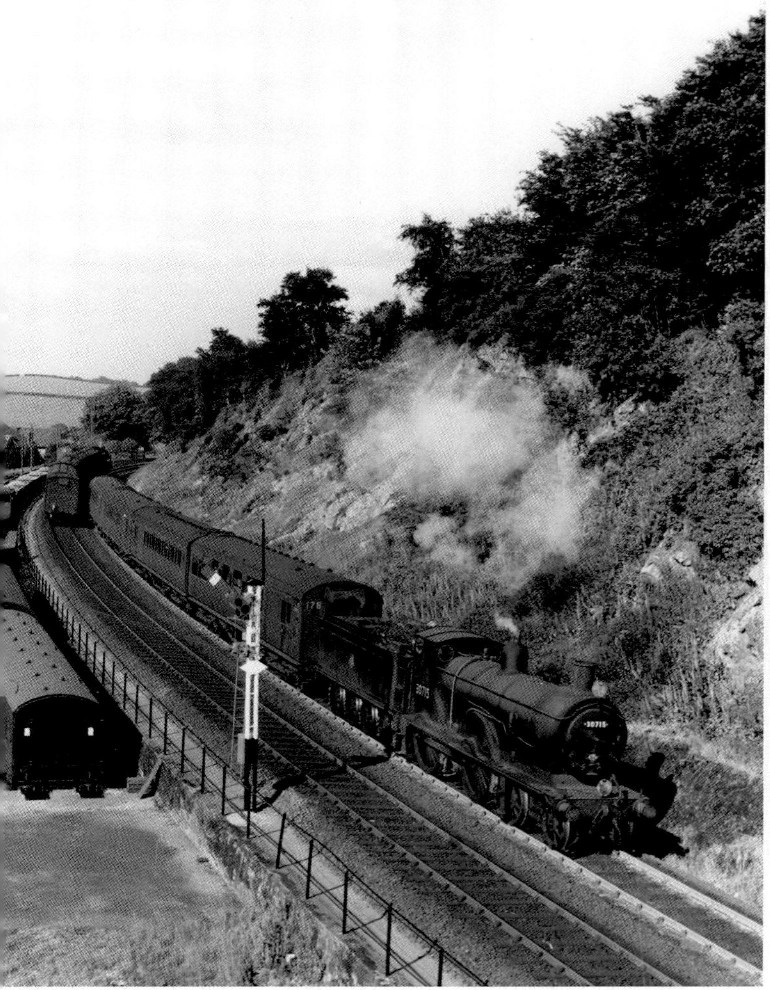

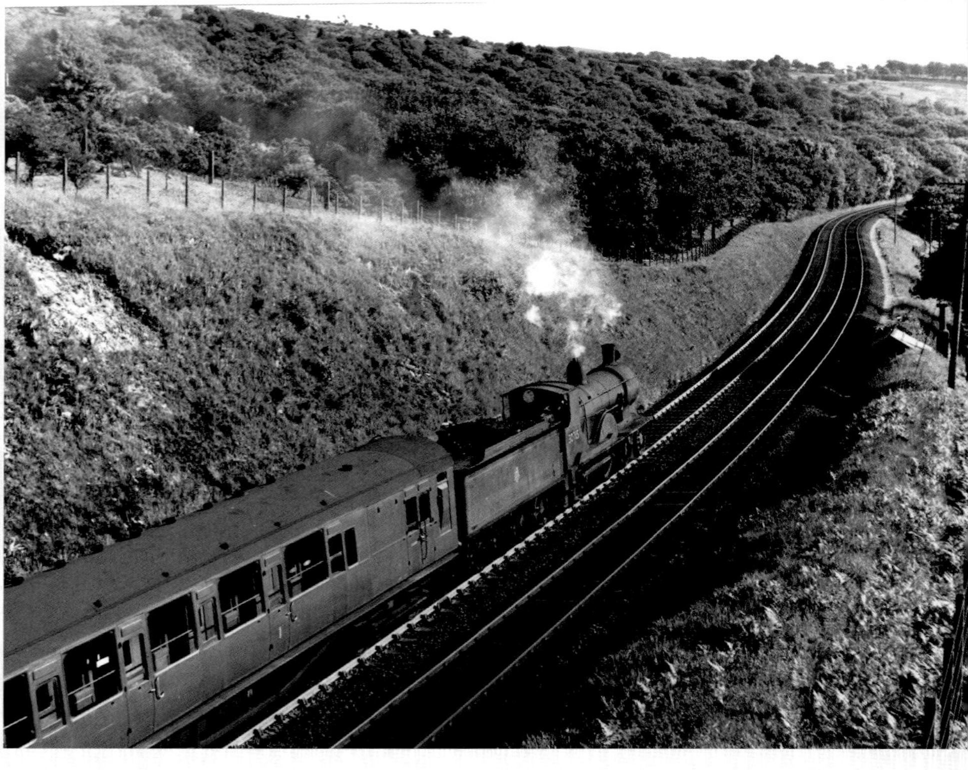

OKEHAMPTON 'T9' 4-4-0 No 30715 heads out of Okehampton with the 5.51pm to Padstow on 16 June 1961. In the first shot an 'N' 2-6-0 can be seen approaching the station with an arrival – a missed chance for a crossing shot, perhaps. By this time 'T9s' at Exmouth Junction were reduced to one cycle of workings, and the successor 'U1s' were coming on the scene.

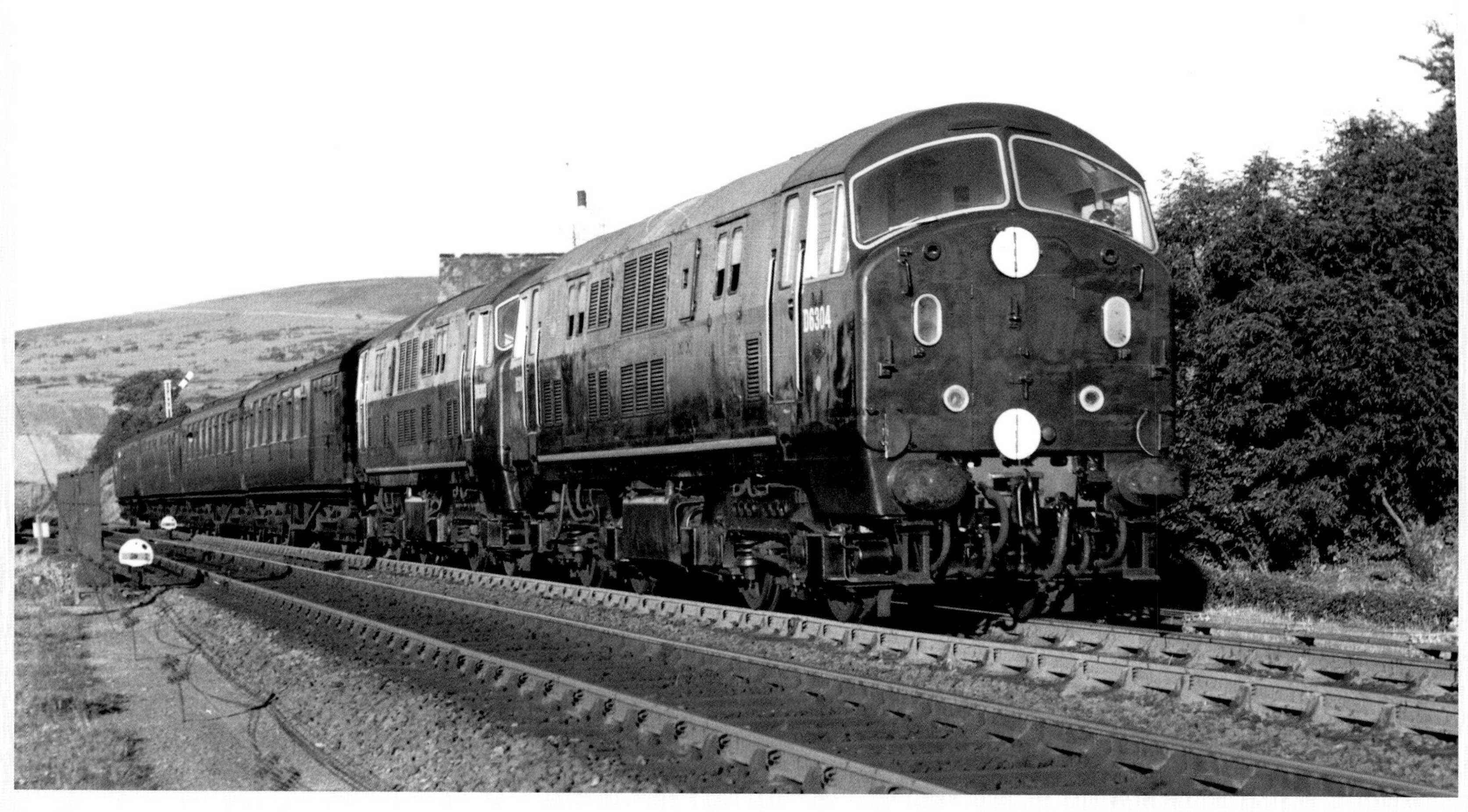

MELDON JUNCTION Diesel-hydraulics Nos D6304 and D6303 approach Meldon Junction with the afternoon WR/SR interchange working from Exeter to Plymouth on 1 August 1959. Could it be that a single North British locomotive of this type could not be relied on to complete such a journey?

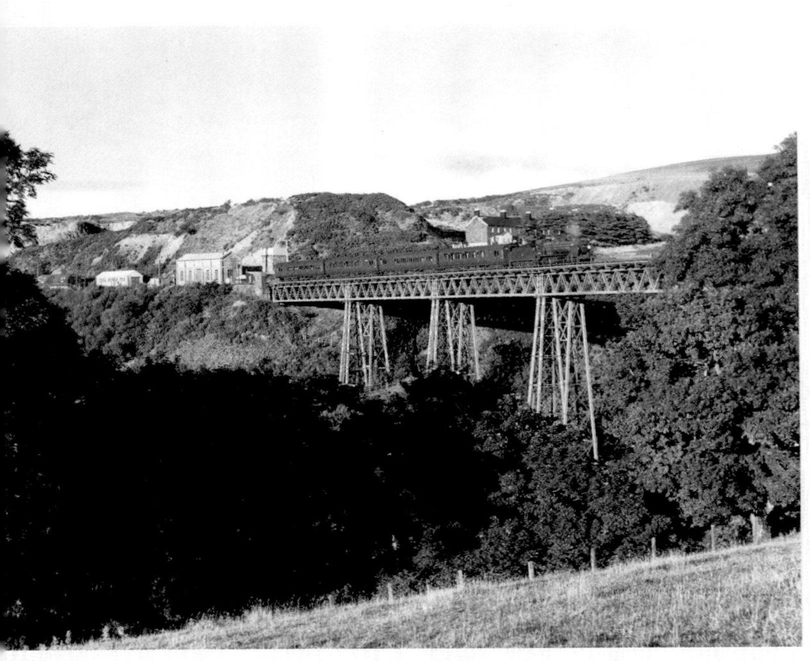

Above: **MELDON VIADUCT** The 7.47pm from Okehampton into North Cornwall is headed across Meldon Viaduct by 'N' 2-6-0 No 31830 on 1 August 1959. Meldon Quarry appears to be shut down for the Bank Holiday weekend.

Right: **BRENTOR** 'N' 2-6-0 No 31835 scurries round the curves south of Brentor station with the Plymouth portion of the down 'Atlantic Coast Express' on 19 April 1963. The ex-GWR Plymouth-Launceston branch is in the foreground, while the church of St Michael de Rupe crowns the skyline.

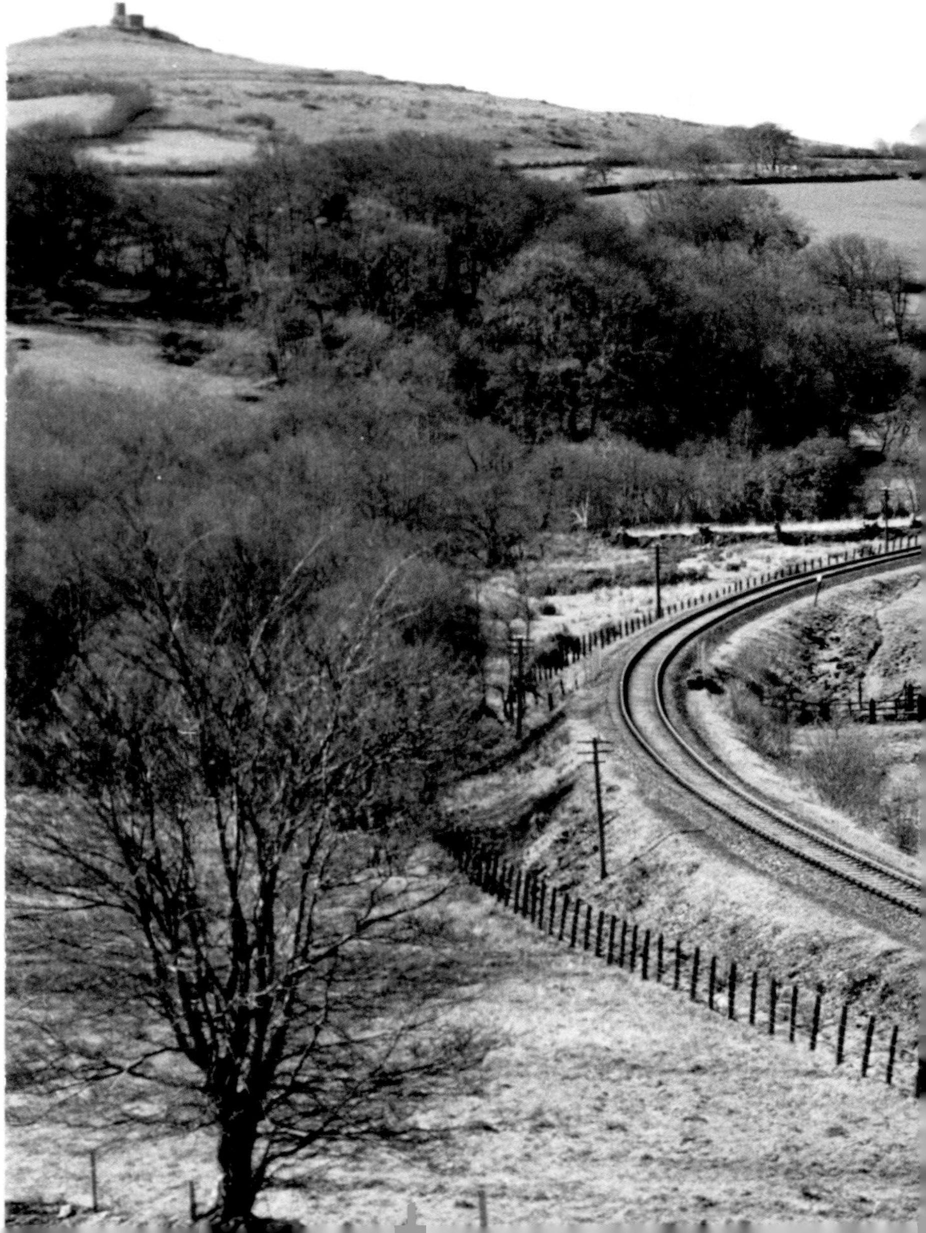

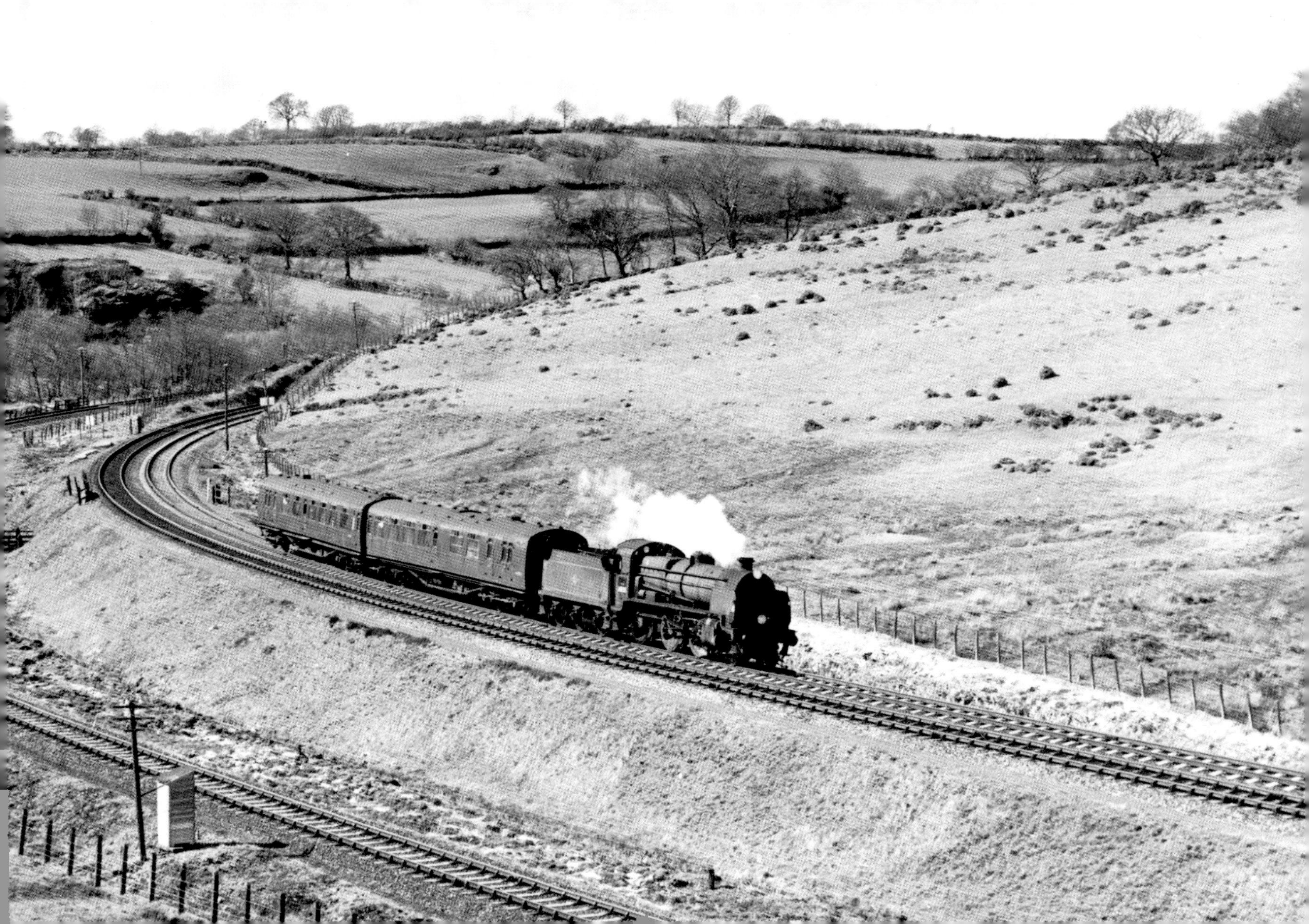

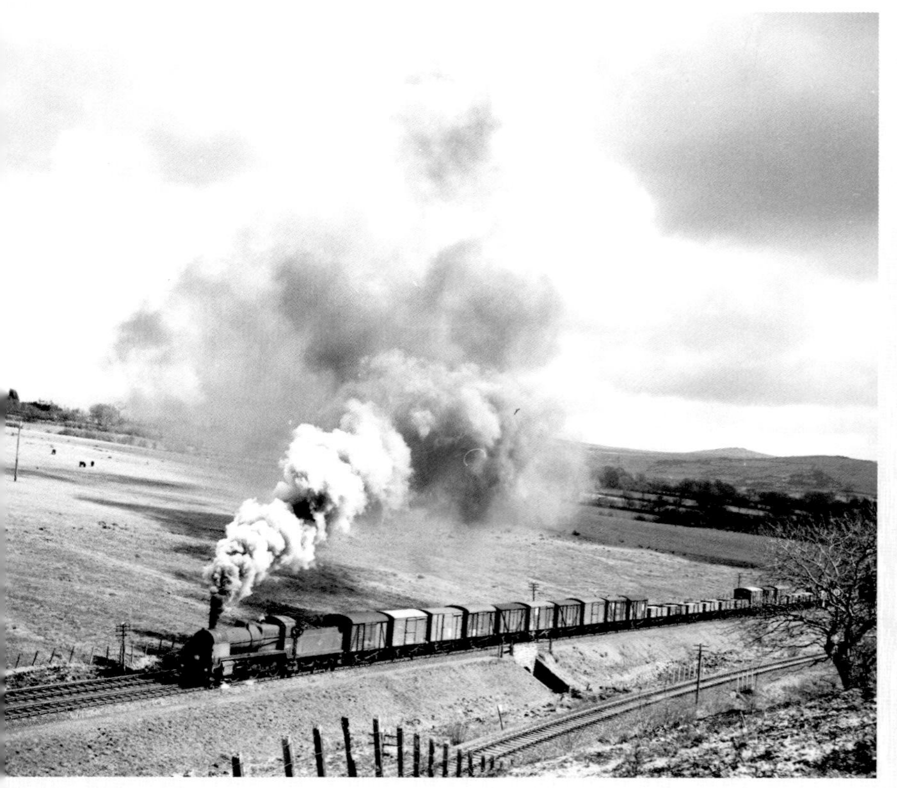

MARY TAVY 'N' 2-6-0 No 31875 gets to grips with the climb round the northern edge of Dartmoor as it hauls the up mid-morning goods train from Plymouth to Exeter on 19 April 1963. The summit near Meldon Junction is still some 9 miles ahead.

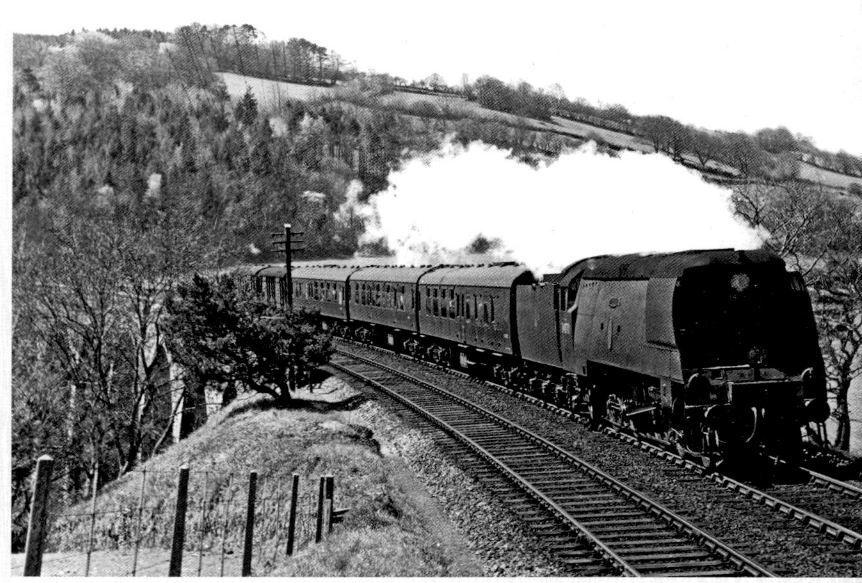

TAVISTOCK 'BB' 4-6-2 No 34070 *Manston* brings the 11.50am (Su) Plymouth-Exeter train off Shillamill Viaduct, 1½ miles south of Tavistock North station, on 29 April 1962.

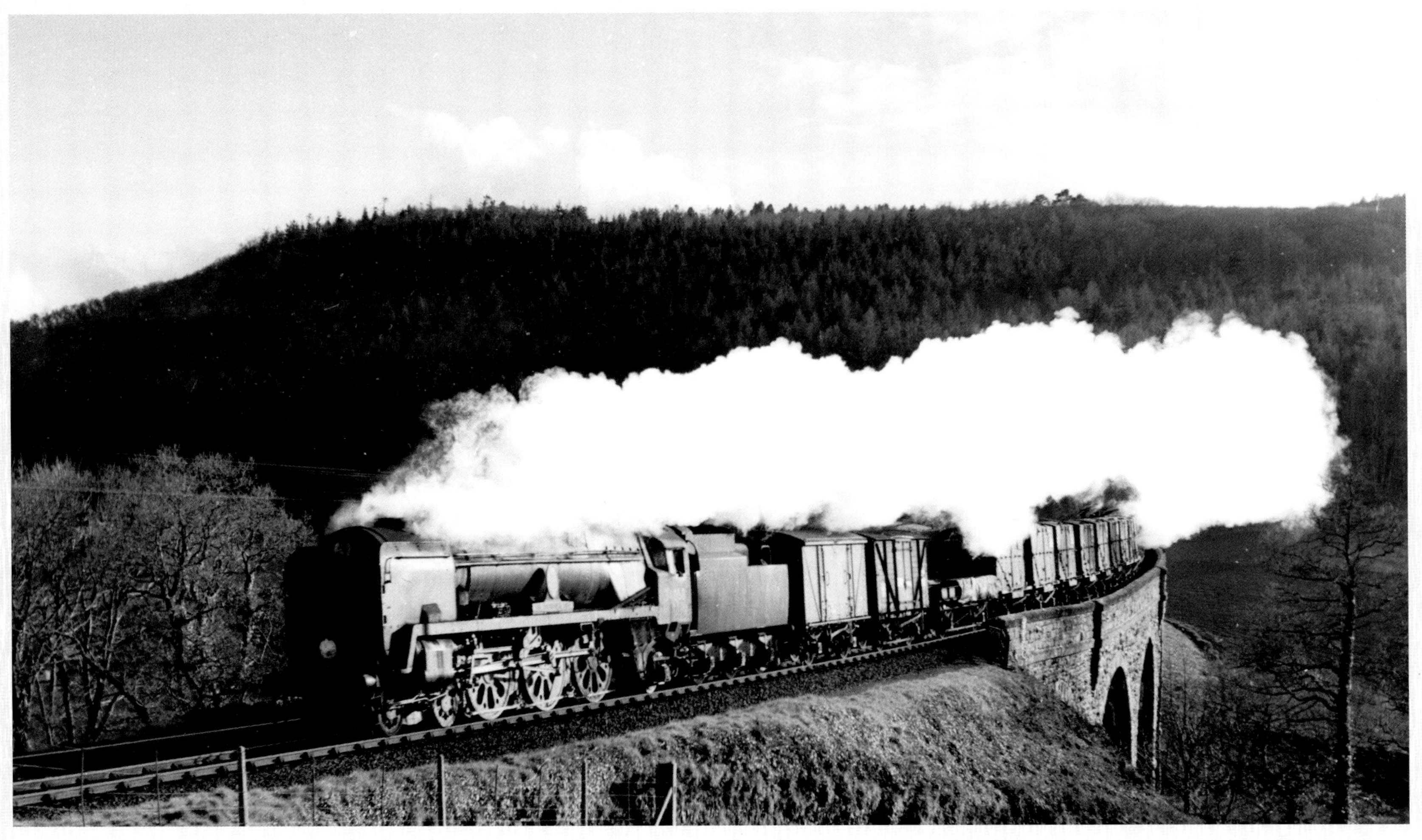

Above: **TAVISTOCK** Also leaving Shillamill Viaduct is 'BB' 4-6-2 No 34058 *Sir Frederick Pile* at the head of the late-afternoon Plymouth-Exeter goods train on 18 April 1963.

Right: **CALSTOCK** Found on Calstock Quay in June 1961, this lifebelt, apparently, had not been relettered for 40 years or more. However, effective it might have been by then as a lifebelt, it can serve as an introduction to the Callington branch.

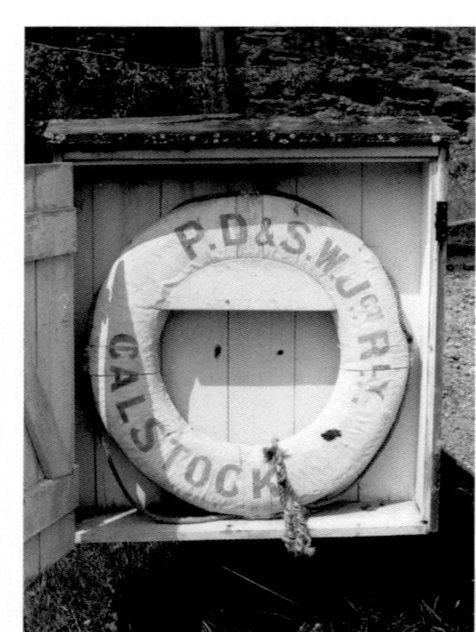

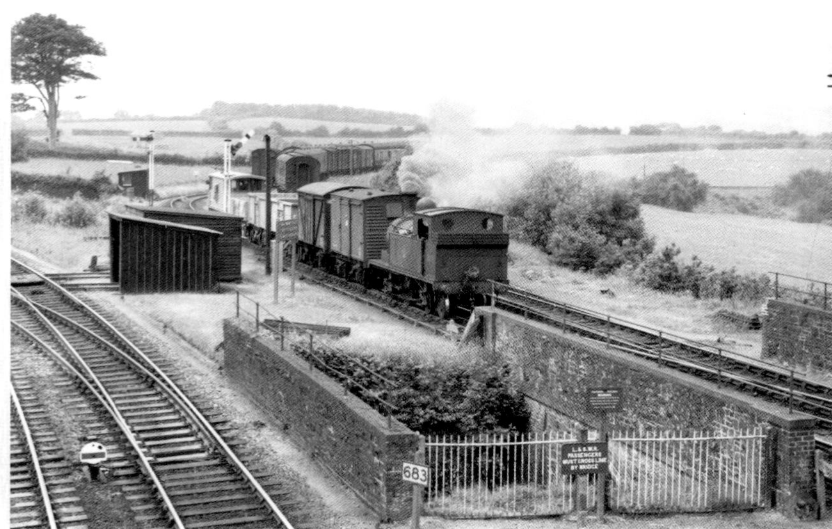

Top far right: **BERE ALSTON** This might be described as a 'grab' shot. I had just arrived by train from Tamerton Foliot and was on the footbridge when something caused me to look down the branch. I saw the branch goods train approaching, and just had time to get ready and take this shot as 'O2' 0-4-4T No 30223 entered Bere Alston station with the midday goods train from Gunnislake on 15 June 1961. The main line to Plymouth is on the left. The locomotive will return to Plymouth on the 12.50pm train from Bere Alston.

Right: **LUCKETT** The 3.15pm Bere Alston-Callington train is approaching Luckett, and 2MT 2-6-2T No 41315 has just shut off steam for the station on 27 April 1962. The course of the line along the hillside in the left background can be clearly seen.

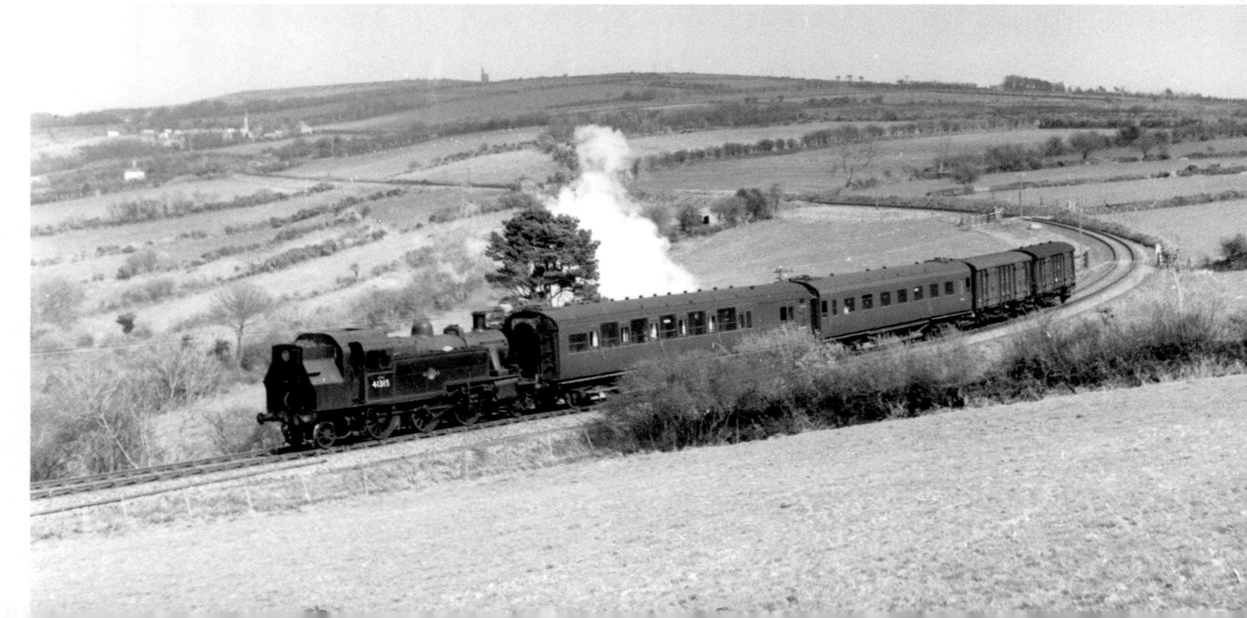

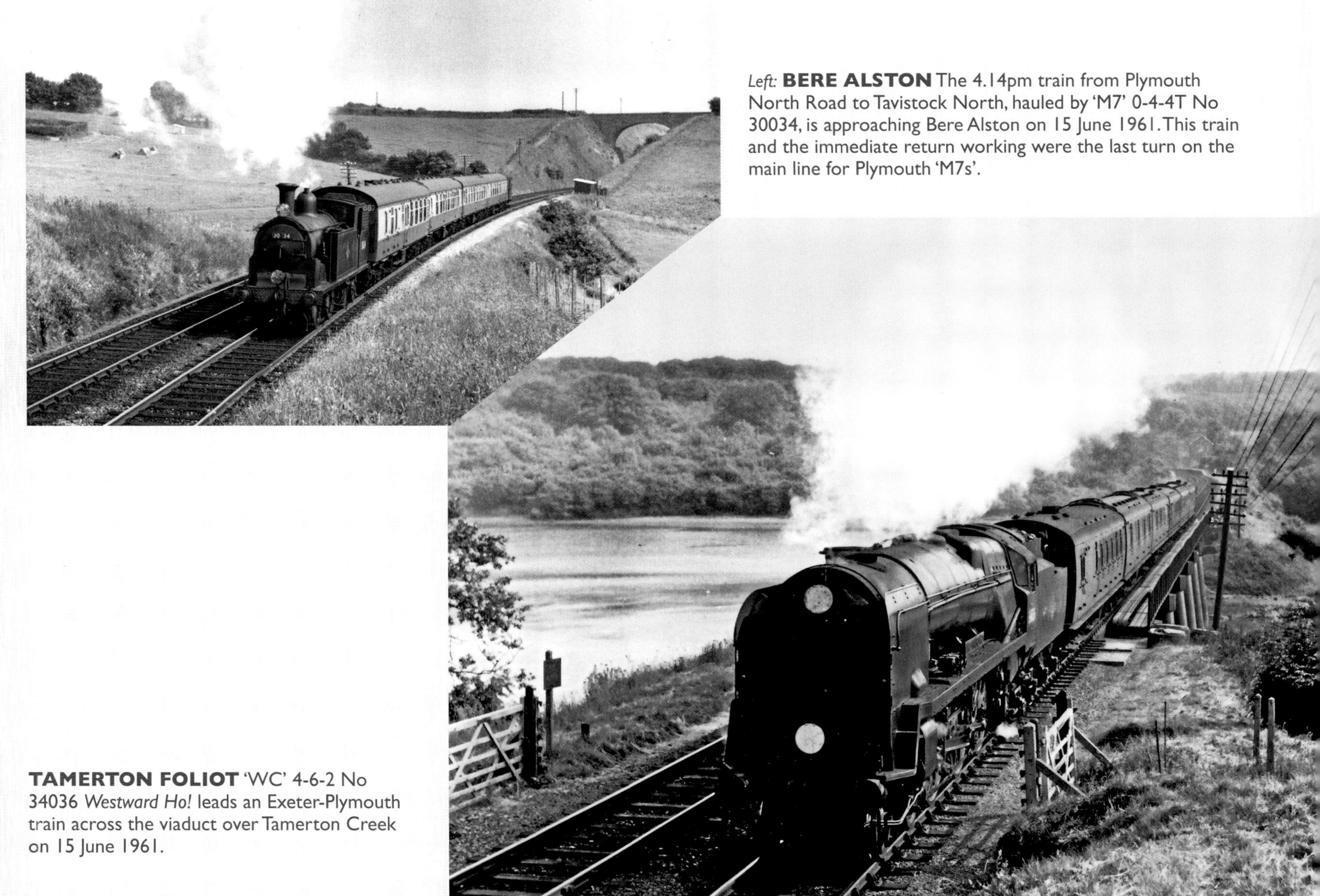

Left: **BERE ALSTON** The 4.14pm train from Plymouth North Road to Tavistock North, hauled by 'M7' 0-4-4T No 30034, is approaching Bere Alston on 15 June 1961. This train and the immediate return working were the last turn on the main line for Plymouth 'M7s'.

TAMERTON FOLIOT 'WC' 4-6-2 No 34036 *Westward Ho!* leads an Exeter-Plymouth train across the viaduct over Tamerton Creek on 15 June 1961.

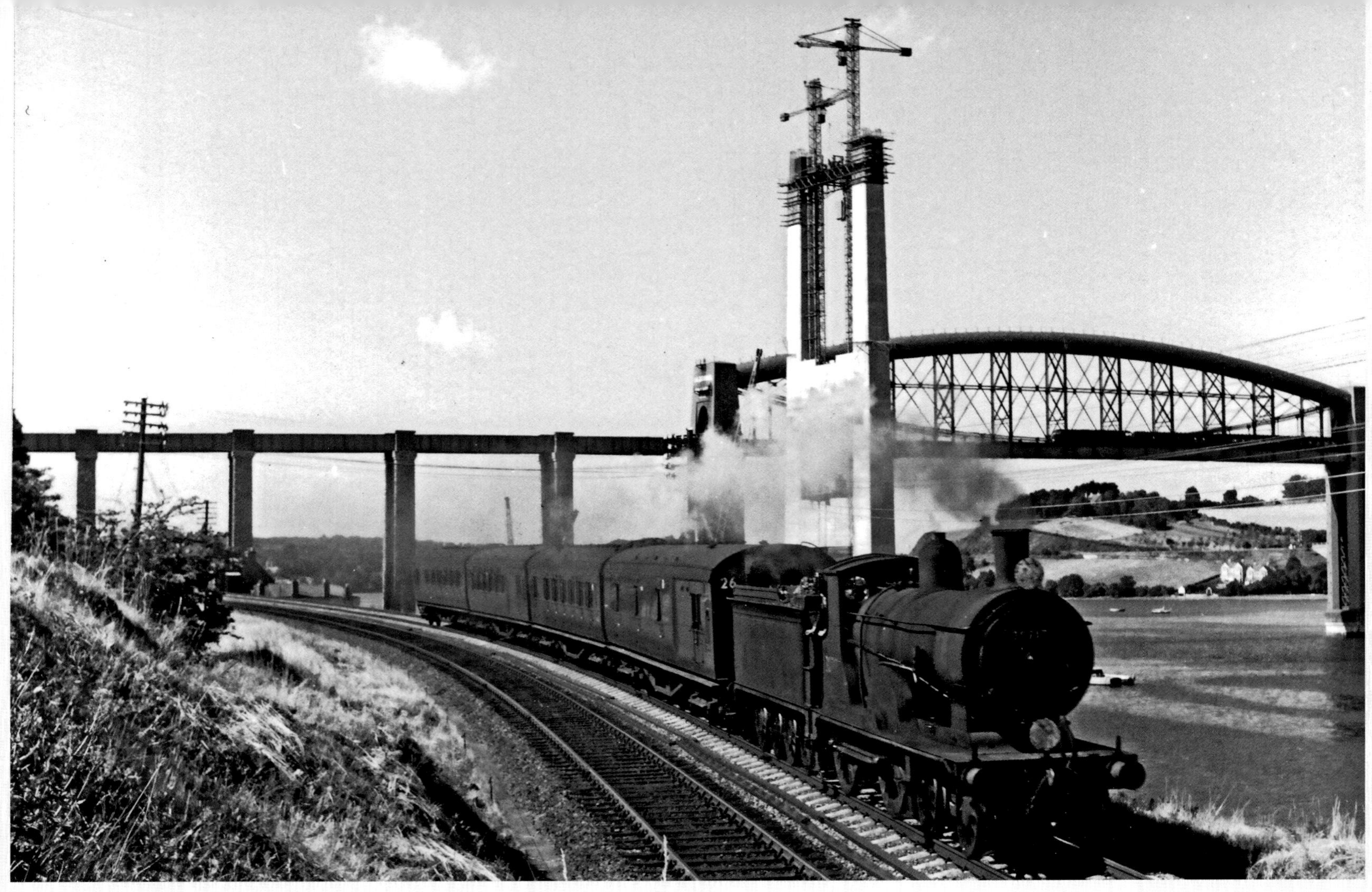

ST BUDEAUX The Royal Albert Bridge stretches across the background, with the start of the parallel road bridge in front of it. A 'Warship' diesel-hydraulic locomotive hauls a train from Cornwall over it, as 'T9' 4-4-0 No 30717 heads the Plymouth portion of the up 'Atlantic Coast Express' through the foreground on 1 July 1960.

Below: **MELDON JUNCTION** 'T9' 4-4-0 No 30715 crosses the bridge over the A30 road with the 3.55pm Okehampton-Padstow service on 1 August 1959. Not merely is the A30 given no more than a standard local road underbridge, but we had been able to stop the car, pile out and grab our shots without impeding other road traffic – on the Saturday of August Bank Holiday weekend!

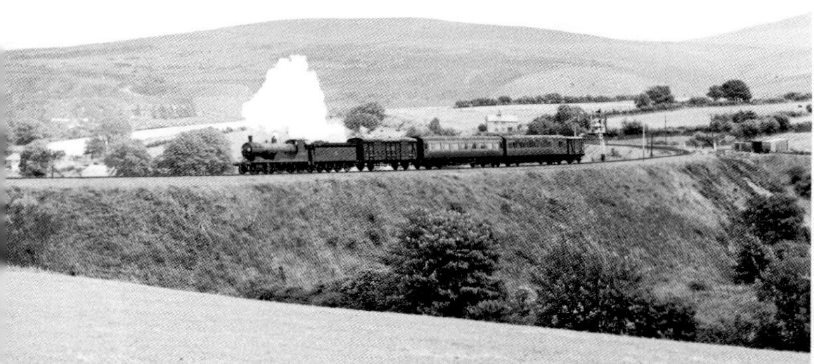

Above: **MELDON JUNCTION** 'T9' 4-4-0 No 30717 pulls away from Meldon Junction at the head of the 1.18pm Okehampton-Bude train on 7 July 1960.

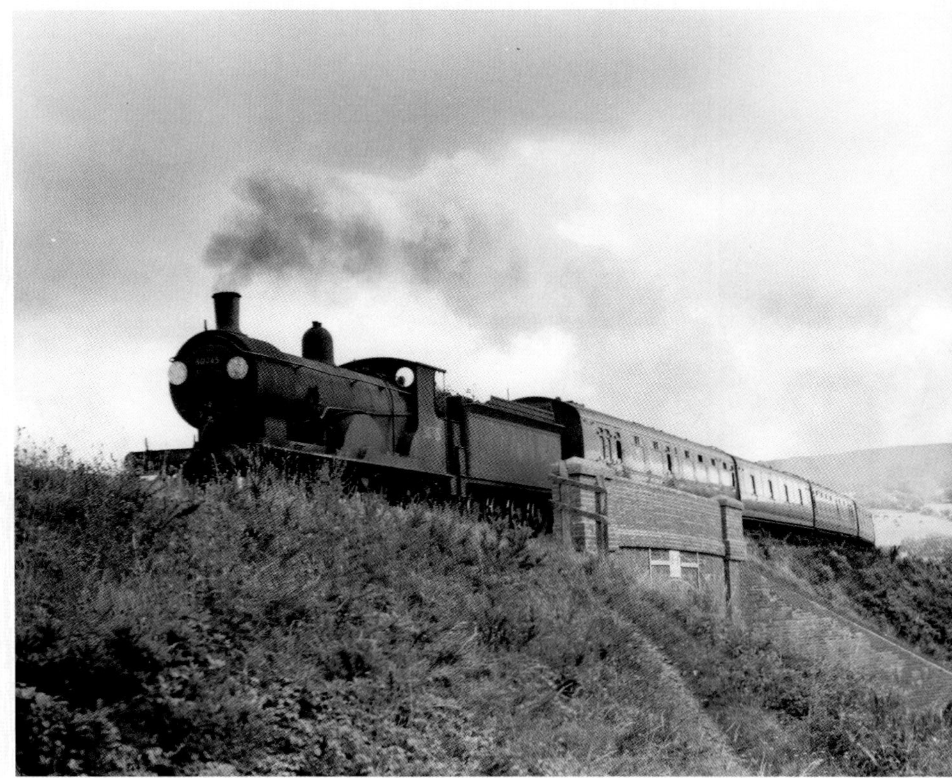

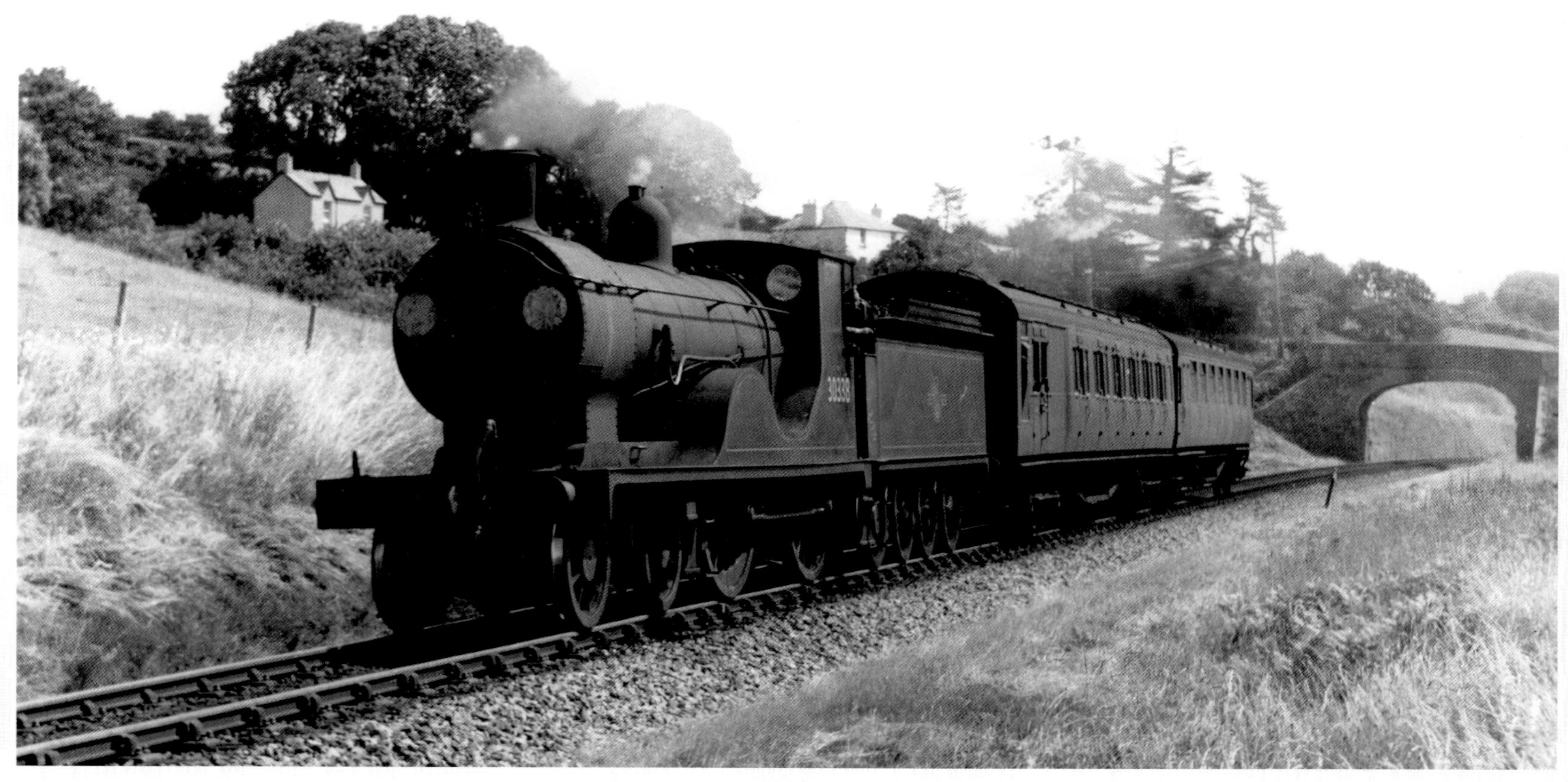

LAUNCESTON 'T9' 4-4-0 No 30338 drifts through the Cornish countryside between Launceston and Egloskerry with the 9.56am Okehampton-Padstow train – all of it, after the Bude portion had been left at Halwill Junction – on 6 July 1960.

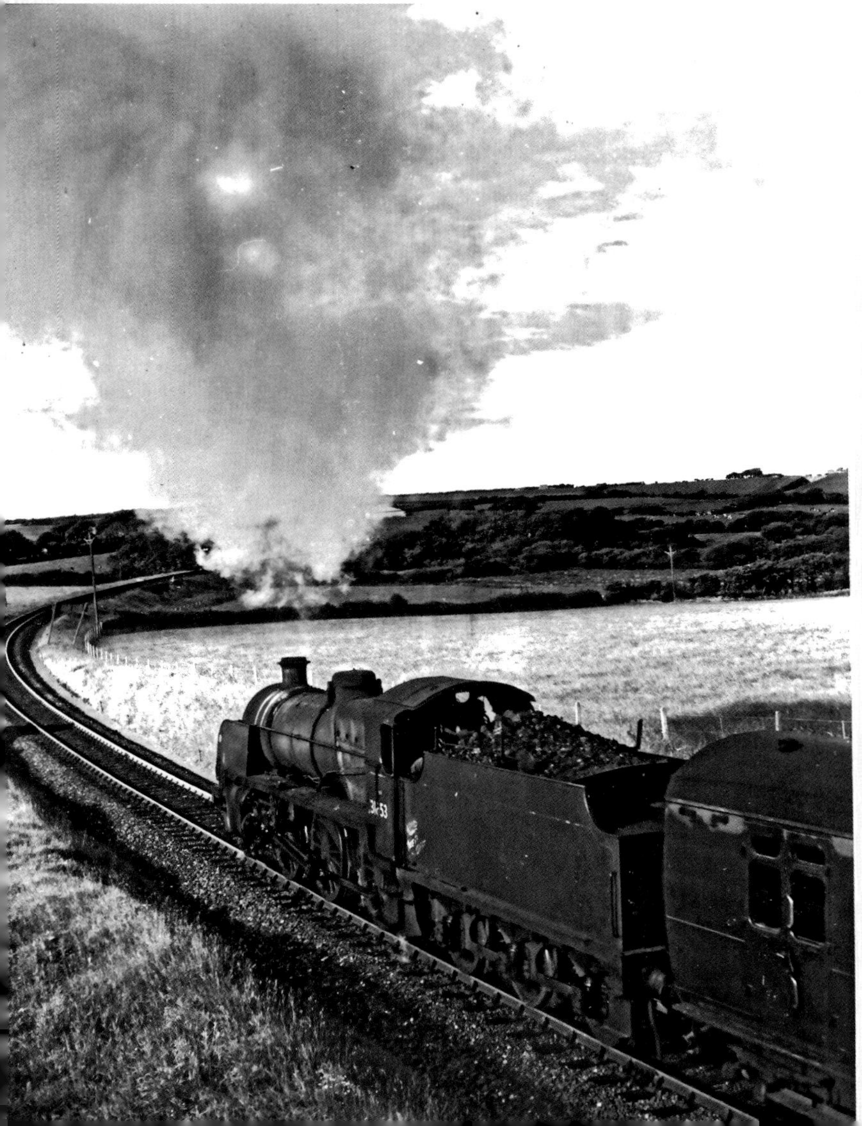

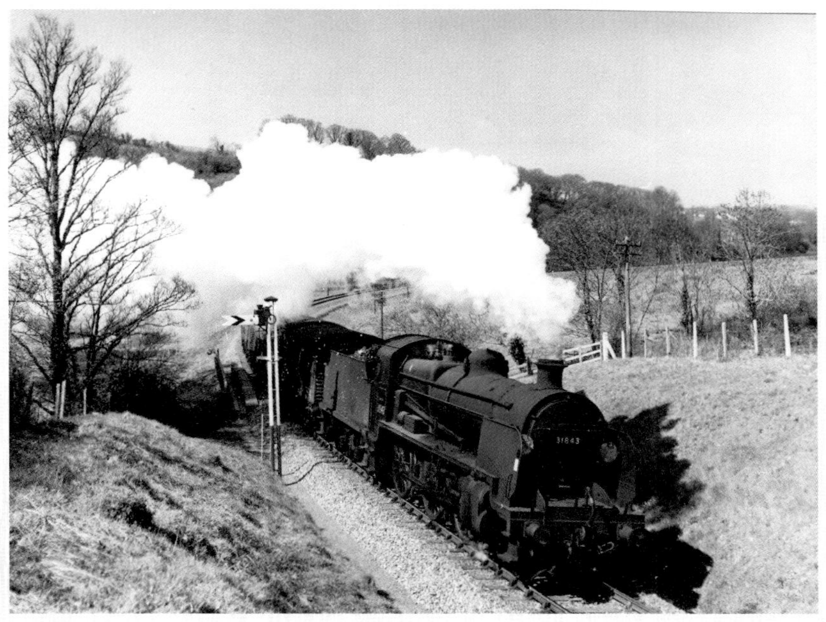

Above: **WADEBRIDGE** A mile out of Wadebridge en route to Okehampton, 'N' 2-6-0 No 31843 has swung across the Camel valley and is starting the climb to Otterham. The train is the 11.35 goods from Wadebridge on 24 April 1962.

Left: **PORT ISAAC ROAD** 'N' 2-6-0 No 31853 restarts the 6.00pm Padstow-Okehampton train from Port Isaac Road station on 9 June 1964. The locomotive shows the grubbier state allowed by the Western Region after its takeover of the line at the end of 1962.

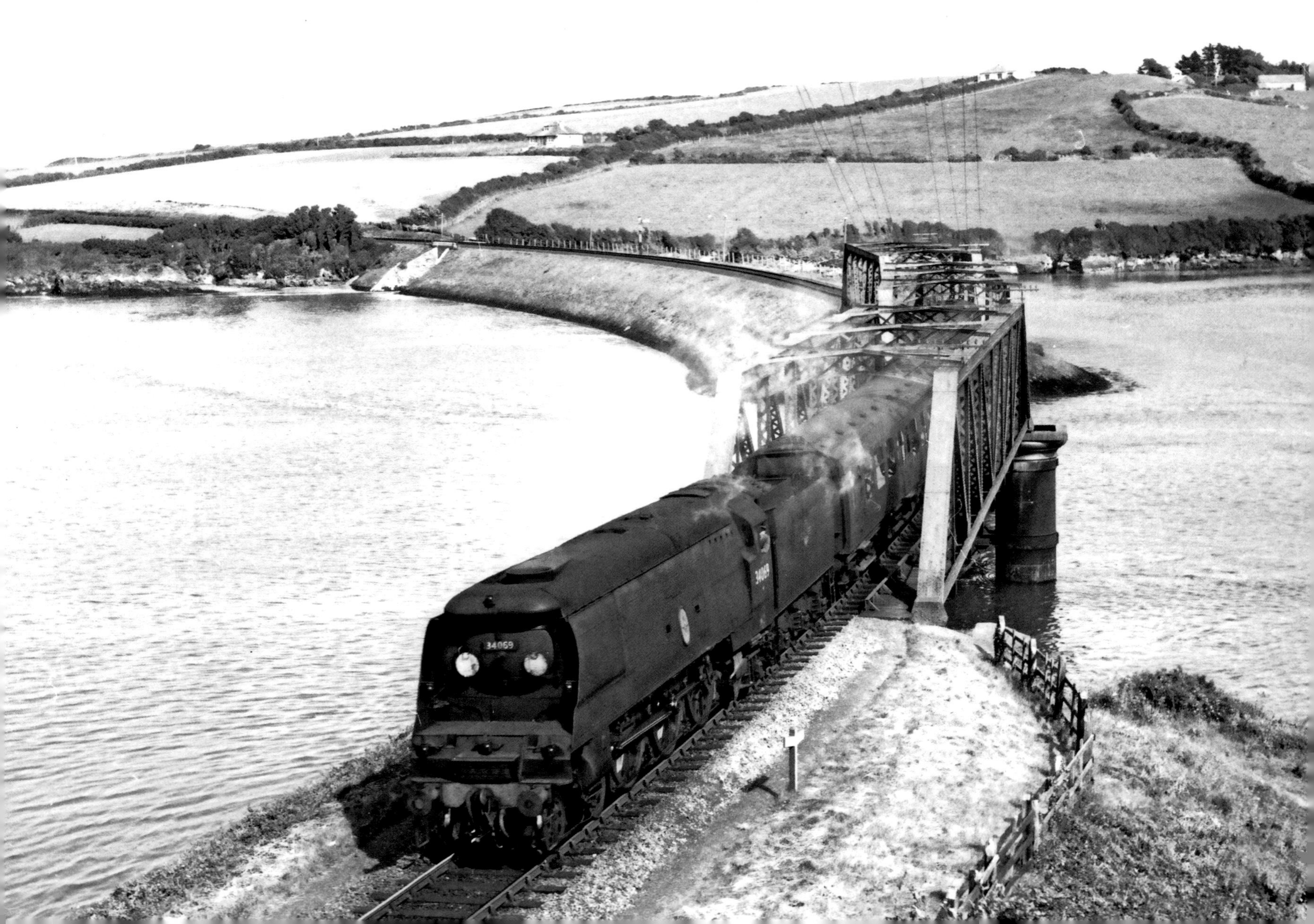

Left: **PADSTOW** The Padstow portion of the down 'Atlantic Coast Express' is headed across the bridge over Little Petherick Creek, half a mile out of the station, by 'BB' 4-6-2 No 34069 *Hawkinge* on 13 June 1961.

Right: **PADSTOW** Also on 13 June 1961, the 6.00pm to Okehampton passes the Padstow outer home signal behind 'T9' 4-4-0 No 30313. The village of Rock can be seen through the smoke across the estuary.

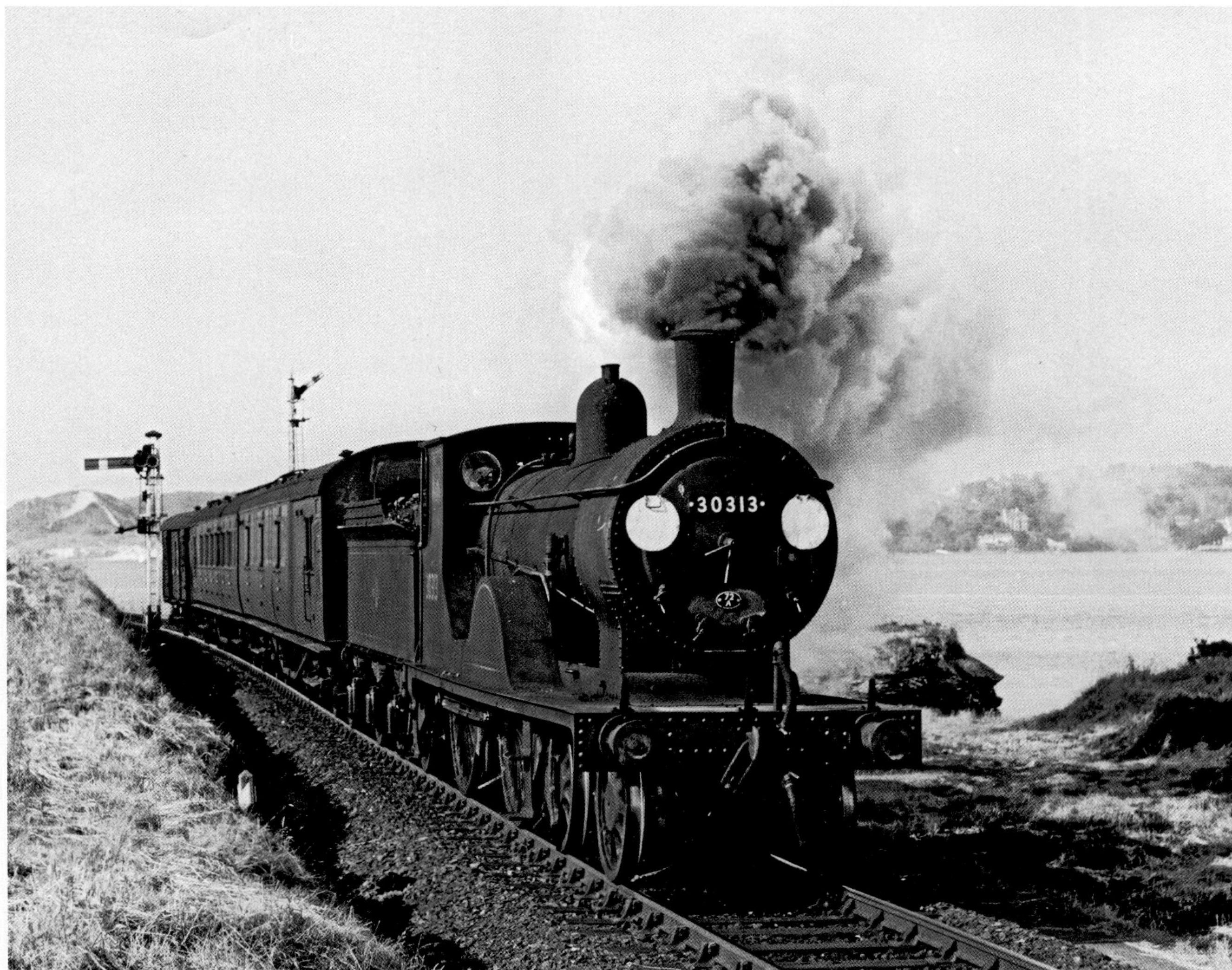

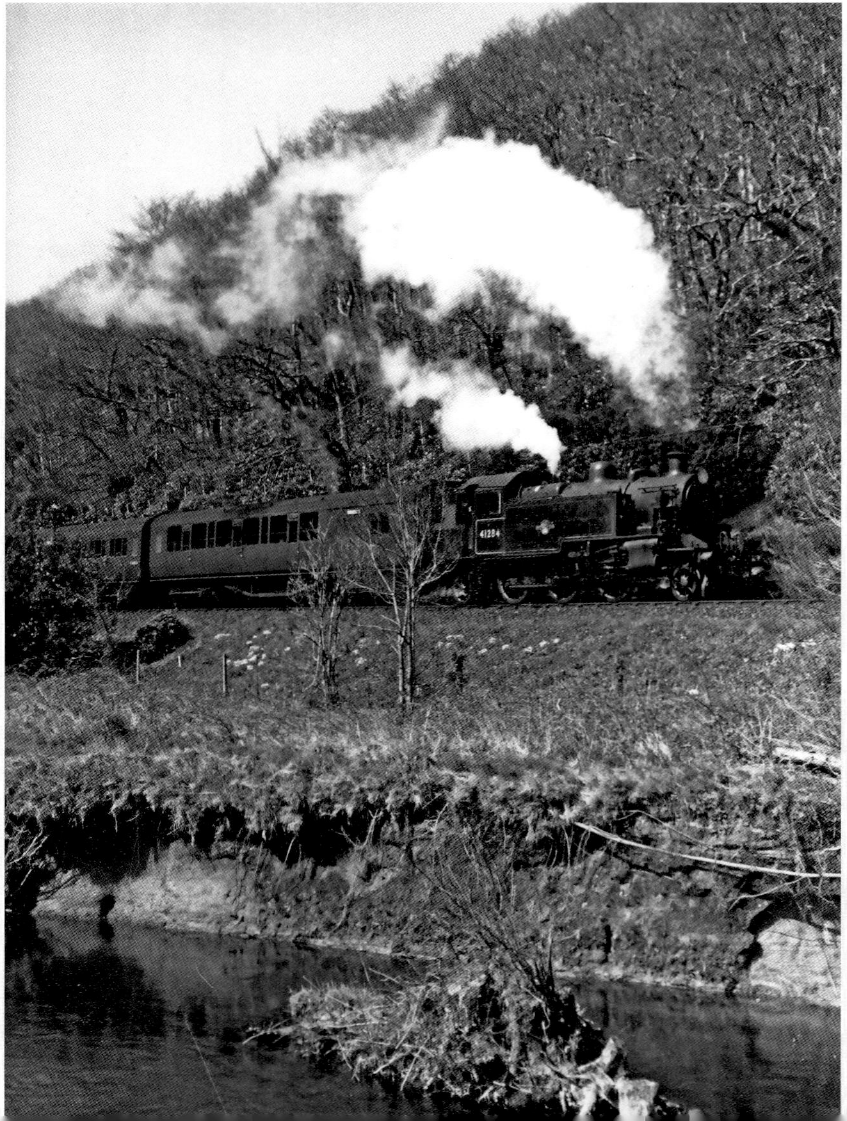

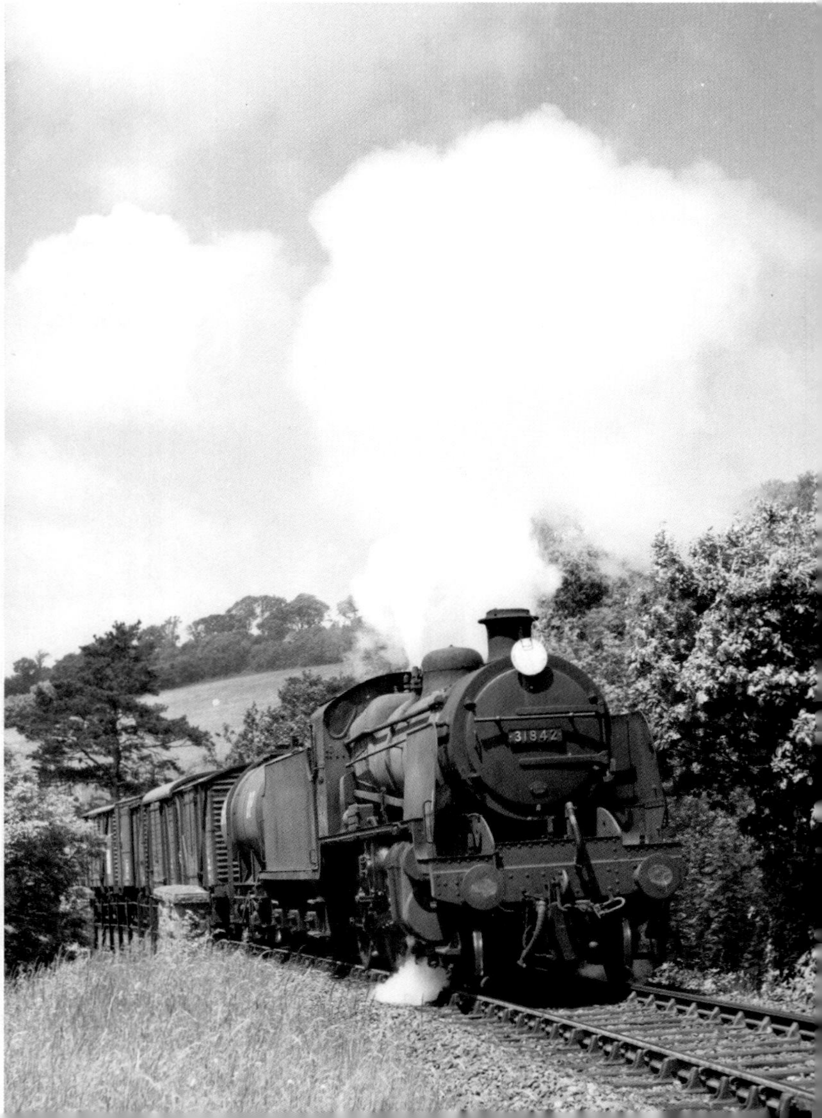

Far left: **WADEBRIDGE** About 3 miles out of Wadebridge, up the valley of the River Camel, 2MT 2-6-2T No 41284 nears Grogley Halt with the 2.52pm Padstow-Bodmin North train on 24 April 1962. A locomotive from an Okehampton-Padstow train will have worked the Padstow-Wadebridge length as part of a fill-in turn; the 2-6-2T will spend most of the day shuttling between Wadebridge and Bodmin North.

Left: **BODMIN** Having shunted in Boscarne Junction sidings, which would also have been shunted earlier in the day by the locomotive of the Wenford train, 'N' 2-6-0 No 31842 sets out to climb the hill to Bodmin General on 10 June 1964 with a goods train for the WR main line.

Right: **WENFORD BRANCH** In the depths of Pencarrow Woods, on the line to Wenford, '0298' 2-4-0WT No 30585 restarts her train of empty china clay wagons from the watering point and sets off for Helland Bridge and Wenford on 14 June 1961. Water supply was by gravity, and levels had to be adjusted upwards when the '1366' 0-6-0PTs took over the working.

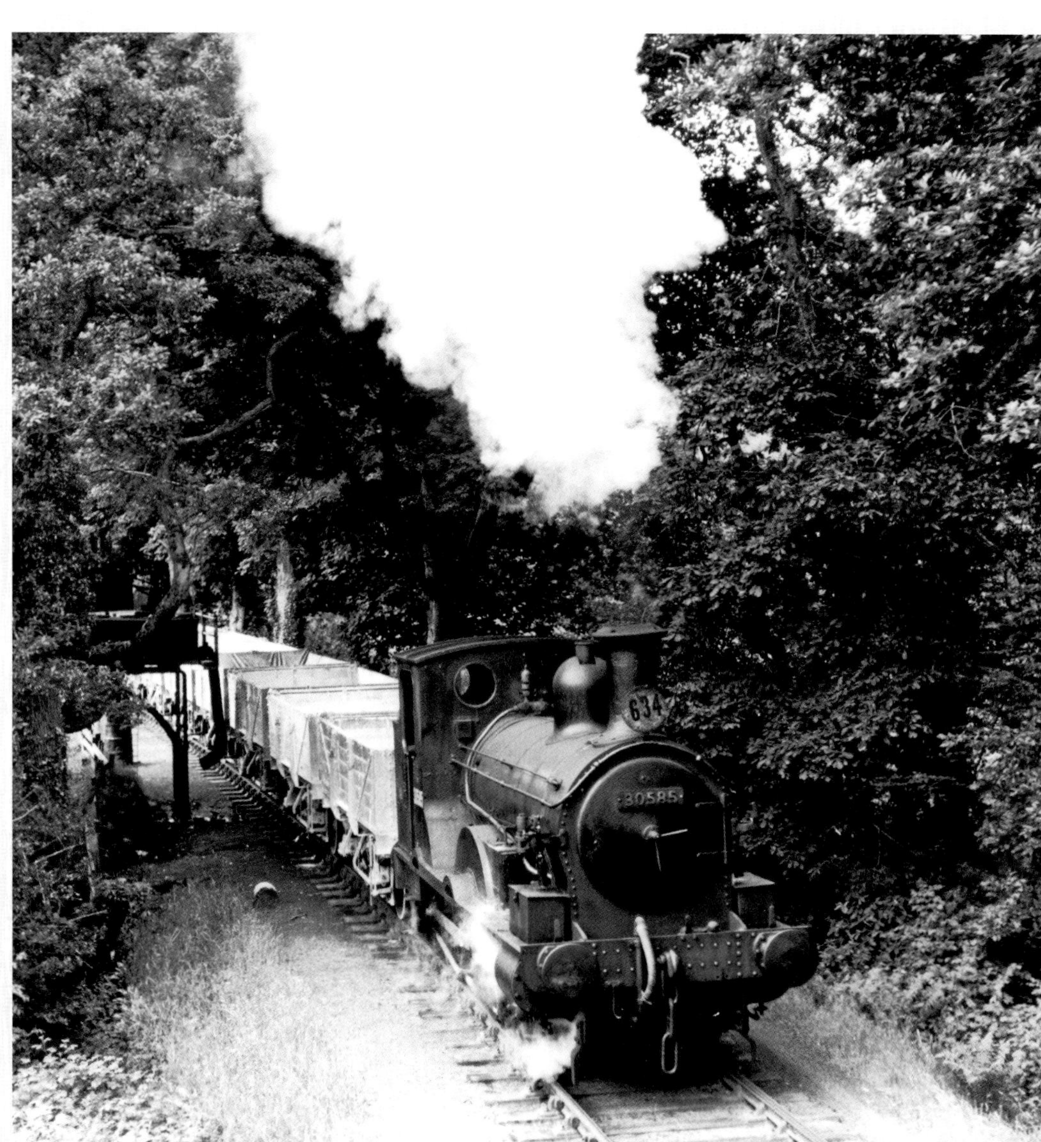

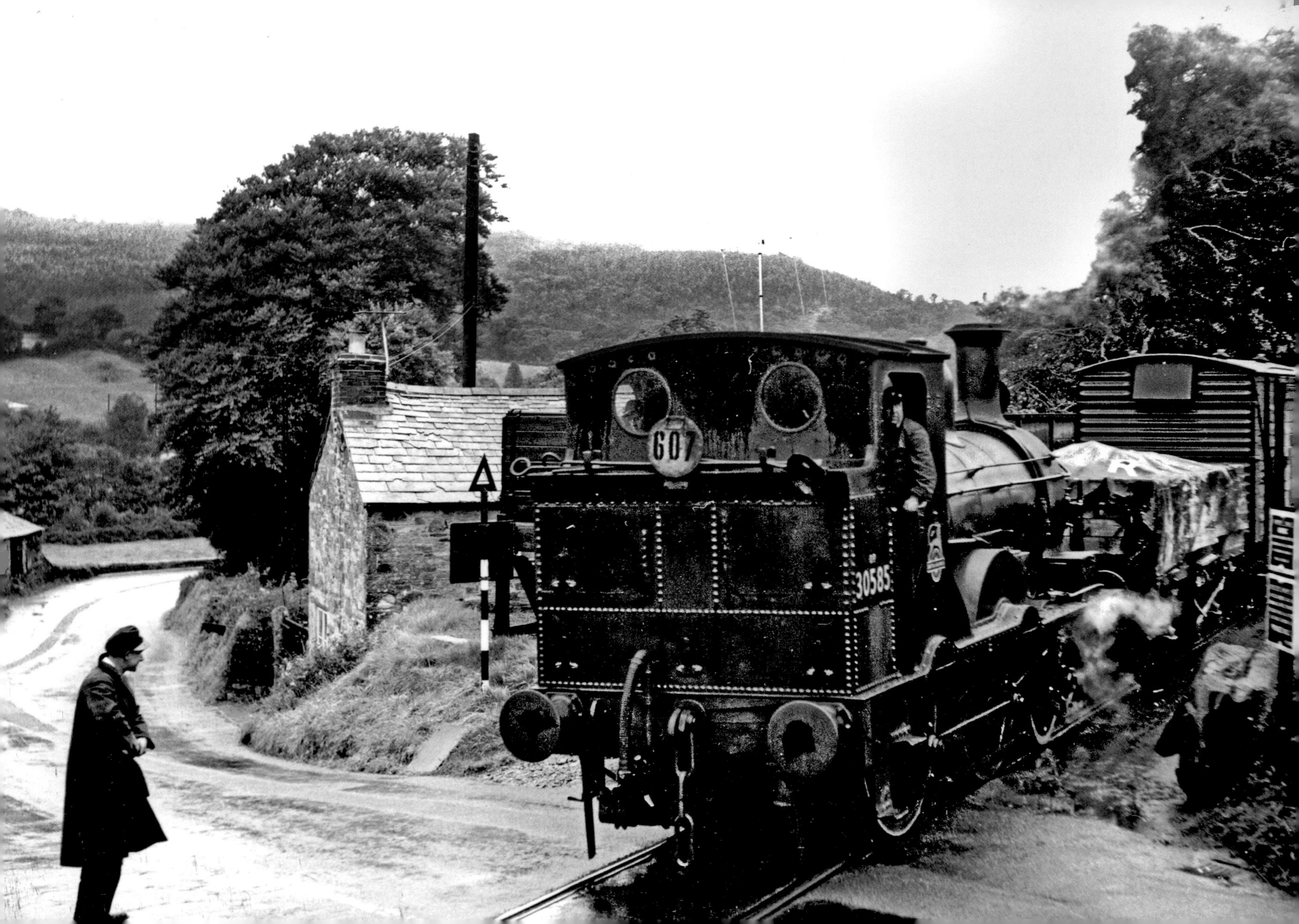

Left: **WENFORD BRANCH** '0298' 2-4-0T No 30585 edges a loaded train from Wenford across the main Bodmin-Wadebridge road on 9 September 1957. It is raining, and the guard, out in the open, clearly wishes the driver would move things along! The rails of the actual level crossing were still causing road traffic to slow as little as ten years ago, when I last visited the area.

Below: **PADSTOW** 'T9' 4-4-0 No 30120 is silhouetted against the Camel estuary as she is turned at Padstow on 13 June 1961. It seems an appropriate ending for this book.

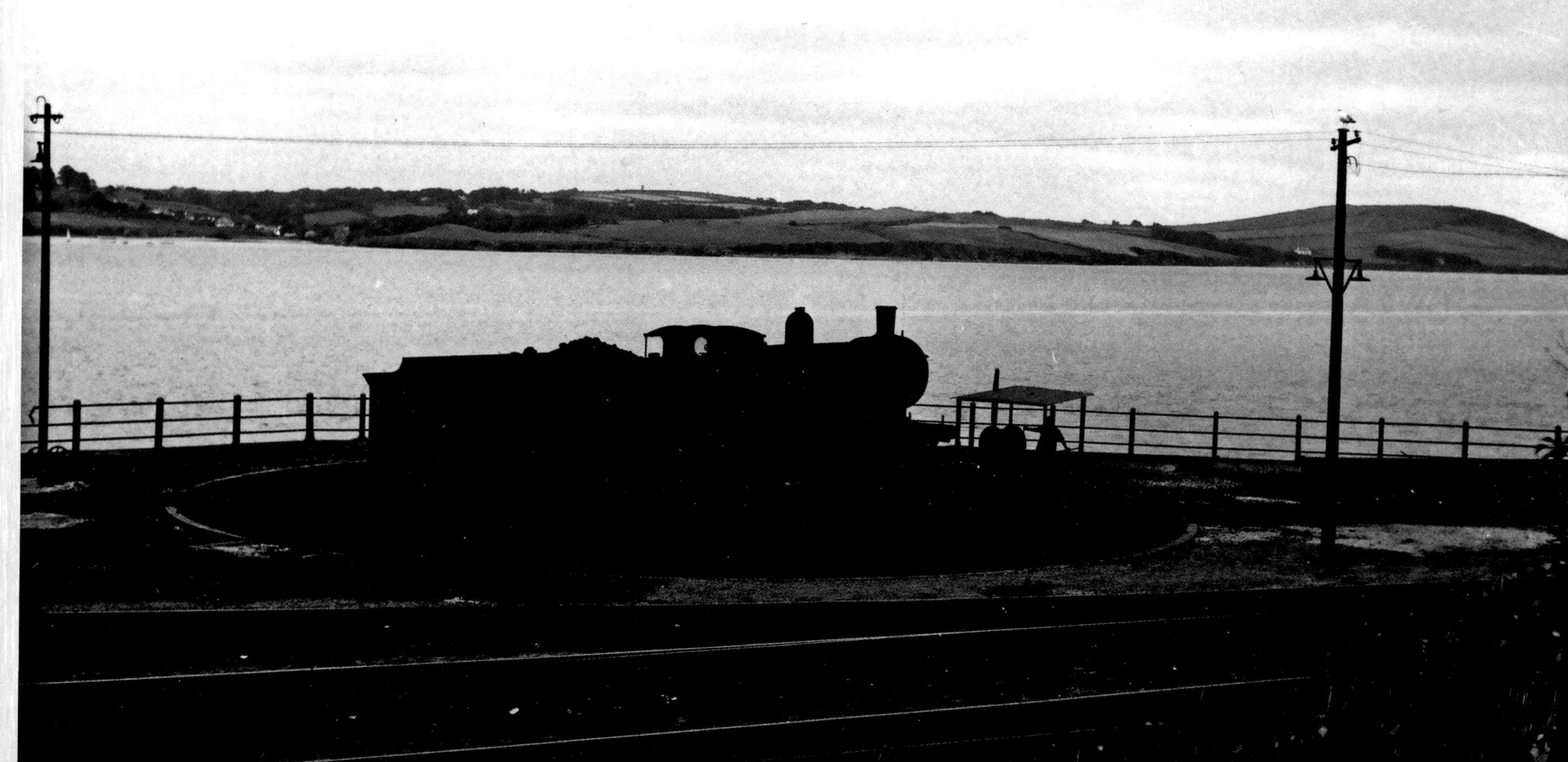

Index of locations